BRITISH RAILWAYS
PRE-GROUPING
ATLAS and GAZETTEER

BRITISH RAILWAYS
PRE-GROUPING
ATLAS and GAZETTEER

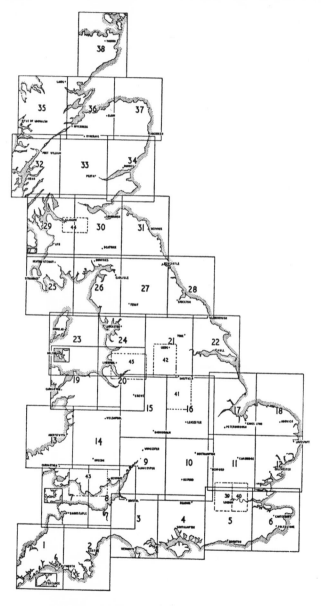

SCALE: EIGHT MILES TO ONE INCH

LONDON

IAN ALLAN LTD

This impression 1980

ISBN 0 7110 0320 3

EX/0176

Published by Ian Allan Ltd, Shepperton, Surrey,
and printed in the United Kingdom by McCorquodale Printers Limited

MAPS OF BRITISH RAILWAYS
BEFORE GROUPING

JUST 35 years ago many of the separate railway companies operating in Britain as self-contained units were grouped into four major systems by the provisions of the Railways Act 1921, and on the 1st January, 1923, these individual units lost their titles in the initials L.M.S.R., L.N.E.R. and S.R., only the G.W.R. keeping its identity although extending its territory by the accretion of the many small railways in Wales. Many of these lines were in fact controlled by the G.W. somewhat earlier than the date above mentioned. Similarly, the L. & Y.R. was amalgamated with the L. & N.W.R. in 1921. It can be noted here that in the sheets that follow, all these railways are shown as independent concerns as a matter of interest but the general picture presented is of the railway system of Britain as it existed in the years prior to 1923.

Taking into account all the minor narrow-gauge lines, the various joint undertakings, committees, etc., there were something like 150 titles extant in the period depicted on these maps and many of these names still live. Through the 25 years of the grouped systems and even now, in Nationalisation days, many of the old names not only are used by members of the railway staffs in day to day working, but such names are currently quoted in official documents, working timetables, etc.

An examination of this Atlas will show that numbers of station names of the 1920's have disappeared, either due to re-naming or to the abandonment of the station through lack of passenger usage. Many branch lines were closed after the amalgamations either to passenger working (a goods and parcel service being maintained) or in their entirety. Since Nationalisation much more has been done in this respect. However, some lines and stations which had in fact been closed by 1922 have been shown in this atlas for the sake of interest and as a record of their existence.

In addition to the inclusion of every railway company at work in the years before 1923 much other matter has been shown. A great many junctions, many still in use as timing points in working timetables, are indicated together with physical features such as the more important viaducts, tunnels, etc., locomotive shed locations and railway workshops. Track water troughs also receive attention and in areas of tourist interest, scenic features in the railway vicinity are indicated. It is hoped that such data will add to the interest and usefulness of this volume.

Many towns with complicated railway layouts have been shown as enlarged insets, and in addition, areas such as London, South Wales, The West Riding, etc., with ramified railway routes and connecting lines points receive attention in separate sheets.

Interpretation of the initials of the various companies will be found in the list of abbreviations shown on pp. 49-51.

Both the checking of the sheets which follow and the compilation of the gazetteer have been undertaken by Mr. U. A. Vincent and the writer is greatly indebted to him for his valued guidance and interest in unearthing obscure matters of cartographic importance and in generally keeping him " on the right lines " in the draughting of these maps.

W. PHILIP CONOLLY.

1   2   3   4   Seven   5

A

B

C

D

E

F

G

PLYMOUTH NORTH RD.

KEYHAM
FORDO
Devonport Jc. ((Joint)
Lipson Jc.
West Jc.   North Rd.Jc.   MUTLEY
Laira Jc.
DEVONPORT
Loco. Shed
Mount Gould Jc.
Friary Jc.
Cattewater Jc.
South Jc.
FRIARY
L.&.S.W. Goods
MILLBAY
STONE-HOUSE POOL
PLYMSTOCK
TURNCHAPEL
ORESTON

CORNWALL

BUDE
L.&.S.W.
HOLSWORTHY
WHITSTONE & BRIDGERULE
DUNSLAND CROSS
HALWILL JUNC. & BEAWORTHY
ASHWATER
ASHBURY
TOWER HILL
OTTERHAM   I.&.S.W.
TRESMEER
CAMELFORD
EGLOSKERRY
LAUNCESTON
LIFTON
CORYTON
LYDFORD
BRENTOR
DELABOLE
MARYTAVY & BLACKDOWN
PORT ISAAC ROAD
CHEESEWRING QUARRY
P. D. & S.W. (B. A. & C.)
TAVISTOCK
MINIONS
WHITCHURCH DOWN PLAT.
ST. KEW HIGHWAY
WENFORD
SOUTH CARADON
LUCKETT
CHILSWORTHY
PADSTOW
Loco. Shed
CALLINGTON
LATCHLEY
GUNNISLAKE
Shillamill Tun.
L.&.S.W. WADEBRIDGE
CALSTOCK
HORRABRIDGE
Grogley Jc.
DUNMERE HALT
BERE ALSTON
GROGLEY HALT
BODMIN
RUTHERN BRIDGE
G.W.
DOUBLEBOIS
BERE FERRERS
Boscarne Jc.   NANSTALLON HALT
BODMIN ROAD
Brownqueen Tun.
Moorswater Jc.
LISKEARD
TAMERTON FOLIOT
NEWQUAY   QUINTRELL DOWNS PLAT.
St. Dennis Jc.
ROCHE
COOMBE
MENHENIOT
ST. BUDEAUX
Tolcarn Jc.
BUGLE
ST. KEYNE
Royal Albert Bridge
FORD NORTH ROAD
GRAVEL HILL
ST. COLUMB RD.
CARB!S
LUXULYAN
LOSTWITHIEL
SALTASH DEFIANCE
TREWERRY & TRERICE HALT
Treverrin Tun.
CAUSELAND
KEYHAM
MELANGOOSE MILL
CAUSELAND G.W. (L. & L.R)
SAINT GERMANS
DEVONPORT
TREAMBLE
MITCHELL & NEWLYN HALT
MELEDOR MILL
GUNHEATH
CARBEAN
GOLANT
Shillingham Tun.
MILLBAY
PERRANPORTH
SHEPHERDS
ST BLAZEY
Loco. Shed
SANDPLACE
TURNCHAPEL
GOONHAVERN HALT
PAR
PLYMOUTH
MITHIAN HALT
BURNGULLOW
ST. AUSTELL
FOWEY
LOOE
GOONBELL HALT
ST. AGNES
MOUNT HAWKE HALT
Polperro Tun.
GRAMPOUND ROAD
CHACEWATER
Loco. Shed
G.W.
Buckshead Tun.
PROBUS & LADOCK PLATFORM
SCORRIER
TRURO
NEWHAM (Goods)
PERRANWELL
Penwithers Jc.
PENRYN
FALMOUTH

PORTREATH (Goods)
CHACEWATER
SCORRIER
ST IVES
Loco. Shed
CARBIS BAY
ROSKEAR
Redruth Jc.
REDRUTH
CAMBORNE
CARN BREA
TRESAVEAN
LELANT
G.W.
GWINEAR ROAD
ST. ERTH
HAYLE
PRAZE
NANCEGOLLAN
Loco. Shed
PENZANCE
MARAZION
TRUTHALL PLATFORM
HELSTON

5   Seven   4   3   2   Eight   1

L. & S.W.

EGGESFORD

TIVERTON

CULMSTOCK   HEMYOCK

G.W.

TIVERTON JUNC.   UFFCULME

LAPFORD

CADELEIGH   CULLOMPTON

A

V   O   N   S   H   I   R   E

MORCHARD ROAD

COPPLESTONE

UP EXE

HELE & BRADNINCH   Summit   Honiton Tun.

THORVERTON   SILVERTON   HONITON

BOW   Coleford Jc.   CREDITON

SAMPFORD COURTENAY   L. & S.W.   NORTH TAWTON   YEOFORD JUNC.   NEWTON ST.CYRES

SIDMOUTH JUNC.

Three

BRAMPFORD SPEKE

STOKE CANON

WHIMPLE

AXMINSTER

SEATON JUNC.

OKEHAMPTON

Cowley Bridge Jc.   ST.   Loco   DAVIDS   Shed   PINHOE   BROAD CLYST

Loco. Shed   Exmouth Jc.

OTTERY ST. MARY

COLYTON

Meldon Jc.   ST.THOMAS   QUEEN STREET

Summit   City Basin Jc.   EXETER

TIPTON ST. JOHN'S   COLYFORD   COMBPYNE

B

Yes Tor

LONGDOWN

IDE

NEWTON POPPLEFORD

SEATON

BRIDESTOWE

MORETON HAMPSTEAD   CHRISTOW   EXMINSTER   TOPSHAM

Watertroughs

WOODBURY ROAD   SIDMOUTH

G.W.

ASHTON   LUSTLEIGH   TRUSHAM

EAST BUDLEIGH

LYMPSTONE

LITTLEHAM

L. & S.W.

BOVEY   CHUDLEIGH

STARCROSS   EXMOUTH   BUDLEIGH SALTERTON

DAWLISH WARREN

HEATHFIELD

DAWLISH

C

TEIGNGRACE   TEIGNMOUTH

PRINCETOWN

TEIGN

NEWTON ABBOT   Works   Loco. Shed   Aller Jc.

ASHBURTON

KINGSKERSWELL

DOUSLAND   YELVERTON

Summit   Dainton Tun.

BUCKFASTLEIGH   TORRE

SHAUGH BRIDGE PLATFORM

STAVERTON   PRESTON PLAT.

TORQUAY

BICKLEIGH

Marley Tun.   Ashburton Jc.

PAIGNTON

D

PLYM BRI. PLAT.   CORNWOOD   BRENT   TOTNES

MARSH MILLS

PLYMPTON   Tavistock Jc.   Summit   IVYBRIDGE   AVONWICK

BITTAFORD PLATFORM   WRANGATON

G.W.

PLYMSTOCK   BILLACOMBE

CHURSTON   BRIXHAM

GARA BRIDGE

ELBURTON CROSS   YEALMPTON

BRIXTON RD.   STEER POINT

KINGSWEAR

LODDISWELL

E

Plymouth to Brest G.W.R.

KINGSBRIDGE

F

G

1   2   3   Eight   4   Nine   5

AVONMOUTH (Gds.)   DOCK (Pass)
PORTISHEAD W.C.& P.   SHIREHAMPTON
PORTISHEAD S. PORTBY RD.   G.W.
CADBURY RD.   PILL   FILTON JUNC.   Westerleigh Jc.
WALTON-IN-GORDANO   CLAPTON   SEA MILLS   STAPLE HILL
WALTON PARK   ROAD   CLIFTON   FISH PONDS   MANGOTSFIELD
CLEVEDON (ALL SAINTS)   PORTBURY   DOWN   WARMLEY   CHIPPENHAM
CLEVEDON   WALTON PARK   BRISTOL   STANLEY BRIDGE HALT
CLEVEDON EAST   CLEVEDON G.W.STA.   CLIFTON BRI.   St. Anne's Pk. Jc.
COLEHOUSE LANE   FLAX BOURTON   TEMPLE MEADS   St. Anne's Park   BITTON   Thingley Jc.
KINGSTON ROAD   HAM LANE   L.S.   St. Anne's Wood Tun.   CALNE
WICK ST. LAWRENCE   NAILSEA & BACKWELL   BRISLINGTON   BOX   CORSHAM   LACOCK HALT
BRISTOL RD.   YATTON   Brislington Tun.   KELSTON FOR SALTFORD   Box Tun.
MILTON RD.   EBDON LANE   Watertroughs   SALTFORD   Middle Hill Tun.   BEANACRE HALT
PUXTON   WORLE TOWN   KEYNSHAM   WESTON   BATHAMPTON   DEVIZES
G.W. STA. WORLE   CONGRESBURY   PENSFORD   Twerton Tun.   Loco   MID. STA.   MELKSHAM   WOODBOROUGH
WESTON-SUPER-MARE   Worle Jc.   BATH   Shed M.R. G.W.   PATNEY & CHIRTON
Uphill Jc.   WRINGTON   Devonshire Tun.   BRADFORD   HOLT   BROUGHTON GIFFORD HALT
BLEADON & UPHILL   LANGFORD   Combe Down Tun.   ON AVON   JUNC.
SANDFORD & BANWELL   BURRINGTON   MIDFORD LIMPLEY STOKE   STAVERTON   SEEND   BROMHAM & ROWDE
WINSCOMBE   BLAGDON   CLUTTON   RADFORD & TIMSBURY   AVONCLIFF HALT   HALT   SEMINGTON HALT
AXBRIDGE   DRAYCOTT   DUNKERTON   FRESHFORD   Bradford Jcs.   TROWBRIDGE   LAVINGTON
CHEDDAR   PAULTON HALT   WELLOW   WESTBURY   EDINGTON & BRATTON
BRENT KNOLL   HALLATROW   G.W.   S.& D.   MELLS ROAD   Watertroughs   Loco. Shed
BURNHAM   LODGE HILL   MIDSOMER NORTON & WELTON   RADSTOCK   WARMINSTER
Level Crossing   WOOKEY   Chilcompton Tun.   S.& D.
HIGHBRIDGE (S.& D.)   Chilcompton S.& D. G.W.   HEYTESBURY
BASON BRIDGE   MASBURY   CHILCOMPTON   FROME
G.W. Loco. Shed (S.& D.)   WELLS (TUCKER STR.) G.W.   BINEGAR   CODFORD
EDINGTON JUNC.   WELLS (PRIORY RD.) S.& D.   Masbury Summit   VOBSTER
DUNBALL   SHAPWICK   POLSHAM   Winsor Hill Tun.   WYLYE
COSSINGTON   ASHCOTT   SHEPTON MALLET   CRANMORE   WISHFORD
BRIDGWATER   GLASTONBURY & STREET   S.& D. Jt. (L.& S.W.)   WANSTROW
WEST PENNARD   PYLLE   EVERCREECH (NEW)   WITHAM   WILTON   G.W.
SOMERSET   EVERCREECH JUNC.   BRUTON   L.& S.W.
Atheney Jc.   CASTLE CARY   COLE   DINTON
ATHELNEY   Castle Cary Jc.   ALFORD HALT
DURSTON   LANGPORT   SOMERTON   KEINTON MANDEVILLE   GILLINGHAM   TISBURY
Curry Rivell Jc.   EAST   CHARLTON MACKRELL   WINCANTON   SEMLEY
LANGPORT WEST   LONG SUTTON & PITNEY   SPARKFORD   Loco. Shed   Buckhorn Weston Tun.
HATCH   MARSTON MAGNA   TEMPLECOMBE JOINT   Goods (S.& D.)   S.& D. STA.
MARTOCK   MILBORNE PORT   DAGGON'S ROAD
MONTACUTE   Loco. Shed (G.W.)   HENSTRIDGE
ILMINSTER   PEN MILL   STALBRIDGE   VERWOOD
L.& S.W. Gds.   TOWN STA. Joint   SHERBORNE
G.W. Gds.   Clifton Maybank   STURMINSTER NEWTON   S.& D. Jt.
YEOVIL JUNC.   SHILLINGSTONE   (L.& S.W. & Mid.)
CHARD (Joint)   SUTTON BINGHAM   YEOVIL   L.& S.W.
L.& S.W. Goods   CLIFTON MAYBANK (Goods) (G.W.)   Loco. Shed (L.& S.W.)
CREWKERNE   YETMINSTER   BLANDFORD   WEST MOORS
CHARD JUNC.   EVERSHOT   SPETISBURY
DORSETSHIRE   WIMBORNE
TOLLER   MAIDEN NEWTON   BAILEY GATE   BOSCOMBE
Corfe Mullen Jc.   BROADSTONE JUNC.   Holes Bay   Gasworks
BRIDPORT   POWERSTOCK   GRIMSTONE & FRAMPTON   Jc.   Loco. Shed
LYME REGIS   EAST STREET   HAMWORTHY JUNC.   BRANKSOME   POOLE   CENTRAL
WEST BAY   DORCHESTER (G.W.)   Goods (L.& S.W.)   PARKSTONE   WEST   BOURNEMOUTH
Loco. Shed (L.& S.W.)   HAMWORTHY (Goods)   L.& S.W.
Dorchester Jc.   MORETON   WOOL   WAREHAM   Worgret Jc.
PORTESHAM   CORYATES HALT   MONKTON & CAME (GOLF LINKS) HALT
ABBOTSBURY   Bincombe Tuns.   CORFE CASTLE
UPWEY   UPWEY WISHING WELL HALT   SWANAGE
Kingswood Jc.   UPWEY JUNC.
RADIPOLE HALT   Loco.Shed (G.W.)
Weymouth Jc.   TOWN STA.
MELCOMBE REGIS   HARBOUR
RODWELL   WEYMOUTH   (L.& S.W. & G.W. Jt.)
WYKE REGIS HALT
PORTLAND
EASTON   Weymouth—Guernsey & Jersey G.W.R.

BRISTOL
CLIFTON DOWN   REDLAND   G.W. & MID. Jt.
MONTPELIER   Ashley Hill Jc.
HOTWELLS   STAPLETON RD.
CANNONS MARSH Gda.   Avonside Wharf   ST. PHILIP'S   Kingswood Jc.
Gds.   Lawrence Hill Jc.
TEMPLE MEADS   LAWRENCE HILL
JOINT PASS   Days Bridge Jc.   St. Anne's Park Jc.
Ashton Jc.   Goods   Feeder Bridge Jc.
Loco Sheds
PYLLE HILL   St. PHILIP'S
BEDMINSTER   MARSH (Gds.)
Bedminster Jc.

WILTS

5 MONKTON COMBE
4 MIDFORD HALT
3 COMBE HAY HALT
2 DUNKERTON COLL. HALT
1 CAMERTON

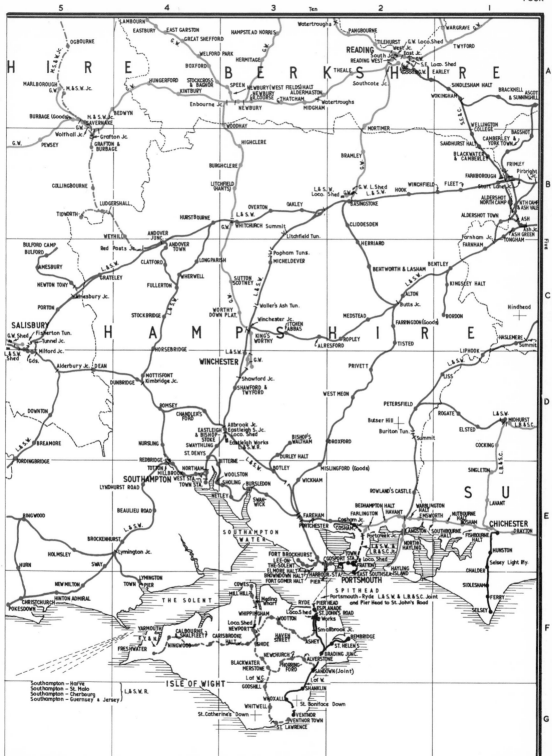

Eleven

(SEE SHEETS THIRTY NINE & FORTY)

5. HAM BRIDGE HALT
4. BUNGALOW TOWN HALT
3. FISHERGATE HALT
2. DYKE JUNC. HALT
1. HOLLAND ROAD HALT

Newhaven-Dieppe L.B. & S.C.

EASTBOURNE

SURREY

SUSSEX

GUILDFORD · BRIGHTON · WORTHING · TUNBRIDGE WELLS · HORSHAM

5 4 3 Twelve 2 1

A

B

C

D

E

F

G

BATTLESBRIDGE
G.E.
WICKFORD
S E G.E. HOCKLEY
RAYLEIGH
ROCHFORD
BURNHAM ON CROUCH
X
MID.
L.T.&S.
PITSEA
BENFLEET LEIGH
WESTCLIFF-ON-SEA
PRITTLEWELL
L.Shed
THORPE BAY
SHOEBURYNESS
SOUTHEND-ON-SEA
Canvey Island
THAMESHAVEN

HIGH HALSTOW HALT
MIDDLE STOKE HALT
GRAIN CROSSING HALT
Hoo Jc.
CLIFFE
SHARNAL STR.
HIGHAM
BELUNCLE HALT
PORT VICTORIA
DOCKYARD
SHEERNESS-ON-SEA
SHEERNESS EAST
MARGATE
SANDS
Rochester Bridge Jc.
ROCHESTER BRIDGE
GILLINGHAM
Loco Shed
QUEENBOROUGH
MINSTER-ON-SEA
EAST MINSTER-ON-SEA
EASTCHURCH
WESTGATE-ON-SEA
BIRCHINGTON-ON-SEA
WEST
EAST
STROOD
Fort Pitt Tun.
CUXTON
ROCHESTER
Gillingham Tun.
RAINHAM
King's Ferry Bri.
BRAMBLEDOWN HALT
HARTY RD. HALT
LEYSDOWN
S.E. & C.
ST.LAWRENCE
BROADSTAIRS
TOWN
HARB. RAMSGATE
Chatham Tun.
CHATHAM
NEWINGTON
West Jc.
SITTINGBOURNE
WHITSTABLE HARB.
HERNE BAY
Minster East Jc.
Minster West Jc.
HALLING
East Jc.
TEYNHAM
TOWN
TANKERTON HALT
MINSTER
GROVE FERRY
Minster 'B' Jc.
SNODLAND
SOUTH STR. HALT
BLEAN & TYLER HILL HALT
STURRY
ASH TOWN
SANDWICH ROAD
SANDWICH
AYLESFORD
FAVERSHAM
Loco. Shed
Faversham Jc.
WEST
GRAVENEY (Goods)
CANTERBURY
STAPLE
TOWN
ROMAN ROAD
MALLING
Preston Hall Tuns.
EAST
BEARSTED & THURNHAM
SELLING
Selling Tun.
EAST
SOUTH
BEKESBOURNE
WINGHAM
WOODNESBOROUGH
EASTRY
EASTRY SOUTH
W.W.
BARMING
TOVIL
BARRACKS
WEST MAIDSTONE
HOLLINGBOURNE
CHILHAM
CHARTHAM
ADISHAM
KNOWLTON
DEAL
EAST FARLEIGH
WATERINGBURY
HARRIETSHAM
LENHAM
BRIDGE
ELVINGTON
EYTHORNE
East Kent Light R.
E N
BISHOPSBOURNE
T
CHARING
BARHAM
SHEPHERDS WELL
Lydden Tun.
WALMER
MARDEN
STAPLEHURST
HOTHFIELD
WYE
ELHAM
KEARSNEY
Guston Tun.
MARTIN MILL
HEADCORN
S.E. & C.
PLUCKLEY
LYMINGE
Buckland Jc.
Charlton Tun.
Priory Tun.
PRIORY Harb. Tun.
HORSMONDEN
FRITTENDEN ROAD
ASHFORD
Loco. Shed
Ashford Works
Archcliffe Jc.
Abbotscliff Tun.
TOWN
GOUDHURST
BIDDENDEN
SMEETH
Martello Tun.
Loco. Shed
DOVER
Dover to Calais, S.E. & C.
CRANBROOK
HIGH HALDEN ROAD
SANDLING JUNC.
Saltwood Tun.
CENT.
Shakespeare Tun.
PIER
TENTERDEN ST. MICHAELS
Sandling Tun.
SMORNCLIFFE CAMP
JUNC. STA.
HARB. FOLKESTONE
HAWKHURST
ROLVENDEN
TENTERDEN TOWN
WESTENHANGER
HYTHE
SANDGATE
Folkestone to Boulogne, S.E. & C.
Kent & East Sussex Light Rly.
HAM STREET & ORLESTONE
ETCHINGHAM
NORTHIAM
WITTERSHAM ROAD
APPLEDORE
BODIAM
JUNCTION ROAD
BROOKLAND
ROBERTSBRIDGE
S.E.A.C.
NEW ROMNEY & LITTLESTONE-ON-SEA
Mountfield Tun.
RYE
LYDD
Tramway
WINCHELSEA
HARB.
CAMBER
BATTLE
DUNGENESS
CROWHURST
Bopeep Tun.
WEST ST. LEONARDS
Loco. Shed
Ore Tun.
ORE
Mount Pleasant Tun.
SIDLEY
WEST
MARINA
HASTINGS
Hastings Tun.
WARRIOR SQUARE
BEXHILL
Bopeep Jc.

Thirteen   Fourteen

1   2   3   4   5

Inset

G.W.   WHITLAND   Cardigan Jc.   ST. CLEARS   SARNAU   CARMARTHEN   DERWYDD ROAD   Y Fan Gihirach

CWM MAWR   CROSS HANDS   LLANDEBIE   CRAIGYNOS (PENWYLLT)   SEE SHEET NO.

FERRYSIDE   Watertroughs   PONTYBEREM   TUMBLE   TIRYDAIL   GARNANT   BRYNAMMAN   GLANAMMAN   CWMLLYNFELL   ABERCRAVE   COLBREN JUNC.

MYNYDD-Y-GARREG   B.P.G.V.   PONT HENRY   CWM BLAWD   AMMANFORD   GWYS   YSTRAD GYNLAIS   ONLLWYN

KIDWELLY   GLYN ABBEY   PONT YATES   PANTYFFYNNON   GURNOS (Gdn)   SEVEN SISTERS

G.W.   TRIMSARAN ROAD   CYNHEIDRE   Ynys-Y-Geinon Jc.   YSTALYFERA   GLYN NEATH

Tycoch Jc.   TRIMSARAN (Gds.)   HOREB   PONTARDULAIS (Joint)   G L A M.

PINGED   PONT LLIW   CRYNANT   RESOLVEN

L. & M.M.   FELIN FOEL   PONTARDAWE

PEMBREY   LLAN-GENNECH L.C.   GROVES END   GLAIS   CILFREW   S.W.M.   BLAENRHONDDA

PEMBREY & BURRY PORT   BYNEA   LLAN-GYFELACH   CLYDACH-ON-TAWE   ABERDYLAIS   BLAEN CWYMM

BURRY PORT   LLANELLY   Dock Goods   GORSEINON   MORRISTON   FELIN FRAN   SKEWEN   NEATH   CAERAU   ABERGWYNFI   TREHERBERT

PENCLAWDD   LOUGHOR   PLAS MARL   LANDORE   NEATH ABBEY   COURT SART   NANTY FFYLLON   HANTYMOEL

LLANMORLAIS   GOWERTON   Summit   UP. BANK   HIGH ST.   BRITON FERRY   CWM AVON BRYN   MAESTEG   CWMDU   PONTY CYMMER

DUNVANT   COCKETT   RUTLAND ST.   JERSEY MARINE   P.T.   TROEDYRHIW GARTH   ORGMORE

KILLAY   SWAN-SEA BAY   COED-Y-GRAIG   ABER-AVON (SEASIDE)   LLANGONOYD   LLETTY BRONGU (LLANGEINOR)   PONT RHYL   LLANGEINOR

MUMBLES ROAD   SWANSEA   PORT TALBOT DOCK   Margam Jc.   BLACK HILL

MUMBLES PIER   Cefn Jc.   KENFIG HILL   TONDU   BRYNMENYN   Bryncethin Jc.

PYLE   G.W.   Coity Jc.

PORTHCAWL   BRIDGEND

SOUTHERNDOWN ROAD   BARRY

Inset map (Pembrokeshire):

G.W.   HAVERFORDWEST   NARBERTH

JOHNSTON   TEMPLETON   KILGETTY

MILFORD HAVEN   SAUNDERSFOOT

NEYLAND   PEMBROKE   DOCK STA.   GOLDEN HILL PLAT.   TOWN STA.   G.W.   MANORBIER   TENBY

LAMPHEY   LYDSTEP   PENALLY

B   R   I   S   T   O   L

ILFRACOMBE   LYNTON   WOODY BAY

Summit   MORTEHOE   PARRACOMBE

BLACKMOOR

L.&S.W.   BRATTON FLEMING

BRAUNTON   WRAFTON   L.&B.   SNAPPER   CHELFHAM

FREMINGTON   TOWN STA.   BARNSTAPLE   JUNC. STA.   Loco. Shed   SWIMBRIDGE   FILLEIGH

APPLEDORE   INSTOW   CHAPELTON   BISHOP'S NYMPTON & MOLLAND   DULVERTON

NORTHAM   WESTWARD HO!   G.W.   SOUTH MOLTON   EAST ANSTEY

B.W.H. & A.   BIDEFORD   UMBERLEIGH

ABBOTSHAM ROAD   PORTSMOUTH ARMS   BAMPTON

TORRINGTON   SOUTH MOLTON ROAD

L.&S.W.   D E V O N S H

EGGESFORD   S O

One   Two

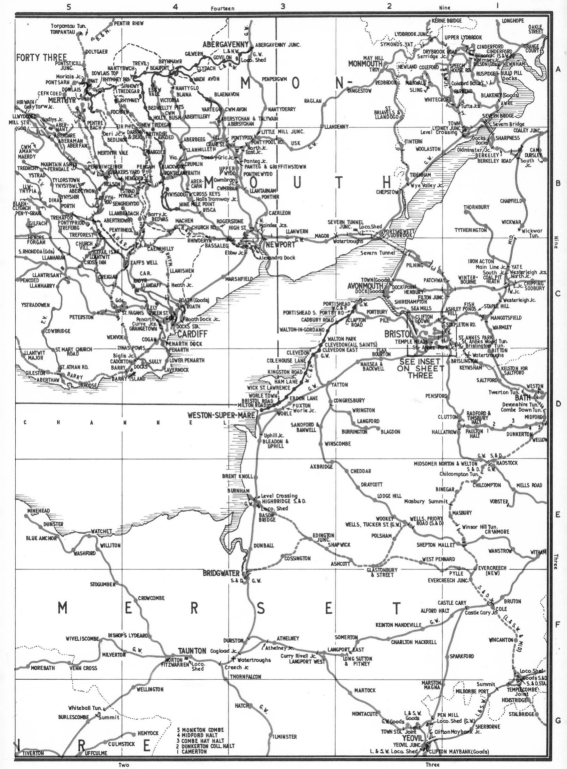

1 2 3 Fifteen 4 5

Fourteen

Eight

WORCESTER

ONIBURY
BROMFIELD
Watertroughs
BITTERLEY
Titterstone Clee
MIDDLETON
CLEE HILL
LUDLOW
STOTTESDON
HIGHLEY
CLEOBURY MORTIMER
CLEOBURY TOWN STA.
ARLEY
WYRE FOREST
HAGLEY
STOURBRIDGE JUNC.
SELLY OAK
BOURNVILLE
HUNNINGTON
KING'S HEATH
HALL
OLTON
MID. HAMPTON-IN-ARDEN
WOOFFERTON
TENBURY WELLS
EASTON COURT
NEEN SOLLARS
NEWNHAM BRIDGE
G.W.
BEWDLEY
KIDDERMINSTER
CHURCHILL & BLAKEDOWN
NORTHFIELD
RUBERY
KING'S NORTON
Northfield Jc.
SHIRLEY
HAZEL WELL
LIFFORD
YARDLEY WOOD PLATFORM
WIDNEY MANOR
SOLIHULL
GRIMES HILL PLATFORM
KNOWLE & DORRIDGE
BERKSWELL
L & N.W.
BERRINGTON & EYE
G.W.
STOURPORT
HARTLEBURY
Summit
EARLSWOOD LAKES
WOOD END PLATFORM
LAPWORTH
DANZEY
Watertroughs E. Jc.
HATTON N. Jc.
HATTON Jc.
LEOMINSTER
FENCOTE
ROWDEN MILL
FERNHILL HEATH
Lickey Incline
BROMSGROVE
Loco. Shed
BLACKWELL
ALVECHURCH
REDDITCH
Goods
HENLEY-IN-ARDEN
N. Jc.
W. Jc.
CLAVERDON
STEENS BRIDGE
FORD BRIDGE
BROMYARD
KNIGHTWICK
Tunnel Jc.
Loco. Shed
Rainbow Hill Jc.
LEIGH COURT
DROITWICH
DUNHAMPSTEAD (Goods)
DROITWICH ROAD (Goods)
STUDLEY & ASTWOOD BANK
COUGHTON
GREAT ALNE
WIXFORD
ALCESTER
BIDFORD-ON-AVON
BEARLEY
N. Jc.
W. Jc.
WILMCOTE
DINMORE
DINMORE Tun.
SUCKLEY
LEOMINSTER Jc.
BRANSFORD ROAD
WORCESTER
Works
FOREGATE STREET
SHRUB HILL (G.W & Mid. Joint)
SPETCHLEY (Goods)
STOULTON
SALFORD PRIORS
BROOM
STRATFORD-ON-AVON
Loco. Shed
BINTON
MILCOTE

HEREFORD

MORETON-ON-LUGG
Barrs Court Jc. N.
CREDENHILL
Brecon Curve Jc.
Shelwick Jc.
WITHINGTON
STOKE EDITH
GREAT MALVERN
MALVERN LINK
NORTON JUNC.
Abbotswood Jc.
WADBOROUGH
PERSHORE
FLADBURY
HARVINGTON
LONG MARSTON
LITTLETON & BADSEY
HONEYBOURNE
EVESHAM
MOORFIELDS (Goods)
BARTON (Gds)
Loco. Shed
BARRS COURT Jc.
Barrs Court Jc. S.
HEREFORD
Rotherwas Jc.
L & N.W.
Red Hill Jc.
ASHPERTON
COLWALL
Malvern Wells G.W.
MALVERN WELLS MID.
DEFFORD
ECKINGTON
BENGEWORTH
WESTON-SUB-EDGE
Campden Tun.
WILLERSLEY HALT
BROADWAY
SHIPSTON-ON-STOUR
LONGDON ROAD
CAMPDEN
STRETTON-ON-FOSSE
TRAM INN
HOLME LACY
LEDBURY
RIPPLE
UPTON-ON-SEVERN
BREDON
ASHTON-UNDER-HILL
LAVERTON HALT
BECKFORD
BLOCKLEY
BALLINGHAM
FAWLEY
DYMOCK
NEWENT
Level Crossing
TEWKESBURY
ASHCHURCH
Greet Tun.
TODDINGTON
MORETON-IN-MARSH
Summit
ROSS-ON-WYE
MITCHELDEAN ROAD
BARBER'S BRIDGE
GRETTON HALT
WINCHCOMBE
CLEEVE
GOTHERINGTON
BISHOP'S CLEEVE
ADLESTROP
KERNE BRIDGE
LONGHOPE
OAKLE STREET
Hunting Butts Tun.
LANSDOWN
ST. JAMES'S
MALVERN ROAD
CHELTENHAM
CHELTENHAM SOUTH & LECKHAMPTON
ANDOVERSFORD
NOTGROVE
STOW-ON-THE-WOLD
BOURTON-ON-THE-WATER
KINGHAM

MONMOUTH

LYDBROOK JUNC.
SYMOND'S YAT
UPPER LYDBROOK
DRYBROOK RD.
CINDERFORD
Bilson Jc.
CINDERFORD (S & W Jt.)
GRANGE COURT
NEWNHAM
Docks
Engine Shed Jc.
GLOUCESTER
Tuffley Jc.
WITHINGTON
CHEDWORTH
MAY HILL
TROY
NEWLAND
COLEFORD
Serridge Jc.
Drybrook Jc.
SPEECH HOUSE RD.
RUSPIDGE
BILSON (Gds)
BULLO PILL
Docks
HARESFIELD
FOSS CROSS
DINGESTOW
REDBROOK
SLING
MILKWALL
Coleford Branch Jc.
PARKEND
BLAKENEY
AWRE (Gds)
Standish Jc.
EBLEY CROSSING HALT
DOWNFIELD CROSSING HALT
STROUD G.W.
BOWBRIDGE CROSSING HALT
ST. MARY'S CROSSING HALT
CIRENCESTER
KELMSCOTT & LANGFORD PLAT.
FAIRFORD
LECHLADE
ST. BRIAVELS & LLANDOGO
WHITECROFT
Tufts Jcs.
SEVERN & WYE Jt. (G.W. & MID.)
TOWN
SEVERN BRIDGE
STONEHOUSE
FROCESTER
RYEFORD
DUDBRIDGE
HAM MILL CROSSING HALT
CHALFORD
Summit
Sapperton Tun.
COATES (GDS.)
CERNEY & ASHTON KEYNES
TINTERN
LYDNEY JUNC.
Loco. Shed
Level Crossing
Docks
SHARPNESS
SEVERN BRIDGE
Oldminster Jc.
BERKELEY ROAD
CAM
COALEY JUNC.
WOODCHESTER
NAILSWORTH
BRIMSCOMBE
BRIMSCOMBE BRI. HALT
RODMARTON PLAT.
KEMBLE JUNC.
KEMBLE
FAIRFORD

GLOUCESTER

WOOLASTON
BERKELEY
South Jc.
DURSLEY
CULKERTON
CERNEY & ASHTON KEYNES
TIDENHAM
Wye Valley Jc.
CHARFIELD
TETBURY
CRICKLADE
HANNINGTON
HIGHWORTH
CHEPSTOW
THORNBURY
WICKWAR
Wickwar Tun.
MALMESBURY
MINETY & ASHTON KEYNES
PURTON
STANTON
BLUNSDON
STRATTON
SHRIVENHAM
SEVERN TUNNEL JUNC.
Loco. Shed
PORTSKEWETT
SUDBROOK
V.P.
Severn Tunnel
TYTHERINGTON
LITTLE SOMERFORD
BRINKWORTH
GREAT SOMERFORD
WOOTTON BASSETT
Works
Highworth Jc.
SWINDON JUNC.
TOWN STA.
Rushey Platt Jc.
RUSHEY PLATT (Goods)
PILNING
IRON ACTON
YATE
CHIPPING SODBURY
Main Line Jc.
Watertroughs
BADMINTON
HULLAVINGTON
HENBURY
PATCHWAY
COALPIT HEATH
N. Jc.
E. Jc.
Westerleigh Jc.
Sodbury Tun.
Alderton Tun.
DAUNTSEY
WOOTTON BASSETT
L.S.
CHISELDON
AVONMOUTH
TOWN (Gds)
DOCK (Gds)
DOCK (Pass)
FILTON JUNC.
WINTERBOURNE
Westerleigh Jc.
SHIREHAMPTON

WILTSHIRE

Eight

Three

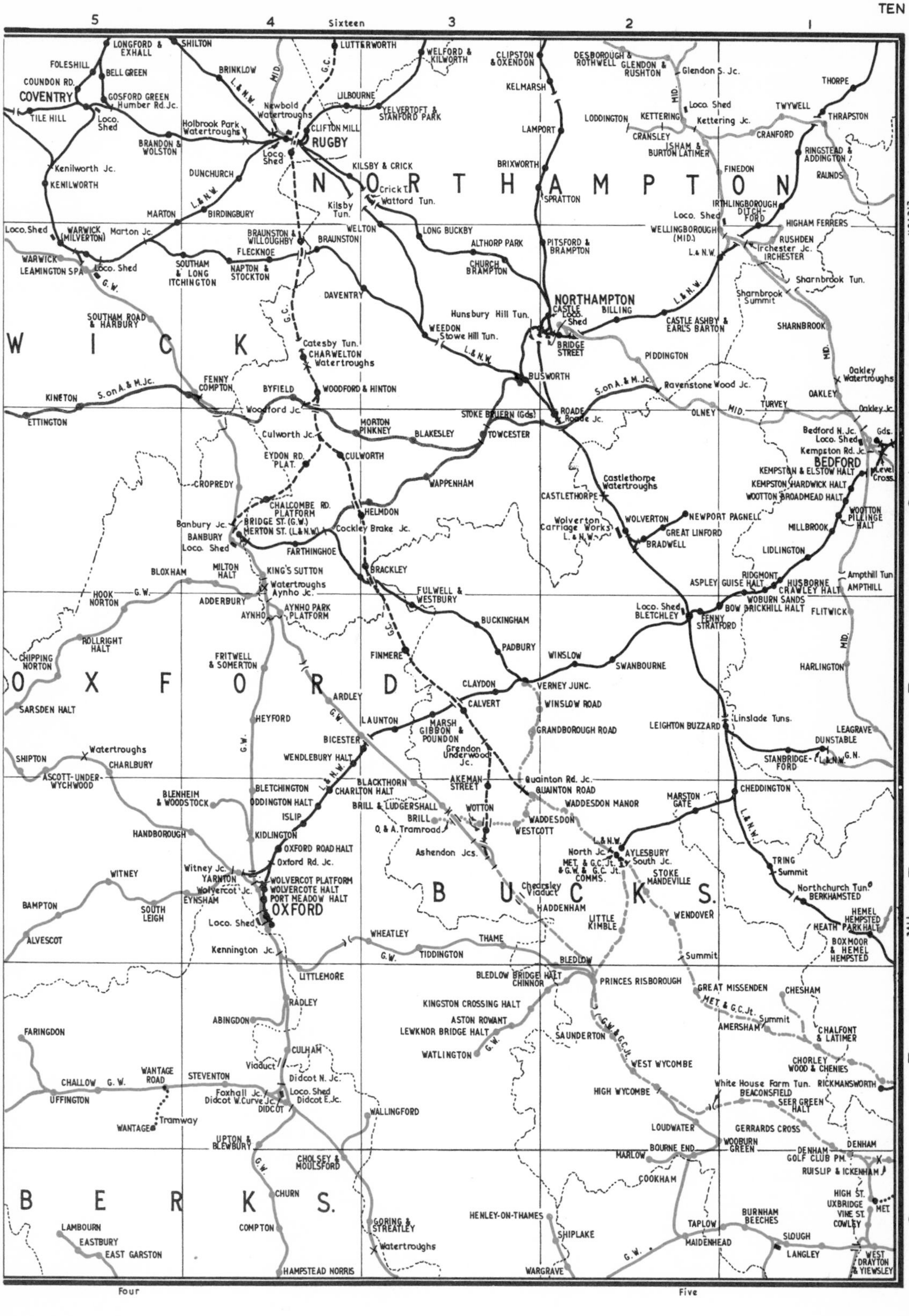
5
4
Sixteen
3
2
1
LONGFORD & EXHALL
SHILTON
LUTTERWORTH
WELFORD & KILWORTH
CLIPSTON & OXENDON
DESBOROUGH & ROTHWELL
GLENDON & RUSHTON
Glendon S. Jc.
THORPE
FOLESHILL
BELL GREEN
BRINKLOW
MID.
G.C.
KELMARSH
COUNDON RD.
COVENTRY
GOSFORD GREEN
Humber Rd. Jc.
L. & N.W.
Newbold Watertroughs
LILBOURNE
YELVERTOFT & STANFORD PARK
LODDINGTON
KETTERING
Loco. Shed
Kettering Jc.
TWYWELL
THRAPSTON
TILE HILL
Loco. Shed
Holbrook Park Watertroughs
CLIFTON MILL
RUGBY
LAMPORT
CRANSLEY
CRANFORD
A
BRANDON & WOLSTON
Loco. Shed
ISHAM & BURTON LATIMER
RINGSTEAD & ADDINGTON
Kenilworth Jc.
KILSBY & CRICK
BRIXWORTH
FINEDON
KENILWORTH
DUNCHURCH
NORTHAMPTON
RAUNDS
Crick T.
Watford Tun.
Kilsby Tun.
SPRATTON
IRTHLINGBOROUGH
DITCHFORD
Eleven
MARTON
BIRDINGBURY
Loco. Shed
HIGHAM FERRERS
Loco. Shed
WARWICK (MILVERTON)
Marton Jc.
WELTON
LONG BUCKBY
WELLINGBOROUGH (MID.)
RUSHDEN
BRAUNSTON & WILLOUGHBY
BRAUNSTON
ALTHORP PARK
PITSFORD & BRAMPTON
L. & N.W.
Irchester Jc.
IRCHESTER
WARWICK
LEAMINGTON SPA
Loco. Shed
SOUTHAM & LONG ITCHINGTON
FLECKNOE
NAPTON & STOCKTON
CHURCH BRAMPTON
Sharnbrook Tun.
G.W.
DAVENTRY
Sharnbrook Summit
NORTHAMPTON
CASTLE
Loco. Shed
BILLING
CASTLE ASHBY & EARL'S BARTON
SOUTHAM ROAD & HARBURY
Hunsbury Hill Tun.
SHARNBROOK
B
WEEDON
Stowe Hill Tun.
BRIDGE STREET
W I C K
Catesby Tun.
CHARWELTON Watertroughs
PIDDINGTON
MID.
BUSWORTH
Oakley Watertroughs
FENNY COMPTON
S. on A. & M. Jc.
Ravenstone Wood Jc.
KINETON
BYFIELD
WOODFORD & HINTON
OAKLEY
ETTINGTON
Woodford Jc.
STOKE BRUERN (Gds)
ROADE
Roade Jc.
OLNEY
TURVEY
Oakley Jc.
MORTON PINKNEY
BLAKESLEY
TOWCESTER
Bedford N. Jc.
Loco. Shed
Gds.
Culworth Jc.
Kempston Rd. Jc.
BEDFORD
EYDON RD. PLAT.
CULWORTH
Castlethorpe Watertroughs
KEMPSTON & ELSTOW HALT
Level Cross.
CROPREDY
WAPPENHAM
KEMPSTON HARDWICK HALT
CASTLETHORPE
WOOTTON BROADMEAD HALT
CHALCOMBE RD. PLATFORM
HELMDON
C
WOOTTON PILLINGE HALT
Banbury Jc.
BRIDGE ST. (G.W.)
MERTON ST. (L. & N.W.)
Cockley Brake Jc.
Wolverton Carriage Works
L. & N.W.
WOLVERTON
NEWPORT PAGNELL
BANBURY
Loco. Shed
GREAT LINFORD
MILLBROOK
FARTHINGHOE
BRADWELL
LIDLINGTON
BLOXHAM
MILTON HALT
KING'S SUTTON
BRACKLEY
Watertroughs
Aynho Jc.
ASPLEY GUISE HALT
RIDGMONT
HUSBORNE CRAWLEY HALT
Ampthill Tun.
AMPTHILL
HOOK NORTON
G.W.
ADDERBURY
FULWELL & WESTBURY
Loco. Shed
BLETCHLEY
WOBURN SANDS
BOW BRICKHILL HALT
AYNHO
AYNHO PARK PLATFORM
FENNY STRATFORD
FLITWICK
ROLLRIGHT HALT
BUCKINGHAM
FRITWELL & SOMERTON
PADBURY
CHIPPING NORTON
FINMERE
WINSLOW
SWANBOURNE
HARLINGTON
O X F O R D
CLAYDON
VERNEY JUNC.
D
ARDLEY
CALVERT
WINSLOW ROAD
SARSDEN HALT
HEYFORD
LAUNTON
MARSH GIBBON & POUNDON
GRANDBOROUGH ROAD
Linslade Tuns.
LEIGHTON BUZZARD
LEAGRAVE
BICESTER
DUNSTABLE
Watertroughs
SHIPTON
WENDLEBURY HALT
Grendon Underwood Jc.
STANBRIDGEFORD
G.N.
CHARLBURY
ASCOTT-UNDER-WYCHWOOD
BLACKTHORN
AKEMAN STREET
Quainton Rd. Jc.
QUAINTON ROAD
CHEDDINGTON
BLENHEIM & WOODSTOCK
BLETCHINGTON
CHARLTON HALT
WADDESDON MANOR
MARSTON GATE
ODDINGTON HALT
BRILL & LUDGERSHALL
WOTTON
ISLIP
BRILL
WADDESDON
HANDBOROUGH
O. & A. Tramroad
WESTCOTT
KIDLINGTON
L. & N.W.
AYLESBURY
North Jc.
MET. & G.C. Jt.
G.W. & G.C. Jt.
COMMS.
South Jc.
OXFORD ROAD HALT
Oxford Rd. Jc.
Ashendon Jcs.
TRING
Summit
WITNEY
Witney Jc.
YARNTON
WOLVERCOT PLATFORM
WOLVERCOTE HALT
PORT MEADOW HALT
OXFORD
Wolvercot Jc.
EYNSHAM
STOKE MANDEVILLE
E
Northchurch Tun.
BERKHAMSTED
Chearsley Viaduct
B U C K S.
BAMPTON
SOUTH LEIGH
HADDENHAM
LITTLE KIMBLE
WENDOVER
HEMEL HEMPSTED
Loco. Shed
HEATH PARK HALT
Five
ALVESCOT
WHEATLEY
THAME
BOXMOOR & HEMEL HEMPSTED
Kennington Jc.
G.W.
TIDDINGTON
Summit
BLEDLOW
LITTLEMORE
BLEDLOW BRIDGE HALT
CHINNOR
PRINCES RISBOROUGH
GREAT MISSENDEN
CHESHAM
MET. & G.C. Jt.
RADLEY
KINGSTON CROSSING HALT
Summit
ABINGDON
ASTON ROWANT
AMERSHAM
CHALFONT & LATIMER
FARINGDON
LEWKNOR BRIDGE HALT
SAUNDERTON
G.W. & G.C. Jt.
CULHAM
WATLINGTON
F
Viaduct
WEST WYCOMBE
CHORLEY WOOD & CHENIES
WANTAGE ROAD
STEVENTON
Didcot N. Jc.
CHALLOW
G.W.
Foxhall Jc.
Didcot W. Curve Jc.
Loco. Shed
Didcot E. Jc.
HIGH WYCOMBE
White House Farm Tun.
RICKMANSWORTH
UFFINGTON
DIDCOT
BEACONSFIELD
SEER GREEN HALT
Tramway
WALLINGFORD
WANTAGE
LOUDWATER
GERRARDS CROSS
UPTON & BLEWBURY
WOOBURN GREEN
DENHAM
BOURNE END
MARLOW
DENHAM GOLF CLUB PM.
CHOLSEY & MOULSFORD
RUISLIP & ICKENHAM
COOKHAM
B E R K S.
CHURN
HIGH ST.
UXBRIDGE
VINE ST.
MET.
G
LAMBOURN
COMPTON
GORING & STREATLEY
HENLEY-ON-THAMES
BURNHAM BEECHES
COWLEY
TAPLOW
SHIPLAKE
EASTBURY
Watertroughs
MAIDENHEAD
SLOUGH
EAST GARSTON
G.W.
LANGLEY
WEST DRAYTON & YIEWSLEY
HAMPSTEAD NORRIS
WARGRAVE
Four
Five

1 2 Seventeen 3 4 5

WANSFORD ROAD
KINGSCLIFFE
WANSFORD
NASSINGTON
ELTON
CASTOR
Yarwell Jc.
ORTON
WATERVILLE
Longville Jc.
Loco. Shed
New England Sidings
Loco. Shed
L.N.W. & G.E. Jc.
PETERBOROUGH
G.E.
FLETTON (Goods)
WHITTLESEA
WEST FEN DROVE
Grassmoor Jc.
WHITEMOOR (Goods)
West Jc.
North Jc.
South Jc.
Loco. Shed
MARCH
March S. Jc.
QUAKERS DROVE
BURNT HOUSE
WHITE FEN
HILGAY
DENVER
RYSTON
ABBEY
STOKE FERRY

A
OUNDLE
BARNWELL
HOLME
YAXLEY & FARCET
BENWICK (Goods)
JONES DROVE
ST. MARY'S
RAMSEY
RAMSEY
WIMBLINGTON
MANEA
STONEA
G.E.
LITTLEPORT
BLACK BANK
LAKENHEATH
BRANDON

B
THORPE
RAUNDS
HUNTINGDON
ABBOTS RIPTON
WARBOYS
SOMERSHAM
HADDENHAM
EARITH BRIDGE
BLUNTISHAM
SUTTON
WILBURTON
STRETHAM
ELY
Dock Jc.
Sutton Branch Jc.
SOHAM
ISLEHAM
MILDENHALL

KIMBOLTON
LONG STOW (Goods) Mid.
HUNTINGDON
GRAFHAM
BUCKDEN
GODMANCHESTER
Jc. Mid.
ST. IVES
Needingworth Jc.
SWAVESEY
LONG STANTON
WATERBEACH
FORDHAM
KENNETT
HIGHAM
SAXHAM & RISBY

C
SHARNBROOK
Oakley Watertroughs
OAKLEY
St. NEOTS
OFFORD & BUCKDEN
TEMPSFORD
OAKINGTON
HISTON
CAMBRIDGE
Coldham Lane Jc.
Mid. Goods
Loco. Shed
G.N. Goods
L.N.W. Goods
GUY
BARNWELL
FULBOURNE
G.E. Goods
CAMBRIDGE
BURWELL
SWAFFHAM PRIOR
BOTTISHAM LODE
Snailwell Jc.
Warren Hill Jc.
NEWMARKET
Chippenham Jc.
SIX MILE BOTTOM
DULLINGHAM

TOFT & KINGSTON (Goods)

D
Oakley Jc.
BEDFORD
North Jc.
Loco. Shed
Kempston Road Jc.
KEMPSTON & ELSTOW HA.
KEMPSTON HARDWICK HALT
WOOTTON BROADMEAD HALT
WOOTTON PILLINGE HALT
MILLBROOK
BLUNHAM
WILLINGTON
St. JOHN'S
Level Crossing
CARDINGTON
SANDY
GAMLINGAY
POTTON
OLD NORTH ROAD
LORD'S BRIDGE
SHELFORD
HARSTON
SHEPRETH
FOXTON
Shepreth Branch Jc.
PAMPISFORD
LINTON
BARTLOW
GREAT CHESTERFORD
ASHDON HALT
HAVERHILL
STURMER
STOKE
BIRDBROOK
C. Valley
YELDHAM
CAVENDISH
CLARE
C.V.

SOUTHILL
BIGGLESWADE
MELDRETH & MELBOURN
WHITTLESFORD

Ampthill Tun.
AMPTHILL
SHEFFORD
HENLOW
ARLESEY
THREE COUNTIES
ROYSTON
ASHWELL & MORDEN
SAFFRON WALDEN
SIBLE & CASTLE HEDINGHAM
HALSTEAD

E
FLITWICK
HARLINGTON
BALDOCK
LETCHWORTH
NEWPORT
AUDLEY END
THAXTED
Cutler's Green Halt

Mid. Goods
HITCHIN
Loco. Shed
STEVENAGE
BUNTINGFORD
WESTMILL
HENHAM HALT
ELSENHAM
Summit
SIBLEY'S

LEAGRAVE
G.N. Goods
LUTON
DUNSTABLE
Langley Watertroughs
Langley Jc.
BRAUGHING
STANDON
STANSTED
EASTON LODGE
DUNMOW
RAYNE
BRAINTREE & BOCKING

KNEBWORTH
BISHOP'S STORTFORD
TAKELEY
FELSTED
CRESSING
WHITE NOTLEY

F
LUTON HOO
CHILTERN GREEN
WHEAT HAMPSTEAD
WELWYN
Welwyn N. Tun.
Welwyn S. Tun.
Welwyn Viaduct
WIDFORD
HADHAM
SAWBRIDGEWORTH

HARPENDEN
Harpenden Jc.
REDBOURN
BEAUMONTS HALT
AYOT
WELWYN GDN. CITY HALT
HERTFORD
St. MARGARETS
HERTINGFORDBURY
COLE GREEN
WARE
MARDOCK
HARLOW
BURNT MILL
HATFIELD PEVEREL

HEMEL HEMPSTEAD
GODWIN'S HALT
St. ALBANS
Loco. Shed
HATFIELD
NAST HYDE HALT
SMALLFORD
HILL END
Ponsbourne Tun.
RYE HOUSE
ROYDON
Broxbourne Jc.
BROXBOURNE & HODDESDON
CHELMSFORD

G
BOXMOOR & HEMEL HEMPSTEAD
HEATH PARK HALT
PARK STREET & FROGMORE
NAPSBURY
POTTERS BAR
CUFFLEY & GOFFS OAK
CHESHUNT
Loco. Shed
THEOBALD'S GROVE
WALTHAM CROSS & ABBEY
NORTHWEALD
BLAKE HALL
ONGAR
INGATESTONE

KINGS LANGLEY & ABBOTS LANGLEY
BRICKET WOOD
RADLETT
Potters Bar Tun.
CREWS HILL
THEYDON BOIS
SHENFIELD & HUTTON
Loco. Shed
BILLERICAY
WOODHAM FERRERS

Watford Tun.
CALLOWLAND
Hadley N. Tun.
Hadley S. Tun.
HIGH BARNET
HADLEY WOOD
GORDON HILL
FORTY HILL
ENFIELD LOCK
CHIGWELL LANE
LOUGHTON
BATTLESBRIDGE

CHORLEY WOOD & CHENIES
High St.
CROXLEY GRN.
Loco. Shed
WATFORD JUNC.
ELSTREE
Elstree Tun.
NEW BARNET
OAKLEIGH PARK
TOTTERIDGE
ENFIELD TOWN
BUSH HILL PARK
BRIMSDOWN
CHURCHBURY
PONDERS END

HUNTINGDON
CAMBRIDGE
BEDFORD
HERTFORD
ESSEX

Five

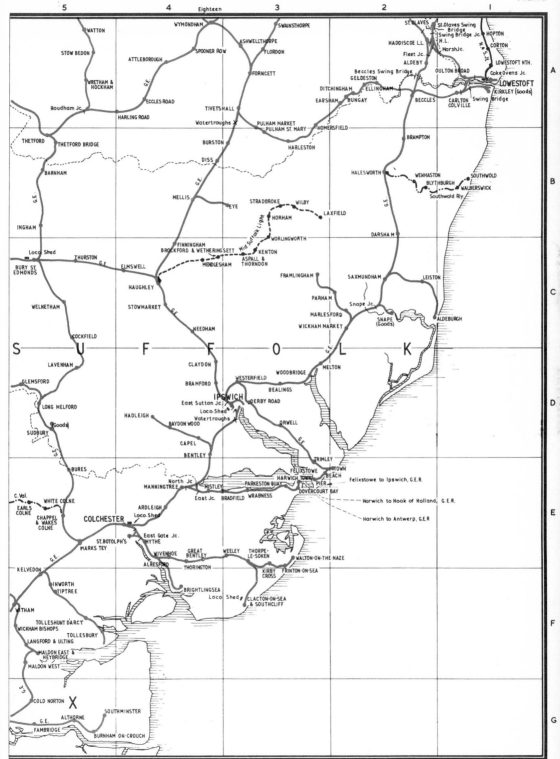

WATTON

STOW BEDON

WRETHAM &
HOCKHAM

WYMONDHAM

SWAINSTHORPE

St.OLAVES
St.Olaves Swing
Bridge
Swing Bridge Jc.
H.L.
Marsh Jc.
HOPTON

CORTON

LOWESTOFT NTH.
Coke Ovens Jc.

ATTLEBOROUGH

SPOONER ROW

ASHWELLTHORPE

FLORDON

FORNCETT

HADDISCOE L.L.

Fleet Jc.
ALDEBY

Beccles Swing Bridge
GELDESTON

OULTON BROAD

Roudham Jc.

HARLING ROAD

ECCLES ROAD

TIVETSHALL

Watertroughs

PULHAM MARKET
PULHAM St.MARY

HOMERSFIELD

DITCHINGHAM   ELLINGHAM

EARSHAM   BUNGAY

BECCLES

CARLTON
COLVILLE

LOWESTOFT

KIRKLEY (Goods)
Swing Bridge

THETFORD

THETFORD BRIDGE

BARNHAM

BURSTON

DISS

HARLESTON

BRAMPTON

A

INGHAM

MELLIS

EYE

STRADBROKE   WILBY

HORHAM   LAXFIELD

Mid Suffolk Light

WORLINGWORTH

HALESWORTH

WENHASTON
BLYTHBURGH
Southwold Rly.

SOUTHWOLD
WALBERSWICK

B

Loco Shed

THURSTON

BURY St.
EDMUNDS

WELNETHAM

ELMSWELL

HAUGHLEY

STOWMARKET

FINNINGHAM
BROCKFORD & WETHERINGSETT
MENDLESHAM

KENTON

ASPALL &
THORNDON

FRAMLINGHAM

PARHAM

MARLESFORD

WICKHAM MARKET

DARSHAM

SAXMUNDHAM

Snape Jc.

SNAPE
(Goods)

LEISTON

ALDEBURGH

C

COCKFIELD

NEEDHAM

S   U   F   F   O   L   K

LAVENHAM

GLEMSFORD

LONG MELFORD

SUDBURY

(Goods)

HADLEIGH

RAYDON WOOD

CAPEL

BENTLEY

CLAYDON

BRAMFORD

IPSWICH

East Sutton Jc.
Loco.Shed
Watertroughs

WESTERFIELD

DERBY ROAD

ORWELL

WOODBRIDGE

BEALINGS

MELTON

D

BURES

North Jc.
MANNINGTREE

East Jc.   BRADFIELD

TRIMLEY

FELIXSTOWE
TOWN
Harwich Town   BEACH
PIER
DOVERCOURT BAY

Felixstowe to Ipswich, G.E.R.

C.Val.
EARLS
COLNE

WHITE COLNE

CHAPPEL
& WAKES
COLNE

COLCHESTER

ARDLEIGH
Loco.Shed

MISTLEY

Parkeston Quay

WRABNESS

Harwich to Hook of Holland, G.E.R.

Harwich to Antwerp, G.E.R

E

KELVEDON

St.BOTOLPH'S
MARKS TEY

East Gate Jc.
HYTHE

WIVENHOE

ALRESFORD

GREAT
BENTLEY

THORINGTON

WEELEY

THORPE-
LE-SOKEN

KIRBY
CROSS   FRINTON-ON-SEA

WALTON-ON-THE-NAZE

WITHAM

INWORTH
TIPTREE

BRIGHTLINGSEA

Loco Shed

CLACTON-ON-SEA
& SOUTHCLIFF

TOLLESHUNT D'ARCY
WICKHAM BISHOPS
LANGFORD & ULTING
TOLLESBURY

MALDON EAST &
HEYBRIDGE
MALDON WEST

F

COLD NORTON

X

ALTHORNE   SOUTHMINSTER

FAMBRIDGE   BURNHAM ON-CROUCH

G

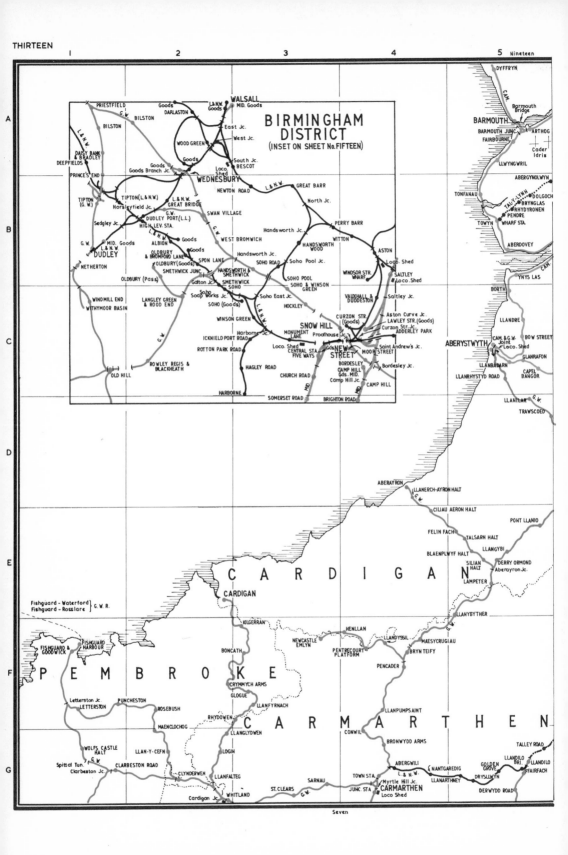

A

B

C

D

E

F

G

BIRMINGHAM DISTRICT
(INSET ON SHEET No. FIFTEEN)

PRIESTFIELD
BILSTON
G.W.
Goods
DARLASTON
L&N.W.
Goods
WALSALL
MID. Goods
BILSTON
L.N.W.
DAISY BANK & BRADLEY
DEEPFIELDS
PRINCE'S END
WOOD GREEN
East Jc.
West Jc.
South Jc.
BESCOT
Loco. Shed
Goods
Goods Branch Jc.
Goods
WEDNESBURY
NEWTON ROAD
GREAT BARR
L.&N.W.
TIPTON (G.W.)
Horsleyfield Jc.
Tipton (L.&N.W.)
L.&N.W.
GREAT BRIDGE
G.W.
DUDLEY PORT (L.L.)
HIGH LEV. STA.
Sedgley Jc.
North Jc.
SWAN VILLAGE
PERRY BARR
G.W.
MID. Goods
L.&N.W.
DUDLEY
NETHERTON
ALBION
OLDBURY & BROMFORD LANE
OLDBURY (Goods)
SMETHWICK JUNC.
Goods
Goods
WEST BROMWICH
Handsworth Jc.
SPON LANE
HANDSWORTH & SMETHWICK
WITTON
Handsworth Jc.
HANDSWORTH WOOD
ASTON
Loco. Shed
OLDBURY (Pass)
Galton Jc.
SMETHWICK SOHO
SOHO ROAD
Soho Pool Jc.
WINDSOR STR. WHARF
SALTLEY & Loco. Shed
WINDMILL END
WITHYMOOR BASIN
LANGLEY GREEN & ROOD END
Soho Jc.
Soap Works Jc.
SOHO (Goods)
Soho East Jc.
SOHO POOL
SOHO & WINSON GREEN
VAUXHALL & DUDDESTON
Saltley Jc.
Aston Curve Jc.
LAWLEY STR. (Goods)
Curzon Str. Jc.
ADDERLEY PARK
HOCKLEY
CURZON STR. (Goods)
G.W.
WINSON GREEN
Harborne Jc.
MONUMENT LANE
SNOW HILL
Proofhouse Jc.
ICKNIELD PORT ROAD
ROTTON PARK ROAD
Loco. Shed
CENTRAL STA. FIVE WAYS
Gds.
NEW STREET
MOOR STREET
Saint Andrew's Jc.
ABERYSTWYTH
OLD HILL
ROWLEY REGIS & BLACKHEATH
HAGLEY ROAD
L.N.W.
CHURCH ROAD
BORDESLEY
CAMP HILL Gds. MID.
Camp Hill Jc.
Bordesley Jc.
CAMP HILL
HARBORNE
SOMERSET ROAD
BRIGHTON ROAD
MID.

DYFFRYN
CAM.
Barmouth Bridge
BARMOUTH
BARMOUTH JUNC.
FAIRBOURNE
ARTHOG
Cader Idris
LLWYNGWRIL
ABERGYNOLWYN
TAL-Y-LLYN
TONFANAU
DOLGOCH
BRYNGLAS
RHYDYRONEN
PENDRE
TOWYN
WHARF STA.
ABERDOVEY
CAM.
YNYS LAS
BORTH
LLANDRE
BOW STREET
CAM. & G.W. Joint
Loco. Shed
GLANRAFON
LLANBADARN
LLANRHYSTYD ROAD
CAPEL BANGOR
LLANILAR
G.W.
TRAWSCOED

ABERAYRON
LLANERCH-AYRON HALT
G.W.
CILIAU AERON HALT
PONT LLANIO
FELIN FACH
TALSARN HALT
BLAENPLWYF HALT
LLANGYBI
SILIAN HALT
DERRY ORMOND
Aberayron Jc.
LAMPETER

CARDIGAN

CARDIGAN
LLANYBYTHER
Fishguard - Waterford
Fishguard - Rosslare
G.W.R.
KILGERRAN
HENLLAN
LLANDYSSIL
MAESYCRUGIAU
NEWCASTLE EMLYN
PENTRECOURT PLATFORM
BRYN TEIFY
FISHGUARD & GOODWICK
FISHGUARD HARBOUR
BONCATH
PENCADER

PEMBROKE

CRYMMYCH ARMS
GLOGUE
Letterston Jc.
LETTERSTON
PUNCHESTON
ROSEBUSH
RHYDOWEN
LLANFYRNACH
LLANPUMPSAINT
TALLEY ROAD
MAENCLOCHOG
LLANGLYDWEN
CONWIL
BRONWYDD ARMS

CARMARTHEN

WOLFS CASTLE HALT
G.W.
LLAN-Y-CEFN
LOGIN
ABERGWILI
NANTGAREDIG
GOLDEN GROVE
LLANDILO BRI.
LLANDILO
FFAIRFACH
Spittal Tun.
Clarbeston Jc.
CLARBESTON ROAD
CLYNDERWEN
LLANFALTEG
SARNAU
TOWN STA.
L.&N.W.
Myrtle Hill Jc.
DRYSLLWYN
LLANARTHNEY
DERWYDD ROAD
WHITLAND
Cardigan Jc.
ST. CLEARS
G.W.
JUNC. STA.
CARMARTHEN
Loco. Shed

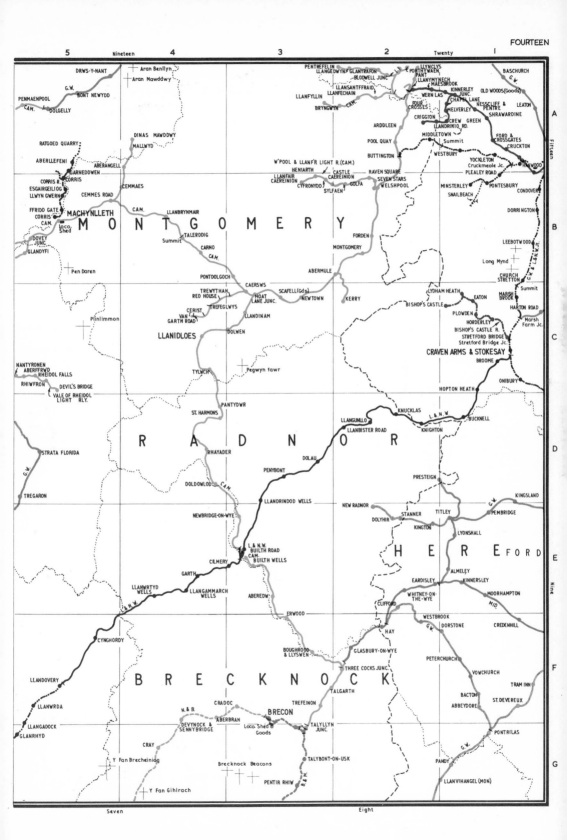

1 Twenty 2 Twenty-one 3 4 5

DERBYs

CHESHIRE

STAFFORD

SHROPSHIRE

(SEE SHEET NO. FORTY FIVE)

MACCLESFIELD

CREWE

STOKE

BURTON-ON-TRENT

BURTON-ON-TRENT
DALLOW LANE WHARF
(SEE INSET)

SHREWSBURY

STAFFORD

WOLVERHAMPTON

(SEE INSET ON
SHEET NO. THIRTEEN)

BIRMINGHAM

Nine

5 Twenty one 4 3 Twenty two 2 1

SHEFFIELD
Tinsley Jc.
VICTORIA
CITY (Gds)
QUEENS RD.(Gds)
HEELEY
BEAUCHIEF
& TOTLEY
DORE & TOTLEY
Dore S. Jc.
Bradway Tun.
DRONFIELD
Totley Tun.
GRINDLEFORD
HIRE
Broomhouse Tun.
SHEEPBRIDGE
CHESTERFIELD
CEN.
MARKET PLACE
BRAMPTON
(Goods)
GRASSMOOR
ROWSLEY
HASLAND (Goods)
HEATH
DARLEY DALE
CLAY CROSS
Goods
MATLOCK
High Tor Tuns.
MATLOCK BATH
STEEPLE
HOUSE
Gds.
Gds.
WIRKS-
WORTH
WHATSTANDWELL
West Jc.
AMBERGATE
South Jc.
IDRIDGEHAY
SHOTTLE
HAZELWOOD
DUFFIELD
LITTLE EATON
Little Eaton Jc.
BREADSALL
DERBY (FRIARGATE)
MICKLEOVER
DERBY
L.N.W. Gds.
PEARTREE &
NORMANTON
ETWALL
EGGINTON (N.S.& G.N. Jt.)
West Jc.
East Jc.
Stenson Jc.
Willington Jc.
REPTON & WILLINGTON
MELBOURNE

TUNNE
DARNALL
TREETON
THURCROFT (Gds)
TREETON
Southern Jc.
Treeton Jc.
G.C.H & B & MID. Jt.
DINNINGTON
LAUGHTON (S. YORKS. Jt.)
RANSKILL
KILLAMARSH
UPPERTHORPE
KILLA.
Branclffe Jc.
SHIREOAKS
ECKINGTON
& RENISHAW
SPINKHILL
STAVELEY
TOWN
CLOWN
WHITWELL
CRESWELL &
WELBECK
ELMTON &
CRESWELL
SHIREBROOK
SCARCLIFFE
WARSOP

NOTT-
ING-
HAM

LINCOLN

GAINSBOROUGH (G.C.)
Pye Wipe Jc.
G.N. Pass
Boultham Jc.
Level Crossing
STURTON
LEA
STOW PARK
LEVERTON
RETFORD
Clarborough Jc.
COTTAM
TORKSEY
Sykes Jc.
LANGWORTH
REEPHAM
SAXILBY
SKELLINGTHORPE
DODDINGTON &
HARBY
HYKEHAM
THORPE-ON-
THE-HILL
HARMSTON
NAVENBY
LEADENHAM

LINCOLN

CLAYPOLE
CAYTHORPE
ANCASTER
SLEAFORD
RAUCEBY
BARKSTON
HOUGHAM
HONINGTON
GRANTHAM

RUTLAND

NORTHAMPTON

LEICESTER

NUNEATON

1   2   Twenty two   3   4   5

A

MARKET RASEN
FOTHERBY HALT
SALTFLEETBY
WICKENBY
LOUTH   Loco. Shed
GRIMOLDBY
THEDDLETHORPE
HALLINGTON
SOUTH WILLINGHAM & HAINTON
WITHCALL
SNELLAND
LEGBOURNE ROAD
MABLETHORPE
EAST BARKWITH
DONINGTON-ON-BAIN
G.N.
WRAGBY
AUTHORPE
ABY
SUTTON-ON-SEA
LANGWORTH
G.N.
KINGTHORPE
ALFORD
MUMBY ROAD
REEPHAM
FIVE MILE HOUSE
WASHINGBORO
WILLOUGHBY

L I N C O L N

B

BRANSTON & HEIGHINGTON
BARDNEY
HORNCASTLE
POTTER HANWORTH
SOUTHREY
SPILSBY
BURGH
STIXWOULD
HALTON HOLGATE
FIRSBY
NOCTON & DUNSTON
WOODHALL SPA
Firsby S. Jc.
SEACROFT
SKEGNESS
BLANKNEY & METHERINGHAM
WOODHALL JUNC.
LITTLE STEEPING
HAVENHOUSE
SCOPWICK & TIMBERLAND
CONINGSBY
Bellwater Jc.
THORPE CULVERT
WAINFLEET
DIGBY
TATTERSHALL
TUMBY WOODSIDE
MIDVILLE
DOGDYKE
NEW BOLINGBROKE
STICKNEY
EAST VILLE
RUSKINGTON
G.N.
G.N.
OLD LEAKE

C

North Jc.
LANGRICK
West Jc.   SLEAFORD
SIBSEY
ANCASTER   South Jc.
HECKINGTON   HUBBERT'S BRIDGE   Loco Shed   BOSTON
RAUCEBY   East Jc.
G.N.   SWINESHEAD   Sleaford Jc.
ASWARBY & SEDRINGHAM
HELPRINGHAM
THE WASH
HUNTANSTON
BILLINGBOROUGH & HORBLING
KIRTON
G.E. DOCKING
HEACHAM
SEDGEFORD

D

G.N. & G.E. JT.
DONINGTON ROAD
ALGARKIRK & SUTTERTON
SNETTISHAM
G.H.
GOSBERTON
DERSINGHAM
RIPPINGALE
SURFLEET
WOLFERTON
CORBY
MORTON ROAD
PINCHBECK
HILLINGTON
M. & G.N. JT.
WHAPLODE
HOLBEACH
FLEET
NORTH WOOTTON
GRIMSTON ROAD
South Jc.   Mid. Goods
SPALDING
MOULTON
M. & G.N. Jt.
GEDNEY
LONG SUTTON
WESTON
SUTTON BRIDGE
Loco Shed   GAYTON ROAD
KING'S LYNN   MIDDLETON

E

COUNTER DRAIN
NORTH DROVE
Cuckoo Jc.
Welland Bank Jc.
Sutton Bridge Jc.
TERRINGTON
East Jc.   TWENTY
WALPOLE   CLENCHWARTON
SOUTH LYNN
Little
Mid Bytham Jc.   BOURNE
West Jc.
HARDWICK ROAD (Goods)
EAST WINCH
CASTLE BYTHAM   LITTLE BYTHAM   THURLBY
LITTLEWORTH   COWBIT
TYDD
N

F

BRACEBORO SPA
ESSENDINE
G.N.
POSTLAND
FERRY
MIDDLE DROVE
MAGDALEN ROAD
NARBOROUGH
RYHALL
TALLINGTON
DEEPING ST. JAMES
WISBECH   WISBECH   EMNETH
SMEETH ROAD
STANFORD   PEAKIRK
FRENCH DROVE   ST. MARY
STOW
Mid.   UFFINGTON & BARNACK
Werrington Watertroughs   Level Crossing   MURROW
WISBECH
ELMBRIDGE
BARNACK   HELPSTON   Werrington Jc.   THORNEY   WRYDE
BOYCES BRI.
KETTON
WALTON   H. & G.N. Jct.
EYE GREEN, FOR CROWLAND   GUYHIRNE
OUTWELL BASIN   Upwell Tramway
OUTWELL VILLAGE
DOWNHAM
UFFORD BRIDGE   G.N.   Loco. Shed
New England Sidings
COLDHAM
DENVER
WANSFORD ROAD
Grassmoor Jc.   WHITEMOOR (Goods)   UPWELL
RYSTON   ABBEY
KINGSCLIFFE   CASTOR   Loco. Shed   PETERBOROUGH   WHITTLESEA
Loco. Shed   North Jc.   HILGAY   STOKE FERRY
NASSINGTON   Yarwell Jc.   L.N.W. & G.E. Jct.   WEST Jc.   MARCH
ORTON   G.E. FLETTON (Goods)   South Jc.   March S. Jc.
WATERVILLE   Fletton Jc.
ELTON   Longville Jc.   QUAKERS DROVE
STONEA
LONGVILLE   WEST FEN DROVE
YAXLEY & FARCET   JONES DROVE   BURNT HOUSE   WIMBLINGTON
LITTLEPORT

G

OUNDLE   G.N.   HOLME   BENWICK (Goods)   WHITE FEN
MANEA
ST. MARY'S
BARNWELL   RAMSEY   CHATTERIS
LAKENHEATH   BRANDON

C A M B R I D G E

BLACK BANK

Sixteen

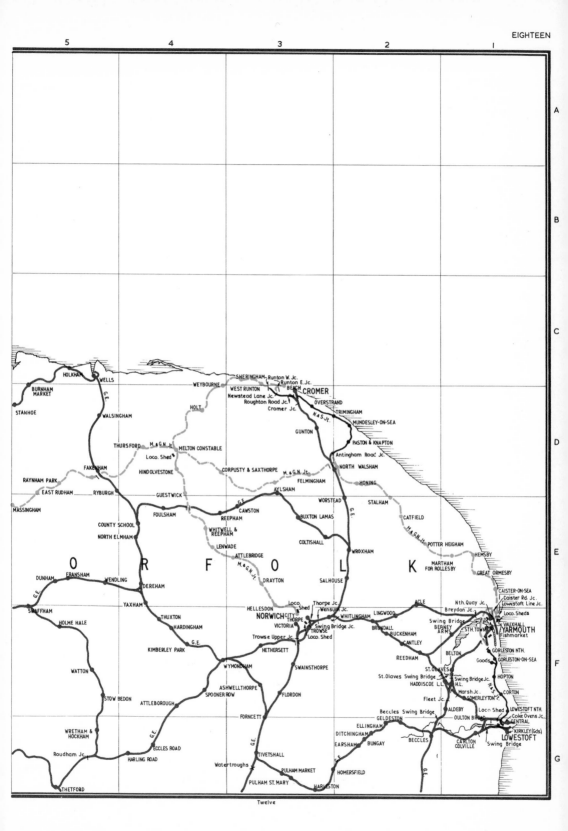

1 2 3 4 5

A

Inset

B

HOLYHEAD
Pier
Loco. Shed
VALLEY
L & N.W.
Holy Island
RHOSNEIGR

C

AMLWCH
RHOSGOCH
LLANERCHYMEDD

ANGLESEY

REDWHARF BAY & BENLLECH
LLANBEDR GOCH
PENTRAETH
LLANGWYLLOG
RHYD-Y-SAINT
LLANGEFNI
CEINT
RHOSNEIGR
TY CROES
HOLLAND ARMS
Britannia Tubular Bridge
LLANFAIR
Belmont Tun.
BODORGAN
Bodorgan Tuns.
L & N.W.
GAERWEN MENAI BR.
BANGOR
Bangor Tun.
Llandegai Tun.
ABER
Aber Watertroughs
PENMAENMAWR
LLANFAIRFECHAN
CONWAY
LLANDUDNO
DEGANWY
LLANDUDNO JUNC.
COLWYN BAY
Penmaenrhos Tun.
LLYSFAEN
MOCHDRE & PABO
OLD COLWYN
GLAN CONWAY
LLANDULAS
ABERGELE
Prestatyn Watertroughs
Pier
Foryd
FORYD
RHYL
PRESTATYN
RHUDDLAN ROAD
MELIDEN
DYSERTH
RHUDDLAN
ST. ASAPH
TREBORTH
FELIN HEN
TREGARTH
PORT DINORWIC
BETHESDA
TAL-Y-CAFN & EGLWYS BACH

D

GRIFFITHS CROSSING
PONT RUG
CARNARVON
PONTRHYTHALLT
CWM-Y-GLO
LLANRWST & TREFRIW
L.&N.W.
TREFNANT
BODFARI
DENBIGH
L & N.W.
LLANRHAIADR
RHEWL
RUTHIN
EYARTH
NANTCLWYD

E

TRYFAN JUNC.
WAENFAWR
LLANBERIS
Y Glydr
Moel Siabod
DINAS JUNC.
BETTWS GARMON
RHOS TRYFAN
BRYNGWYN
QUELLYN LAKE
SNOWDON MOUNTAIN RLY.
SNOWDON
BETTWS-Y-COED
LLANWNDA
GROESLON
PENYGROES
NORTH WALES N.G.R.
NANTLE
PONT-Y-PANT
DOLWYDDELEN
ROMAN BRIDGE
DERWEN
DENBIGH

CARNARVON

PANT GLAS
BEDGELERT
Festiniog Tun.
GWYDDELWERN
CORWEN
CYNWYD
BRYNKIR
YNYS
BLAENAU FESTINIOG
L.&N.W.
DUFFWS
G.W.
DINAS
TAN-Y-GRISIAU
CROESOR R.
MANOD
FEST.
FESTINIOG
LLANGYBI
CHWILOG
WERN (Goods)
PORTMADOC
MINFFORDD
TAN-Y-BWLCH
DUALLT
FESTINIOG RLY.
FEST.
PENRHYNDEUDRAETH
MAENTWROG ROAD
ARENIG
G.W.
FRONGOCH
LLANDRILLO
G.W.
AFONWEN
CRICCIETH
CAM.
TALSARNAU
CWM PRYSOR
TRAWSFYNYDD
BALA
BALA JUNC.
LLANDDERFEL
Llandderfel Tun.
PWLLHELI
ABERERCH

F

HARLECH
CAM.
Bala Lake

MERIONETHSHIRE

LLANUWCHLLYN
G.W.
LLANGYNOG
TANAT VAL.
PENYBONTFAWR
PEDAIR-FFORDD

G

LLANBEDR & PENSARN
Rhobell fawr
DYFFRYN
DRWS-Y-NANT
Aran Benllyn
Aran Mawddwy

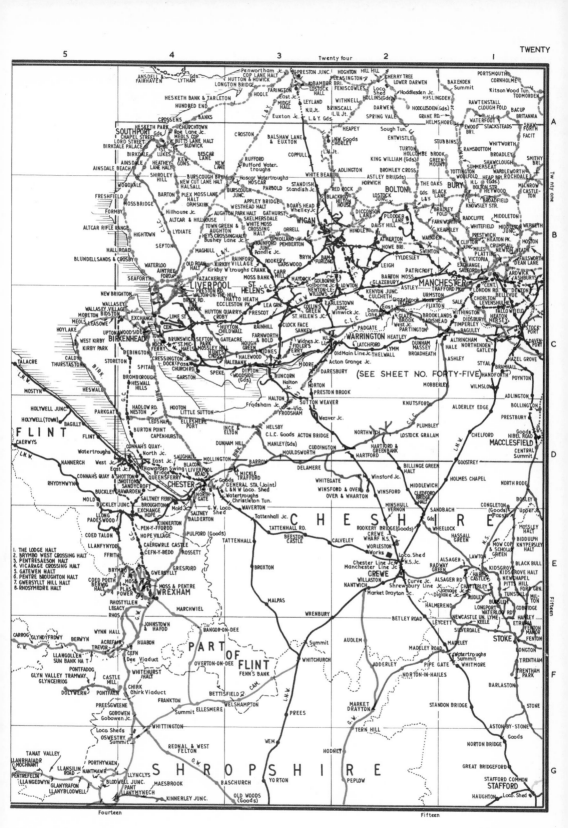

Y O R K S

LEEDS

STALYBRIDGE

YORK

HARROGATE

BRADFORD

HALIFAX

HUDDERSFIELD

OLDHAM

BARNSLEY

DONCASTER

SHEFFIELD

WAKEFIELD

ROTHERHAM

SEE SHEET NO. FORTY TWO

Askrigg, Redmire, Wensley, Leyburn, Constable Burton, Finghall Lane, Jervaulx, Crakehall, Ainderby, Scruton, Northallerton, Cordio Jcs., Kirby Moorside, Nawton, Aysgarth, Leeming Bar, Newby Wiske, Otterington, Severus Jc., Poppleton Jc., Bootham Jc., Burton Lane Jc., Helmsley, Layerthorpe, Foss Islands (Goods), Nunnington, Hovingham Spa, Slingsby, Flaxton, Strensall, Warthill, Haxby, Earswick, Murton Lane, Holtby, Wheldrake, Cottingwith, Escrick, Thorganby, Skipwith & N. Duffield, Riccall, Cawood, Church Fenton, Bolton Percy, Ulleskelf, Stutton (Goods), Tadcaster, Newton Kyme, Thorp Arch, Wetherby, Collingham Bridge, Bardsey, Copmanthorpe, Naburn, Swing Bridge, Dunnington Halt, Dunnington (for Kexby), Elvington, Pannal, Spofforth, Wetherby W. Jc., Wetherby E. Jc., Chaloner's Whin Jc., Poppleton Jc., Severus Jc., Holgate Bridge Jc.

(many further station and junction names on map)

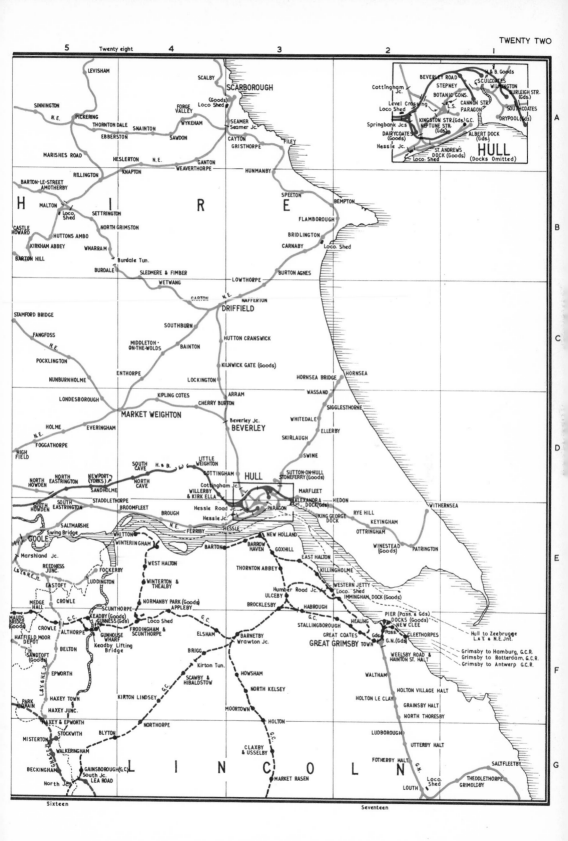

5   Twenty eight   4   3   2   1

Hull inset (top right):

BEVERLEY ROAD
STEPNEY
Cottingham Jc.
BOTANIC GDNS.
Level Crossing
Loco Shed
H.& B. Goods
SCULCOATES
WILMINGTON
BURLEIGH STR. (Gds)
SOUTHCOATES
CANNON STR
PARAGON
L.S.
DRYPOOL (Gds)
KINGSTON STR (Gds) G.C.
NEPTUNE STR. (Gds)
Springbank Jcs
DAIRYCOATES (Goods)
Hessle Jc.
ST. ANDREWS
DOCK (Goods)
Loco. Shed
ALBERT DOCK (Gds)
HULL (Docks Omitted)

LEVISHAM
SCALBY
SCARBOROUGH
(Goods)
Loco Shed

SINNINGTON
N.E.
PICKERING
FORGE VALLEY
SEAMER
Seamer Jc.
THORNTON DALE
SNAINTON
WYKEHAM
EBBERSTON
SAWDON
CAYTON
GRISTHORPE
FILEY
MARISHES ROAD
HESLERTON
N.E.
GANTON
WEAVERTHORPE
HUNMANBY
RILLINGTON
KNAPTON

BARTON-LE-STREET
AMOTHERBY
SPEETON
BEMPTON

H   I   R   E

MALTON
Loco. Shed
SETTRINGTON
FLAMBOROUGH
CASTLE HOWARD
HUTTONS AMBO
NORTH GRIMSTON
BRIDLINGTON
CARNABY
Loco. Shed
KIRKHAM ABBEY
WHARRAM
BARTON HILL
BURDALE Tun.
SLEDMERE & FIMBER
BURTON AGNES
BURDALE
WETWANG
LOWTHORPE
GARTON
N.E.
NAFFERTON
STAMFORD BRIDGE
DRIFFIELD
FANGFOSS
SOUTHBURN
HUTTON CRANSWICK
N.E.
MIDDLETON-ON-THE-WOLDS
BAINTON
POCKLINGTON
KILNWICK GATE (Goods)
ENTHORPE
NUNBURNHOLME
LOCKINGTON
HORNSEA BRIDGE
HORNSEA
LONDESBOROUGH
KIPLING COTES
ARRAM
WASSAND
HOLME
EVERINGHAM
CHERRY BURTON
SIGGLESTHORNE
MARKET WEIGHTON
Beverley Jc.
WHITEDALE
ELLERBY
FOGGATHORPE
N.E.
BEVERLEY
SKIRLAUGH
HIGH FIELD
LITTLE WEIGHTON
SWINE
NORTH HOWDEN
SOUTH CAVE
H.& B.
Cottingham
HULL
NEWPORT (YORKS)
NORTH CAVE
WILLERBY & KIRK ELLA
Cottingham Jc.
SUTTON-ON-HULL
STONEFERRY (Goods)
NORTH EASTRINGTON
SANDHOLME
STADDLETHORPE
MARFLEET
SOUTH HOWDEN
SOUTH EASTRINGTON
BROOMFLEET
Hessle Road Jc.
ALEXANDRA DOCK (Gds)
HEDON
BROUGH
PARAGON
KING GEORGE DOCK
RYE HILL
SALTMARSHE
N.E.
Hessle Jc.
FERRIBY
HESSLE
KEYINGHAM
WITHERNSEA
Swing Bridge
GOOLE
WHITTON
BARTON
NEW HOLLAND
OTTRINGHAM
Marshland Jc.
WINTERINGHAM
BARROW HAVEN
GOXHILL
WINESTEAD (Goods)
PATRINGTON
REEDNESS JUNC.
FOCKERBY
WEST HALTON
EAST HALTON
L. & N.E. Jt.
EASTOFT
LUDDINGTON
KILLINGHOLME
CROWLE
WINTERTON & THEALBY
THORNTON ABBEY
WESTERN JETTY
Loco. Shed
IMMINGHAM DOCK (Goods)
MEDGE HALL
NORMANBY PARK (Goods)
APPLEBY
Humber Road Jc.
SCUNTHORPE
BROCKLESBY
PIER (Pass. & Gds)
DOCKS (Goods)
NEW CLEE
MAUDS BRIDGE (Goods)
CROWLE
KEADBY (Goods)
KEADBY (Guinness) (Gds)
Loco Shed
FRODINGHAM & SCUNTHORPE
G.C.
ULCEBY
HABROUGH
STALLINGBOROUGH
HEALING
Pass.
CLEETHORPES
HATFIELD MOOR DEPOT
ALTHORPE
GUNHOUSE WHARF
Keadby Lifting Bridge
ELSHAM
BARNETBY
Wrawton Jc.
GREAT COATES
Gds.
G.N. (Gds)
BELTON
BRIGG
GREAT GRIMSBY TOWN
SANDTOFT (Goods)
Kirton Tun.
HOWSHAM
WEELSBY ROAD & HAINTON ST. HALT
EPWORTH
SCAWBY & HIBALDSTOW
NORTH KELSEY
WALTHAM
PARK DRAIN
HAXEY TOWN
KIRTON LINDSEY
MOORTOWN
HOLTON VILLAGE HALT
HAXEY JUNC.
HOLTON LE CLAY
GRAINSBY HALT
HAXEY & EPWORTH
STOCKWITH
NORTHORPE
HOLTON
NORTH THORESBY
MISTERTON
BLYTON
LUDBOROUGH
WALKERINGHAM
CLAXBY & USSELBY
UTTERBY HALT
BECKINGHAM
GAINSBOROUGH (G.C.)
South Jc.
LEA ROAD
North Jc.
MARKET RASEN
FOTHERBY HALT
Loco. Shed
SALTFLEETBY
THEDDLETHORPE
GRIMOLDBY
LOUTH

L   I   N   C   O   L   N

Hull to Zeebrugge L.& Y. & N.E.Jnt.
Grimsby to Hamburg, G.C.R.
Grimsby to Rotterdam, G.C.R.
Grimsby to Antwerp, G.C.R.

1   2   3   4   5

ISLE OF MAN

SULBY BRIDGE
LEZAYRE
BALLAUGH
SULBY GLEN
RAMSEY
I. of Man S. P. Co. Ltd.

KIRK MICHAEL

Manx Electric Tramway

SNAE FELL

ST. GERMAINS

PEEL · PEEL ROAD
LAXEY
ST. JOHN'S
WATERFALL
I. of M. Rly.
CROSBY
UNION MILLS
FOXDALE
DOUGLAS
MID. R.   To Heysham
PORT SODERICK
SANTON
L. of Man Steam Packet Co., Ltd.
BALLABEG
COLBY
BALLASALLA
PORT ERIN · PORT ST. MARY
CASTLETOWN

AMLWCH
L.N.W.
RHOSGOCH

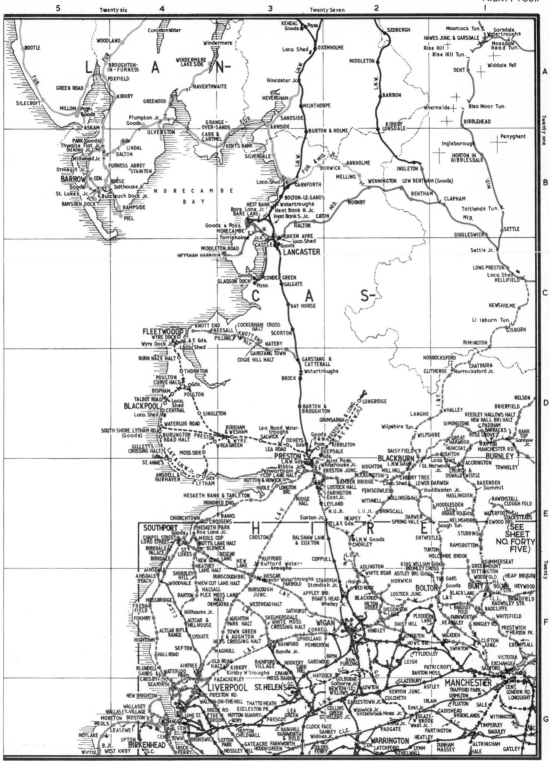

1　　　　2　　　　3　　Twenty nine　　4　　　　5

A

Tunnel
PINMORE

PINWHERRY

A Y R

BARRHILL

Summit

K I R K C U D

Larne & Stranraer Steamship Comm.

B

To Larne

GLENWHILLY

Loch Skerrow

W I G T O W N

NEWTON-
STEWART

Cairnsmore

Loch
Ryan

NEW LUCE

PALNURE

GATEHOUSE
OF FLEET

Summit

Harbour

Loco. Shed
STRANRAER

CASTLE
KENNEDY

PORTPATRICK & WIGTOWNSHIRE JOINT

KIRKCOWAN

CREETOWN

C

COLFIN

DUNRAGIT
Challoch Jc.

GLENLUCE

WIGTOWN

PORTPATRICK

KIRKINNER

WHAUPHILL

SORBIE

MILLISLE

GARLIESTON

WHITHORN

D

E

F

ISLE OF MAN

G

SULBY
BRIDGE

LEZAYRE

BALLAUGH

SULBY
GLEN

RAMSEY

I. of M.

KIRK MICHAEL

Twenty three

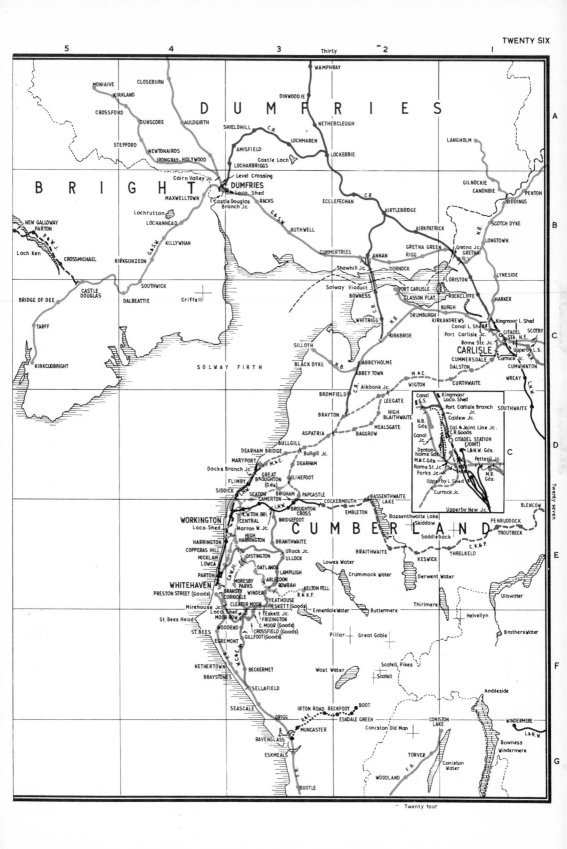

1   Thirty one   2   3   4   5

A

STEELE ROAD
KIELDER
FONTBURN
EWESLEY
WIDDRINGTON
LONG WITTON
PLASHETTS
N.B.
FALSTONE
LONGHIRST
NEWCASTLETON
THORNEYBURN
WOODBURN
SCOTSGAP
PEGSWOOD
ASHINGTON
TARSET
BELLINGHAM
KNOWESGATE
MIDDLETON
MORPETH
NORTH SEATON
HEPSCOTT
N.B.
N.E.
KERSHOPE FOOT
ANGERTON
MELDON
CHOPPINGTON
BEDLINGTON
BEBSIDE

NORTHUMBERLAND
STANNINGTON
PLESSEY

B

WARK
BARRASFORD
PONTELAND
N.E.
CRAMLINGTON
ANNITSFORD
CALLERTON
CHOLLERTON
HUMSHAUGH
DARRAS HALL
KILLINGWORTH
COXLODGE
FOREST HALL
FOURSTONES
WALL
KENTON
WEST GOSFORTH
BENTON
GILSLAND
GREENHEAD
BARDON MILL
HAYDON BRIDGE
N.E.
SOUTH GOSFORTH
HEDDON-ON-THE-WALL
NEWBURN
W. JESMOND
JESMOND
LOW ROW
HALTWHISTLE
NORTH WYLAM
LEMINGTON
SCOTSWOOD
CENTRAL
NAWORTH
FEATHERSTONE PARK
Haltwhistle Tun.
HEXHAM
PRUDHOE
WYLAM
RYTON
BRAMPTON TOWN
LANGLEY
ELRINGTON
Corbridge Tun.
BLAYDON
BRAMPTON JUNC.
COANWOOD
STAWARD
RIDING MILL
STOCKSFIELD
SWALWELL
BENSHAM
LOW FELL
AMBLEY
NEWCASTLE
ROWLANDS GILL

C

HOW MILL
ALLENDALE
HIGH WESTWOOD
UNTZ GREEN
LAMESLEY
BIRTLEY
HEADS NOOK
WETHERAL
EBCHESTER
SHIELD ROW
BEAMISH
PELTON
COTEHILL
SLAGGYFORD
SHOTLEY BRIDGE
W. STANLEY (Gds.)
BLACKHILL
LEADGATE
CHESTER LE STREET
CONSETT
ANNFIELD PLAIN
KNITSLEY
PLAWSWORTH
ROWLEY
LANCHESTER
WITTON GILBERT

D

ARMATHWAITE
Armathwaite Tun.
ALSTON
WASKERLEY (Goods)
BURN HILL
DURHAM
Baron Wood Tuns.
PARKHEAD (Goods)
ALDIN GRANGE
CALTHWAITE
WEARHEAD
USHAW MOOR
Relly Mill Jc.
LAZONBY & KIRKOSWALD
EASTGATE
STANHOPE
TOW LAW
WATERHOUSES
BRANDON
Lazonby Tun.
ST. JOHN'S CHAPEL
WESTGATE-IN-WEARDALE
FROSTERLEY
BRANCEPETH
PLUMPTON
WOLSINGHAM
CROOK
WILLINGTON
CROXDALE
LITTLE SALKELD
HARPERLEY
SPENNYMOOR
LANGWATHBY
BEECHBURN
BYERS GREEN
HUNWICK
WITTON-LE-WEAR
WEAR VALLEY JUNC.
COUNDON
Waste Bank Tun.
WEAR VALLEY JUNC.
Culgaith Tun.
CULGAITH
ETHERLEY
Loco. Shed
PENRITH
NEW BIGGIN
BISHOP AUCKLAND
SHILDON
RedHills Jc.
Eamont Bri. Jc.
Eden Valley Jc.
CLIFTON
TEMPLE SOWERBY
BUTTERKNOWLE
EVENWOOD
WEST AUCKLAND
CLIBURN
KIRKBY THORE
COCKFIELD

DURHAM

E

CLIFTON & LOWTHER
LONG MARTON
MIDDLETON-IN-TEESDALE
MICKLETON
HEIGHINGTON
APPLEBY
ROMALDKIRK
WESTMORLAND
ORMSIDE
COTHERSTONE
WINSTON
GAINFORD
Merrybent Jc.
N.E.
WARCOP
LARTINGTON
BARNARD CASTLE
BROOMIELAW
Forcett Jc.
PIERCEBRIDGE

F

SHAP
Helm Tun.
BOWES
N.E.
SHAP SUMMIT
MUSGRAVE
FORCETT DEPOT
BARTON (Goods)
BARRAS
Stainmore Summit
CROSBY GARRETT
SMARDALE
Belah Viaduct
Loco. Shed
KIRKBY STEPHEN & RAVENSTONEDALE
KIRKBY STEPHEN
MOULTON
GAISGILL
RAVENSTONEDALE
Birkett Tun.
SCORTON
Loco. Shed
TEBAY
RICHMOND
CATTERICK BRIDGE
Dillicar Watertroughs
Wild Boar Fell
High Seat
STAVELEY
Blease Fell
Aisgill Summit
Great Shunner Fell
BURNESIDE
LOW GILL
GRAYRIGG
Baugh Fell
Shotlock Hill Tun.
Y O R K

G

KENDAL Gds.
Loco. Shed
OXENHOLME
SEDBERGH
HAWES JUNC. & GARSDALE
Moorcock Tun.
Mossdale Head Tun.
REDMIRE
WENSLEY
LEYBURN
CONSTABLE BURTON
Watertroughs
M.R.
ASKRIGG
SPENNITHORNE
FINGHALL LANE
CRAKEHALL
MIDDLETON
Rise Hill Tun.
HAWES
N.E.
AYSGARTH
JERVAULX
BEDALE

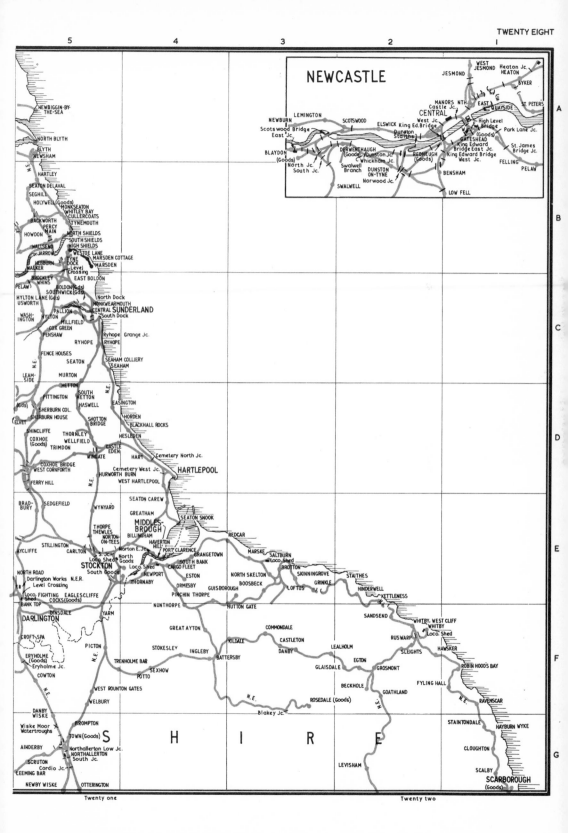

NEWCASTLE

WEST JESMOND
HEATON Jc.
HEATON
JESMOND
BYKER
MANORS NTH.
Castle Jc.
EAST
QUAYSIDE
ST. PETERS
CENTRAL
West Jc.
High Level
Bridge
LEMINGTON
SCOTSWOOD
ELSWICK King Ed.Bridge
Park Lane Jc.
NEWBURN
Scotswood Bridge
GATESHEAD
Dunston
Station
King Edward
Bridge East Jc.
ST. James
Bridge Jc.
Scotswood
East Jc.
West Jc.
DERWENTHAUGH
(Goods)
Dunston Jc.
REDHEUGH
(Goods)
King Edward Bridge
West Jc.
BLAYDON
(Goods)
North Jc.
South Jc.
Whickham Jc.
Swalwell
Branch
DUNSTON
ON-TYNE
FELLING
PELAW
BENSHAM
SWALWELL
Norwood Jc.
LOW FELL

NEWBIGGIN-BY-THE-SEA
NORTH BLYTH
BLYTH
NEWSHAM
HARTLEY
SEATON DELAVAL
SEGHILL
HOLYWELL(Goods)
MONKSEATON
WHITLEY BAY
CULLERCOATS
TYNEMOUTH
BACKWORTH
PERCY
MAIN
HOWDON
NORTH SHIELDS
SOUTH SHIELDS
HIGH SHIELDS
WALLSEND
JARROW
WESTOE LANE
TYNE
DOCK
MARSDEN COTTAGE
HEBBURN
(Level)
Crossing
MARSDEN
WALKER
BROCKLEY
WHINS
EAST BOLDON
PELAW
BOLDON(Gds)
North Dock
HYLTON LANE (Gds)
SOUTHWICK (Gds)
USWORTH
MONKWEARMOUTH
WASH-INGTON
PALLION
CENTRAL SUNDERLAND
South Dock
HYLTON
MILLFIELD
COX GREEN
PENSHAW
RYHOPE
Ryhope Grange Jc.
RYHOPE
FENCE HOUSES
SEAHAM COLLIERY
SEAHAM
SEATON
MURTON
LEAM-SIDE
HETTON
PITTINGTON
SOUTH
HETTON
HASWELL
EASINGTON
(Gds)
SHERBURN COL.
SHERBURN HOUSE
HORDEN
(ELVET)
SHOTTON
BRIDGE
BLACKHALL ROCKS
SHINCLIFFE
THORNLEY
WELLFIELD
HESLEDEN
COXHOE
(Goods) TRIMDON
CASTLE
EDEN
HART
Cemetery North Jc.
WINGATE
COXHOE BRIDGE
Cemetery West Jc.
HARTLEPOOL
WEST CORNFORTH
HURWORTH BURN
FERRY HILL
WEST HARTLEPOOL
BRAD-BURY
SEDGEFIELD
SEATON CAREW
WYNYARD
SEATON SNOOK
GREATHAM
MIDDLES-BROUGH
THORPE
THEWLES
NORTON-ON-TEES
BILLINGHAM
REDCAR
AYCLIFFE
STILLINGTON
CARLTON
Norton E. Jc.
HAVERTON
HILL
PORT CLARENCE
MARSKE
SALTBURN
Loco. Shed
S. Jc.
North
Goods
GRANGETOWN
SOUTH BANK
BROTTON
NORTH ROAD
STOCKTON
Loco. Shed
CARGO FLEET
NORTH SKELTON
SKINNINGROVE
STAITHES
Darlington Works N.E.R.
South Goods
NEWPORT
ESTON
BOOSBECK
GRINKLE
Level Crossing
THORNABY
ORMESBY
GUISBOROUGH
LOFTUS
LOCO. Shed
FIGHTING
EAGLESCLIFFE
PINCHIN THORPE
HINDERWELL
BANK TOP
COCKS(Goods)
KETTLENESS
DARLINGTON
DINSDALE
YARM
NUNTHORPE
HUTTON GATE
SANDSEND
CROFT SPA
GREAT AYTON
COMMONDALE
WHITBY, WEST CLIFF
WHITBY
Loco. Shed
PICTON
KILDALE
CASTLETON
RUSWARP
ERYHOLME
(Goods)
STOKESLEY
INGLEBY
DANBY
LEALHOLM
SLEIGHTS
HAWSKER
Eryholme Jc.
TRENHOLME BAR
BATTERSBY
EGTON
GROSMONT
COWTON
SEXHOW
GLAISDALE
ROBIN HOOD'S BAY
POTTO
BECKHOLE
GOATHLAND
FYLING HALL
WEST ROUNTON GATES
WELBURY
ROSEDALE (Goods)
RAVENSCAR
DANBY
WISKE
Blakey Jc.
Wiske Moor
Watertroughs
BROMPTON
STAINTONDALE
HAYBURN WYKE
TOWN(Goods)
S   H   I   R   E
AINDERBY
Northallerton Low Jc.
CLOUGHTON
SCRUTON
NORTHALLERTON
South Jc.
LEVISHAM
Cordio Jc.
LEEMING BAR
SCALBY
NEWBY WISKE
OTTERINGTON
SCARBOROUGH
(Goods)

1 2 3 Thirty Two 4 5

A

To INVERARY To ARROCHAR Ben Lomond ABERFOYLE DOUNE
LOCHGOILHEAD Summit ROWARDENNAN GARTMORE N.B. KIPPEN
CRARAE Loch Goil Loch Long PORT OF MENTEITH GARGUNNOCK BUCHLYVIE

CARRICK CASTLE WHISTLEFIELD Loch Lomond BALMAHA S T I R L
GARELOCHHEAD BALFRON I N G
ARDENTINNY SHANDON DRYMEN GARTNESS KILLEARN
KILMUN Gare Loch DUMBARTON ROW CALDARVAN DUMGOYNE Campsie Fells GARTSHORE (Goods)
BLAIRMORE HELENSBURGH (UPPER) JAMESTOWN BLANEFIELD STRATHBLANE (Pass.) KILSYTH (Gds)
ARDNADAM COVE HELENSBURGH Loco. Shed BALLOCH CAMPSIE GLEN LENNOXTOWN GAVELL
CRAIGENDORAN ALEXANDRIA MILTON OF CAMPSIE

ORMIDALE KIRN GOUROCK PORT MATILDA CATHCART STR. DALREOCH DUMBARTON MILNGAVIE TORRANCE KIRKINTILLOCH GARTSHORE (Goods)
DUNOON FORT MATILDA PRINCES PIER GREENOCK W. CARTSDYKE DUMBARTON EAST (Gds) BALMORE BARDOWIE
RAVENSCRAIG CARDROSS BRENTON DUMBUCK (Gds) BOWLING HILLFOOT Waterside
LYNEDOCH INCH GRN (Goods) KILPATRICK SINGER BEARSDEN LENZIE Campsie Bridgend Jc.
OVERTON CARTSDYKE PORT GLASGOW OLD KILPATRICK DALMUIR Milngavie Jc. SUMMERS TON BISHOPBRIGGS
UPPER PORT GLASGOW (Goods) LANGBANK KILBOWIE CLYDEBANK MARYHILL STEPPS RD.
INELLAN INVERKIP YOKER SCOTSTOUN HILL SPRINGBURN PK. GARNKIRK
KILMACOLM BISHOPTON SCOTSTOUN BUCHANAN ST. ROBROYSTON
HOUSTON PARTICK ST. ROLLOX W. BLAIRHILL
PORT BANNATYNE Blackstone RENFREW QUEEN ST. ST. ENOCH SHETTLESTON
BRIDGE OF WEIR PAISLEY ABERCORN CENTRAL BARGEDDIE
TIGHNABRUAICH BUTE N.JOHNSTONE LINWOOD GOVAN CARNTYNE MT. VERNON BROOMHO
KILBARCHAN IBROX CROOKSTON CATHCART PROVINHO
To TARBERT Etc. FIRTH OF CLYDE Hill of Stake MILLIKEN PARK JOHN STONE ELDERSLIE DYKEBAR CROSSMYLOOF RUTHERGLEN
POTTERHILL CAMBUSLANG KIRKHILL NEWTON
ROTHESAY LOCHWINNOCH HOWWOOD BARRHEAD CEN. NITSHILL MUIREND CAMYLE BLANTYRE HIGH BLANTYRE
LARGS LOCHSIDE CALDWELL NEILSTON THORNLIEBANKS GIFFNOCK CLARKSTON BUSBY BOTH L. Shed

KILCHATTAN BAY MILLPORT Pier KILBIRNIE BEITH G.&S.W. NETHERTON (Goods) WHITECRAIGS THORNTONHALL
FAIRLIE GLENGARNOCK BEITH (Joint) LUGTON POPLAWMOOR PATTERSON HAIRMYRES EAST KILBRIDE MEIKLE EARNOCK
WEST KILBRIDE BARRMILL Edst Jc. SEE SHEET NO. FORTY FOUR QUARTER
BRACKEN HILLS GIFFEN DUNLOP GLASSFORD
To CAMPBELTOWN DALRY GREE (Gds) L A
LOCHRANZA Dalry Jc. AUCHENMADE STEWARTON STRATHAVEN NTH. CEN.
LISSENS (Goods) RYELAND CEN.
CORRIE ARDROSSAN SALTCOATS MONTGREENAN CUNNINGHAMHEAD
Montgomerie Pier Stubbs Jc. KILMAURS KILMARNOCK NEWMILNS LOUDOUNHILL DRUMCLOG
WINTON PIER STEVENSTON BOGSIDE CROSSHOUSE Kaypark Jc. DARVEL County Boundary Jc.
ARRAN SOUTH BEACH IRVINE G.&S.W. SPRINGSIDE HURLFORD GALSTON
BRODICK DREGHORN ST.MARNOCKS GATEHEAD Bellfield Jc. MUIRKIRK
DRYBRIDGE RICCARTON & CRAIGIE (Gds) GARROCHBURN (Goods) Loco. Shed
GAILES BARASSIE MAUCHLINE CATRINE CRONBERRY
LAMLASH TROON Gds MONKTON Mossblown Jc. TARBOLTON LUGAR
KING'S CROSS Lochgreen Jc. PRESTWICK Brackenhill Jc. COMMONDYKE AUCHINLECK OLD CUMNOCK Logan Jc.
WHITING BAY Falkland Jc. ANNBANK TRABBOCH SKARES DUMFRIES HOUSE CUMNOCK
NEWTON-ON-AYR Blackhouse Jc. AUCHINCRUIVE OCHILTREE
AYR Goods Hawkhill Jc. DRONGAN BELSTON Jc. NEW CUMNOCK
To CARRADALE Etc. To MACHRIE BAY Etc. HEADS OF AYR Alloway Jc. GREENAN CASTLE (Goods) HOLLYBUSH RANKINSTON Watertroughs
DUNURE ALLOWAY Dalrymple Jc. HOLEHOUSE
DALRYMPLE PATNA Blackcraig Hill

CLYDE STEAMER ROUTES
— — N.B.
······· G. & S. W.
— ·· N.B. & CAL.
— — CAL.

KINTYRE
LINTMILL HALT
MACHRIHANISH CAMPBELTOWN
PLANTATION HALT
TROOGAL HALT MOSS RD. HALT
DRUMLEMBLE HALT
MACHRIHANISH FARM HALT
MACHRIHANISH & CAMP-BELTOWN LIGHT RLY.

KNOWESIDE A Y R S H I R E
CASSILLIS
MAYBOLE WATERSIDE
GLENSIDE
MAIDENS DALMELLINGTON
TURNBERRY KILKERRAN
DIPPLE (Goods) DAILLY
KILLOCHAN
GIRVAN

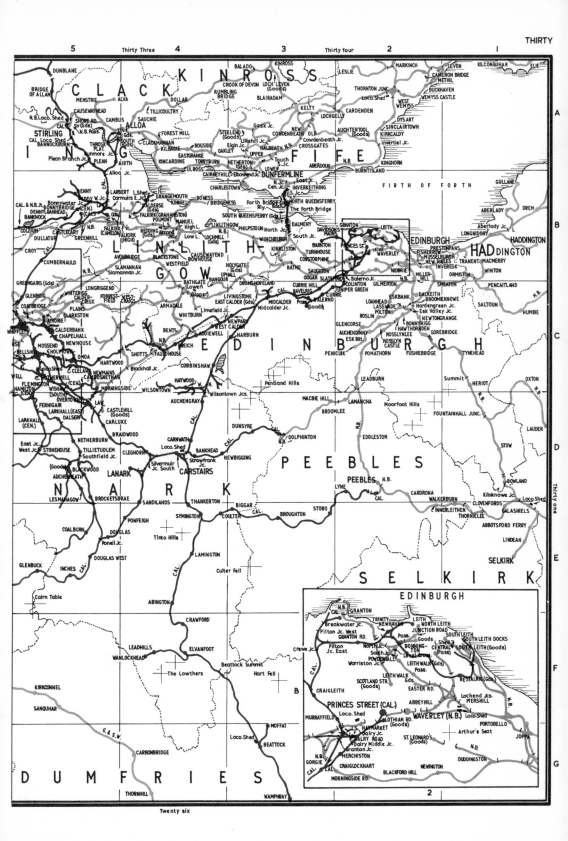

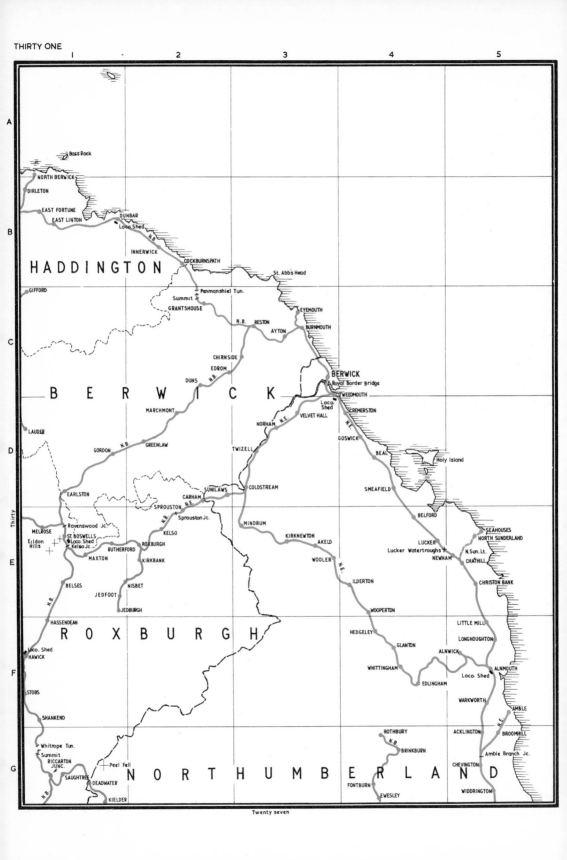

1   2   3   4   5

A

Bass Rock

NORTH BERWICK
DIRLETON

EAST FORTUNE
EAST LINTON   DUNBAR
B   Loco. Shed   N.B.
          INNERWICK
                    COCKBURNSPATH
HADDINGTON   St. Abb's Head

GIFFORD   Penmanshiel Tun.
                Summit
                GRANTSHOUSE   EYEMOUTH
                    N.B. RESTON   BURNMOUTH
                          AYTON
C
                    CHIRNSIDE
                    EDROM
          DUNS   N.B.   BERWICK
B E R W I C K   Royal Border Bridge
          MARCHMONT   TWEEDMOUTH
                          NORHAM N.E. Loco. Shed
                                VELVET HALL SCREMERSTON
LAUDER   GOSWICK
                    TWIZELL   BEAL
          GORDON N.B. GREENLAW   Holy Island
D
                    SUNILAWS COLDSTREAM   SMEAFIELD
EARLSTON
          SPROUSTON N.E.
MELROSE   Ravenswood Jc. Sprouston Jc.   BELFORD
Eildon ST BOSWELLS N.B. KELSO   MINDRUM
Hills   Loco. Shed ROXBURGH   KIRKNEWTON   SEAHOUSES
        Kelso Jc. RUTHERFORD   AKELD   NORTH SUNDERLAND
E   MAXTON   KIRKBANK   WOOLER N.E. LUCKER N.Sun. Lt.
                                    Lucker Watertroughs NEWHAM CHATHILL
        BELSES   ILDERTON   CHRISTON BANK
        JEDFOOT NISBET   WOOPERTON
                JEDBURGH
HASSENDEAN   LITTLE MILL
N.B. R O X B U R G H   HEDGELEY   LONGHOUGHTON
    Loco. Shed   GLANTON   ALNWICK
HAWICK   WHITTINGHAM   ALNMOUTH
F   Loco. Shed
STOBS   EDLINGHAM WARKWORTH
                                                AMBLE
SHANKEND   ROTHBURY   ACKLINGTON BROOMHILL
        Whitrope Tun.   N.B.
        Summit   BRINKBURN   Amble Branch Jc.
        RICCARTON   CHEVINGTON
G   JUNC.   Peel Fell N O R T H U M B E R L A N D
        SAUGHTREE DEADWATER   FONTBURN   WIDDRINGTON
N.B.   KIELDER   EWESLEY

Thirty

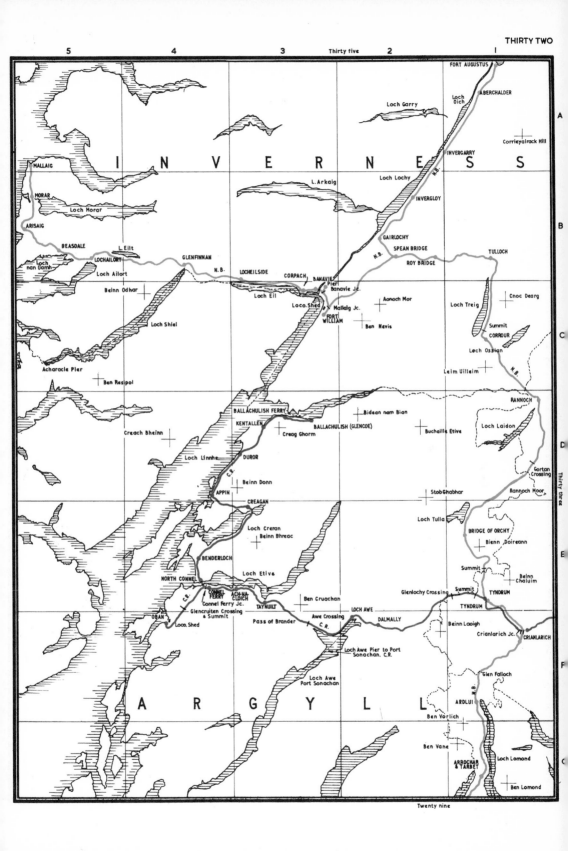

FORT AUGUSTUS
Loch Garry
Loch Oich
ABERCHALDER
Corrieyairack Hill
INVERGARRY
N.B.
I N V E R N E S S

MALLAIG
MORAR
Loch Morar
L. Arkaig
Loch Lochy
INVERGLOY
ARISAIG
BEASDALE
L. Eilt
GLENFINNAN
N.B.
GAIRLOCHY
SPEAN BRIDGE
TULLOCH
Loch nan Uamh
LOCHAILORT
Loch Ailort
LOCHEILSIDE
CORPACH
BANAVIE
N.B.
ROY BRIDGE
Beinn Odhar
N.B.
Loch Eil
Pier
Banavie Jc.
Aonach Mor
Loch Treig
Cnoc Dearg
Loch Shiel
Loco. Shed
Mallaig Jc.
FORT WILLIAM
Ben Nevis
Summit
CORROUR
Loch Ossian
Acharacle Pier
Ben Resipol
Leim Uilleim
N.B.
RANNOCH

BALLACHULISH FERRY
Bidean nam Bian
Loch Laidon
Creach Bheinn
KENTALLEN
BALLACHULISH (GLENCOE)
Buchaille Etive
Creag Ghorm
Loch Linnhe
DUROR
C.R.
Gortan Crossing
Beinn Donn
Stob Ghabhar
Rannoch Moor
APPIN
CREAGAN
Loch Tulla
Loch Creran
Beinn Bhreac
BRIDGE OF ORCHY
BENDERLOCH
Beinn Doireann
Loch Etive
Summit
NORTH CONNEL
Beinn Chaluim
CONNEL FERRY
ACH-NA-CLOICH
Glenlochy Crossing
Summit
C.R.
Connel Ferry Jc.
TAYNUILT
Ben Cruachan
TYNDRUM
OBAN
Glencruiten Crossing & Summit
Awe Crossing
LOCH AWE
TYNDRUM
Loco. Shed
Pass of Brander
C.R.
DALMALLY
Beinn Laoigh
Crianlarich Jc.
CRIANLARICH
Loch Awe Pier to Port Sonachan, C.R.
Glen Falloch
N.B.
Loch Awe
Port Sonachan
A R G Y L L
ARDLUI
Ben Vorlich
Ben Vane
Loch Lomond
ARROCHAR & TARBET
Ben Lomond

1 2 3 Thirty six 4 5

A

KINCRAIG
Loch Insh
Carn Mairg
H.R.
NEWTONMORE
KINGUSSIE
The Cairngorms

I N V E R N E S S   A B E

Inchlea Crossing

B

DALWHINNIE
Carn na Caim
Loch Ericht
Druimuachdar Summit
DALNASPIDAL
Loch Garry

C

H.R.
BLAIR ATHOLL
STRUAN
KILLIECRANKIE
Killiecrankie Tun.
Ben Vrackie
Pass of Killiecrankie

RANNOCH

P E R T H

PITLOCHRY
Moulinearn Crossing
GRANDTULLY
H.R.
BALLINLUIG

D

Gortan Crossing
Rannoch Moor
ABERFELDY
GUAY
DALGUISE
Inchmagranachan Crossing
Inver Tun.
DUNKELD
BLAIRGOWRIE
ROSEMOUNT

Kenmore Pier

Loch Tay
Ben Lawers
Kingswood Crossing
Kingswood Tun.
Summit
WOODSIDE & BURRELTON
MURTHLY
Kingswood Tun.
BANKFOOT
CARGILL
BALLATHIE (Goods)
STANLEY JUNC.
C.R.
STRATHORD
LUNCARTY

E

LOCH TAY
KILLIN Pier
Killin Pier to Kenmore Pier, C.R.
Ben Chonzie
KILLIN JUNC.
LUIB
C.R.
Glen Ogle
METHVEN
RUTHVEN ROAD, ALMOND BANK
Almond Valley Jc.
Methven Jc.
PERTH
GENERAL
Loco. Shed
N.B. Goods
D.&P.J.C.
PRINCES STR.
KINFAUNS
GLENCARSE
CRIANLARICH
LOCHEARNHEAD
C.R.
ST. FILLANS
DALCHONZIE PLATFORM
COMRIE
BALGOWAN
TIBBERMUIR
MADDERTY
ABERCAIRNY
CRIEFF
INNERPEFFRAY
HIGHLANDMAN
FORGANDENNY
Hilton Jc.
BRIDGE OF EARN
Moncrieff Tun.
Balmano Jc.
ABERNETHY N.B.

F

Balquhidder Jc.
Loch Earn
BALQUHIDDER
KINGSHOUSE
Ben Vorlich
STRATHYRE
MUTHILL
FORTEVIOT
DUNNING
C.R.
GLENFARG
Summit
GATESIDE

Benvane
Loch Lubnaig
Uamh Bheag
TULLIBARDINE
AUCHTERARDER
GLENEAGLES
Summit
MAWCARSE
MILNATHORT
Loch Katrine
St. Bride's Crossing
Pass of Leny
CALLANDER
C.R.
BLACKFORD
GREENLOANING
KINROSS N.B.
BALADO N.B.
LOCH LEVEN

G

Ben Ledi
Drumvaich Crossing
KINBUCK
CROOK OF DEVON
LOCH LEVEN (Goods)
Loch Achray
Loch Venachar
DOUNE
DUNBLANE
RUMBLING BRIDGE
ABERFOYLE
Lake of Menteith

K I N R O S S

Thirty two

5   4   Thirty seven   3   2   1

TORPHINS
GLASSEL
DESS
ABOYNE
DINNET
G.N.of S.
CAMBUS O'MAY
BALLATER
MILLTIMBER
G.N. of S.
CULTER
DRUM
PARK
CRATHES
BANCHORY
Summit
COVE BAY
Portlethen
C.R.
NEWTONHILL
MUCHALLS

R   **D**   **E**   **E**   **N**

STONEHAVEN

K I N C A R D I N E

CARMONT
DRUMLITHIE
Summit
FORDOUN
LAURENCEKIRK
GORDOUN
BERVIE
N.B.
JOHNSHAVEN
BIRNIE ROAD
C.R.
LAURISTON
ST. CYRUS
EDZELL
MARYKIRK
NORTH WATER BRIDGE
STRACATHRO
CRAIGO
Kinnaber Jc.
HILLSIDE
DUBTON JUNC.
Broomfield Jcs.
CARESTON
BRECHIN
MONTROSE
BRIDGE OF DUN

A   **N**   **G**   **U**   **S**

TANNADICE
C.R.
JUSTINHAUGH
FARNELL ROAD
KIRRIEMUIR
Loco Shed
CLOCKSBRIGGS
AULDBAR ROAD
LUNAN BAY
FORFAR
Kirriemuir Jc.
KINGSMUIR
GLASTERLAW
N.B.
INVERKEILOR
GLAMIS
GUTHRIE
FRIOCKHEIM
ALYTH
JORDANSTONE
LEYSMILL
CAULDCOTS
EASSIE
COLLISTON
LETHAM GRANGE
MEIGLE
CARMYLLIE
KIRKBUDDO
ALYTH JUNC.
DENHEAD
St. Vigean's Jc.
Ardler Jc.
NEWTYLE
CUTHLIE
Harbour Branch Jc.
ARBROATH
ARDLER
ARBIRLOT
COUPAR ANGUS
MONIKIE
ELLIOT
ELLIOT JUNC.
AUCHTERHOUSE
C.R.
ROSEMILL (Goods)
BALDRAGON
KINGENNIE
EAST HAVEN
DRONLEY
CARNOUSTIE
LOCHEE
BALDOVAN
BUDDON
BARRY LINKS
LOCHEE WEST
MARYFIELD
BARNHILL
LIFF
D. & A. Joint
MONIFIETH
INVERGOWRIE
DUNDEE
INCHTURE VILLAGE
LONGFORGAN
Ninewells Jc.
TAYPORT
INCHTURE
ESPLANADE
EAST NEWPORT
The Tay Bridge
WEST NEWPORT
ERROL
WORMIT (Goods)
ST. FORT
C.R.
INCHCOONANS (Goods)
LEUCHARS OLD STA.
N.B.
KILMANY
LEUCHARS JUNC.
NEWBURGH
LUTHRIE
GUARD BRIDGE
LINDORES
DAIRSIE
ST. ANDREWS
Glenburnie Jc.
Lindores Loch
COLLESSIE
N.B.
CUPAR
MOUNT MELVILLE
AUCHTERMUCHTY
SPRINGFIELD
STRAVITHIE
BOARHILLS
STRATHMIGLO
LADYBANK
KINGSBARNS
KINGSKETTLE
LARGOWARD (Goods)
FALKLAND ROAD
LOCHTY (Goods)
CRAIL
MONTRAVE (Goods)
ANSTRUTHER
KENNOWAY (Goods)
LARGO
N.B.
KILCONQUHAR
PITTENWEEM
LESLIE
MARKINCH
CAMERON BRIDGE
LUNDIN LINKS
ST. MONANS
LEVEN
ELIE
METHIL
THORNTON JUNC.
W. WEMYSS
BUCKHAVEN
WEMYSS CASTLE

F   **I**   **F**   **E**

4 — DUNDEE (inset)

DUNDEE
BROUGHTY FERRY
WEST FERRY
STANNERGATE (Goods)
Camperdown E. Jc.
EAST
D. & A. Joint
Cal. Loco. Shed
Buckingham W. Jc.
WEST
N.B. Loco. Shed
N.B. Pier
Ninewells Jc.
TAY BRIDGE (Goods)
MAGDALEN GREEN
ESPLANADE
TAYPORT
WEST NEWPORT
EAST NEWPORT
The Tay Bridge
N.B.
WORMIT (Goods)
WORMIT (Pass)

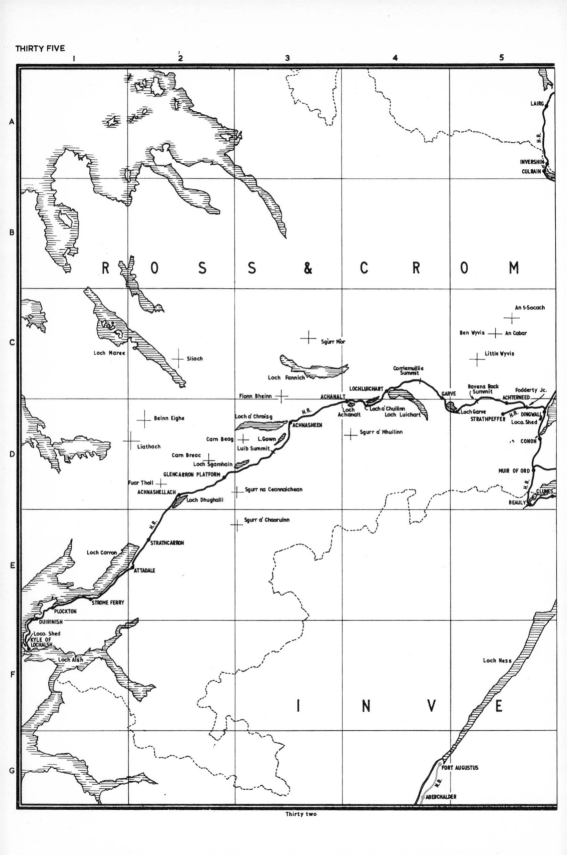

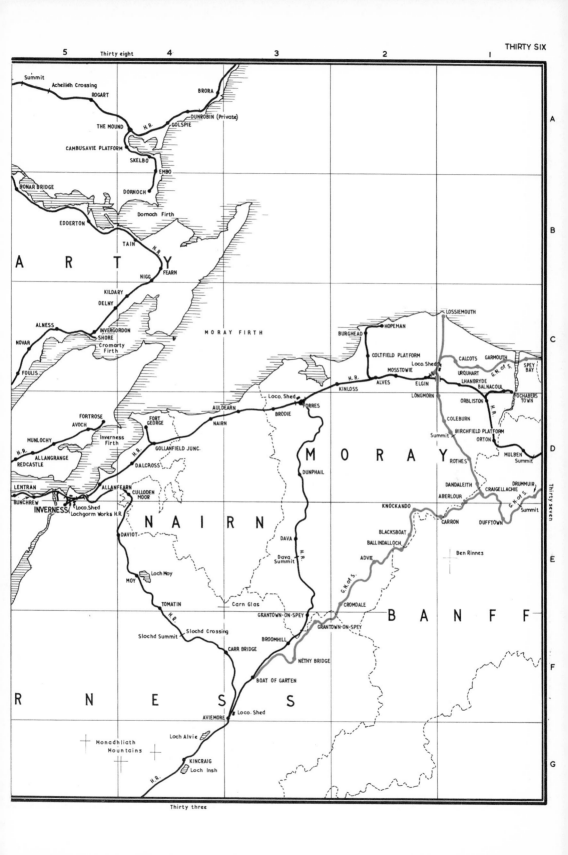

Summit
Acheilidh Crossing
ROGART
BRORA
THE MOUND
H.R.
GOLSPIE
DUNROBIN (Private)
CAMBUSAVIE PLATFORM
SKELBO
EMBO
BONAR BRIDGE
DORNOCH
Dornoch Firth
EDDERTON
TAIN
H.R.
A R T Y
NIGG
FEARN
KILDARY
DELNY
ALNESS
INVERGORDON
NOVAR
SHORE
Cromarty
Firth
FOULIS
M O R A Y   F I R T H

LOSSIEMOUTH
HOPEMAN
BURGHEAD
COLTFIELD PLATFORM
Loco. Shed
CALCOTS
GARMOUTH
G.N. of S.
SPEY
BAY
MOSSTOWIE
URQUHART
H.R.
ALVES
ELGIN
LHANBRYDE
BALNACOUL
KINLOSS
LONGMORN
FOCHABERS
TOWN
Loco. Shed
FORRES
ORBLISTON
BRODIE
H.R.
COLEBURN
AULDEARN
BIRCHFIELD PLATFORM
FORT
GEORGE
NAIRN
Summit
ORTON
M O R A Y
ROTHES
MULBEN
Summit
FORTROSE
AVOCH
MUNLOCHY
Inverness Firth
GOLLANFIELD JUNC.
DUNPHAIL
DANDALEITH
DRUMMUIR
H.R.
ALLANGRANGE
REDCASTLE
DALCROSS
ABERLOUR
CRAIGELLACHIE
Thirty seven
LENTRAN
ALLANFEARN
CULLODEN
MOOR
KNOCKANDO
G.N. of S.
Summit
BUNCHREW
INVERNESS
Loco. Shed
Lochgorm Works H.R.
N A I R N
CARRON
DUFFTOWN
DAVIOT
DAVA
BLACKSBOAT
Ben Rinnes
BALLINDALLOCH
Dava
Summit
ADVIE
H.R.
MOY
Loch Moy
G.N. of S.
TOMATIN
Carn Glas
CROMDALE
B A N F F
GRANTOWN-ON-SPEY
SLOCHD Crossing
GRANTOWN-ON-SPEY
Slochd Summit
BROOMHILL
CARR BRIDGE
NETHY BRIDGE
R N E S S
BOAT OF GARTEN
AVIEMORE
Loco. Shed
Loch Alvie
Monadhliath
Mountains
KINCRAIG
H.R.
Loch Insh

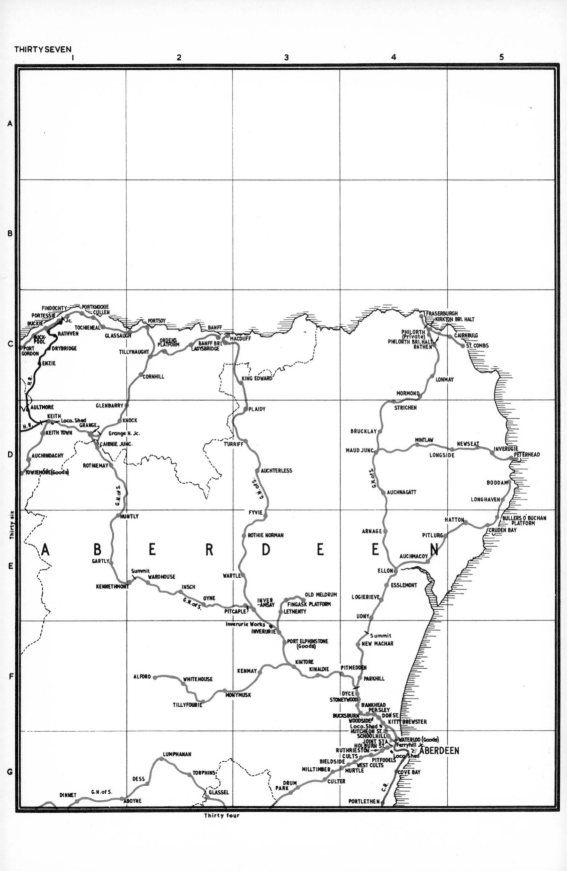

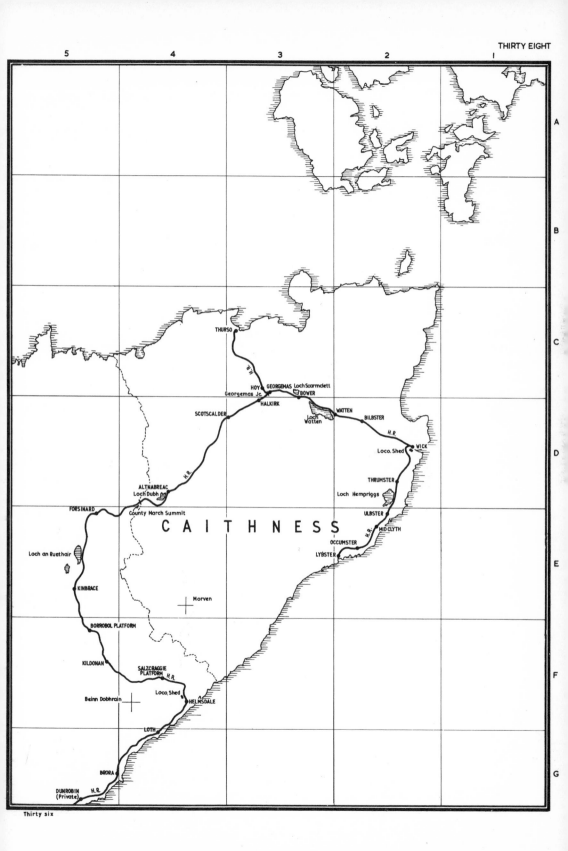

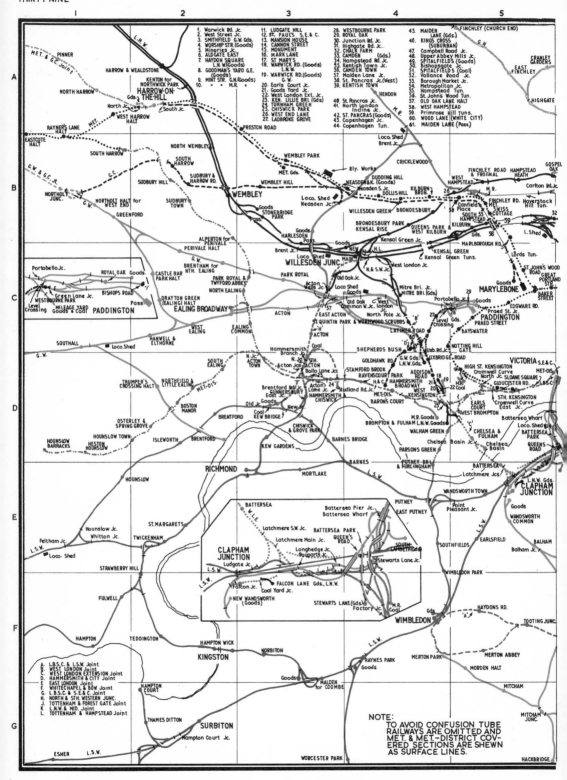

1. Warwick Rd. Jc.
2. West Street Jc.
3. SMITHFIELD G.W. Gds.
4. WORSHIP STR.(Goods)
5. Minories.
6. ALDGATE EAST
7. HAYDON SQUARE (N.Wgoods)
8. GOODMAN'S YARD G.E. (Goods)
9. MINT STR. G.N(Goods)
10. M.R.

11. LUDGATE HILL
12. ST. PAUL'S S.E.& C.
13. MANSION HOUSE
14. CANNON STREET
15. MONUMENT
16. MARK LANE
17. ST MARY'S
18. WARWICK RD.(Goods) L.N.W.
19. WARWICK RD.(Goods) G.W.
20. Earls Court Jc.
21. Goods Yard Jc.
22. West London Ext.(Gds)
23. KEN. LILLIE BRI.(Gds)
24. TURNHAM GREEN
25. CHISWICK PARK
26. WEST END LANE
27. LADBROKE GROVE

28. WESTBOURNE PARK
29. ROYAL OAK
30. Junction Rd. Jc.
31. Highgate Rd. Jc.
32. CHALK FARM
33. CAMDEN (Gds.)
34. Hampstead Jc.
35. Kentish Town Jc.
36. CAMDEN TOWN
37. Maiden Lane Jc.
38. St. Pancras Jc.(West)
39. KENTISH TOWN
40. St. Pancras Jc.
41. North London Incline Jc.
42. ST. PANCRAS(Goods)
43. Copenhagen Jc.
44. Copenhagen Jc.

45. MAIDEN LANE (Gds.)
46. KINGS CROSS (SUBURBAN)
47. Campbell Road Jc.
48. Upper Abbey Hills Jc.
49. SPITALFIELD'S (Goods)
50. Bishopsgate Jc.
51. SPITALFIELD'S (Coal)
52. Vallance Road Jc.
53. Borough Market Jc.
54. Metropolitan Jc.
55. Hampstead Tun.
56. St. John's Wood Tun.
57. OLD OAK LANE HALT
58. WEST HAMPSTEAD
59. Primrose Hill Tuns.
60. WOOD LANE (WHITE CITY)
61. MAIDEN LANE (Pass.)

A. L.B.S.C. & L.S.W. Joint
B. WEST LONDON Joint
C. WEST LONDON EXTENSION Joint
D. HAMMERSMITH & CITY Joint
E. EAST LONDON Joint
F. WHITECHAPEL & BOW Joint
G. L.B.S.C & S.E.& C. Joint
H. NORTH & STH. WESTERN JUNC.
J. TOTTENHAM & FOREST GATE Joint
K. L.N.W. & MID. Joint
L. TOTTENHAM & HAMPSTEAD Joint

NOTE:
TO AVOID CONFUSION TUBE
RAILWAYS ARE OMITTED AND
MET. & MET.-DISTRICT COV-
ERED SECTIONS ARE SHEWN
AS SURFACE LINES.

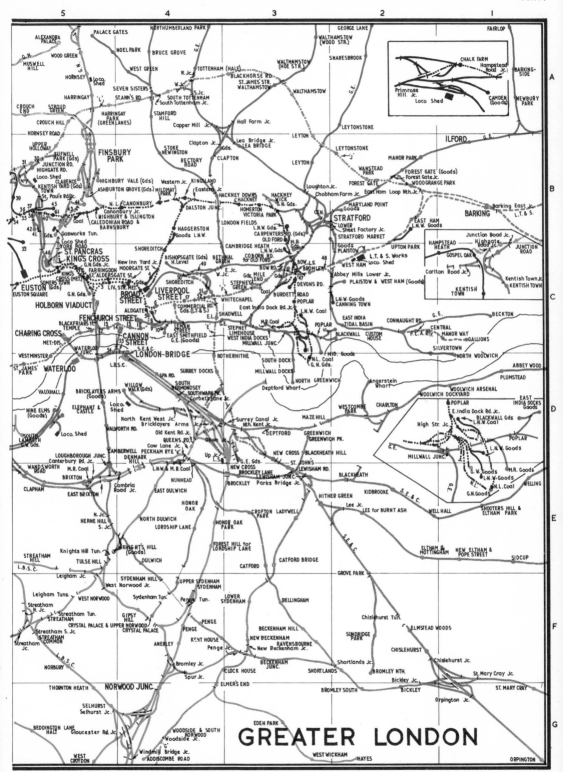

GREATER LONDON

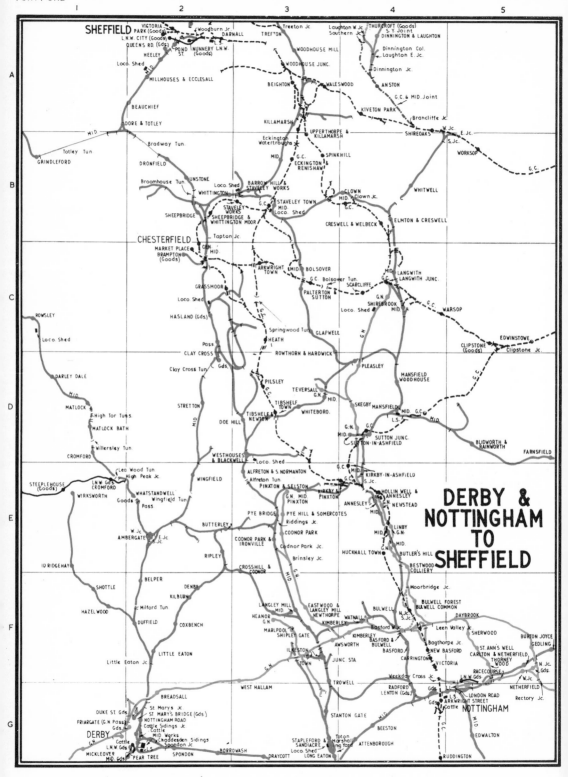

DERBY & NOTTINGHAM TO SHEFFIELD

5   4   3   2   1

A

Summit
HORSFORTH
MID. BINGLEY
BINGLEY
Bingley Jc.
Thackley Tun.
APPERLEY BRI. & RAWDON
BAILDON
THACKLEY
Apperley Jc.
CALVERLEY & RODLEY
Summit
SALTAIRE
STATION RD. (MID. P.)
IDLE
N.E.
NEWLAY & HORSFORTH
MID.
SCHOLES
Bingley Tun.
Hewenden Via.
WILSDEN
CULLINGWORTH
SHIPLEY
GOODS BRIDGE STREET (G.N.)
G.N.
KIRKSTALL
HEADINGLEY
CARDIGAN ST. (Goods)
LEEDS
WELLINGTON (Pass.)
CROSS GATES
N.E.
GARFORTH
MICKLEFIELD
FRIZINGHALL
Loco. Shed
ECCLESHILL
STANNINGLEY, for FARSLEY
BRAMLEY
St. Gds.
WELLINGTON
CENTRAL
HOLBECK
NEW
MARSH LANE
Cross Gates Jc.
DENHOLME
MANNINGHAM
MARKET STR.
PUDSEY LOWTOWN
ARMLEY & WORTLEY
HUNSLET (Gds.)

B

BRADFORD
EXCHANGE
St. DUNSTANS
LAISTERDYKE
PUDSEY GREENSIDE
COPLEY HILL
FARNLEY & WORTLEY
HUNSLET LANE (Gds.)
THORNTON
GREAT HORTON
HORTON PARK Gds.
DUDLEY HILL
Loco. Shed
BEESTON
HUNSLET
Loco. Shed
Stourton Jc.
MID.
WOODLESFORD
KIPPAX
LEDSTON
BURTON SALMON
CLAYTON
BOWLING JUNC.
BIRKENSHAW & TONG
G.N.
GILDERSOME
CHURWELL
MORLEY (LN·W)
ROTHWELL
E. & W. YORKS.
UNION
ROBIN HOOD
QUEENSBURY
BOWLING
Loco. Shed
LOW MOOR
G.N. Gds.
DRIGHLINGTON & ADWALTON
Morley Tun.
MORLEY (G.N.)
TINGLEY
Ardsley Tun.
Ardsley J.S.
METHLEY (MID.)
Methley Jc.
METHLEY (Joint)
METHLEY (L·Y)
FRYSTON (Goods)
Queensbury Tun.
HALIFAX & OVENDEN JNT. (G.N. & L. & Y.)
New Furnace Tun.
Wyke Tun.
GOMERSAL
UPPER BATLEY
WOODKIRK
Colliery Jc.
N. Jc.
METHLEY JOINT
(G.N., L.Y., N.E.)
CASTLEFORD (N.E.)
HOLMFIELD
OVENDEN
WHEATLEY (Goods)
Lea Bank Tun.
WYKE & NORWOOD GREEN
Oakenshaw Tun.
BIRSTAL
MORLEY (G.N.)
LOFTHOUSE & OUTWOOD (G.N.)
STANLEY
ALTOFTS & WHITWOOD
Altofts Jc.
CASTLEFORD (L. & Y.)
Cutsyke Jc.
WHEATLEY Tun.
PELLON
Old Lane Tun.
NORTH BRI.
Lightcliffe Tun.
CLECKHEATON L. & Y.
CARLINGHOW L.N.W.
BATLEY (L·N·W)
METHLEY JOINT
(Joint)
Whitwood Jc.

C

St. PAUL'S
Milner Royd (J.S. Gds.)
Pass.
HIPPERHOLME
LIGHTCLIFFE
Bailiff Bri. Tun.
LIVERSEDGE L. & Y.
STAINCLIFFE & BATLEY CARR
FLUSHDYKE
WAKEFIELD
NORMANTON
Loco. Shed
Goose Hill Jc.
FERRY BRIDGE (S. & K.)
HALIFAX
COPLEY
Dryclough Jc.
Beacon Hill Tun.
CLIFTON ROAD
HECKMONDWIKE
BATLEY CARR
DEWSBURY
ALVERTHORPE
WESTGATE Jnt.
KIRKGATE Jnt.
Ings Rd. Jc.
Wrenthorpe Jc.
Gds. Jnt.
PONTEFRACT (MONKHILL)
TANSHELF
SOWERBY BRIDGE
Bank House Tun.
GREETLAND
ELLAND
Salterhebble Tun.
BRIGHOUSE
COOPER BRIDGE
Bradley Wood Jc.
RAVENSTHORPE
NORTHORPE
BATTYEFORD
Loco. Shed
THORNHILL
OSSETT
EARLSHEATON
HORBURY & OSSETT
HORBURY JUNC.
Watertraughs
SANDAL
Oakenshaw (Gds.)
Crofton West
SNYDALE Jc.
OAKENSHAW (Gds.)
SHARLSTON
CROFTON
L. & Y.
PONTEFRACT (BAGHILL)
FEATHERSTONE
WEST VALE
STAINLAND & HOLYWELL GREEN
Elland Tun.
Bradley Tun.
Heckmondwike Jc.
BRADLEY
Heaton Lodge Jc.
MIRFIELD
L.N.W. Jc.
RAVENSTHORPE & THORNHILL
MIDDLESTOWN Jc.
HORBURY JUNC.
MIDDLESTOWN
MID.
Hare Pk. Jc.
Hare Pk. Jc.
HARE PARK & CROFTON
East Jc.
Nostell N.Jc.
Nostell S.Jc.
Wintersett Jc.
NOSTELL
ACKWORTH
SWINTON & KNOTTINGLEY JNT.
(MID. & N.E.)
Brackenhill Jc.
ACKWORTH MOOR TOP (Goods)

D

Kirkburton Branch Jc.
HILLHOUSE (Goods)
HUDDERSFIELD
L. & Y. & L.N.W. Jnt.
DEIGHTON
MID. Goods
Springwood Tun.
KIRKHEATON
SANDAL & WALTON
CRIGGLESTONE
Crigglestone Tun.
BRACKENHILL LIGHT
Hemsworth Col.
ACKWORTH MOOR TOP (Goods)
LONGWOOD & MILNSBRIDGE
GOLCAR
Netherton Tun.
LINTHWAITE (Gds)
SLAITHWAITE
NETHERTON
Springwood Jc.
LOCKWOOD
Meltham Branch Jc.
Butternab Tun.
BERRY BROW
FENAY BRI. & LEPTON
L.N.W.
Crigglestone Jc.
CRIGGLESTONE
RYHILL
RYHILL HALT
New Monkton Main Col.
HEMSWORTH
UPTON & NTH. ELMSALL
East Jc.
Moorthorpe
HEALEY HOUSE
Healey House Tun.
Robin Hood Tun.
Honley Tun.
HONLEY
KIRKBURTON
Woo Iley Tun.
Royston Jc.
NOTTON & ROYSTON
HEMSWORTH & STH. KIRKBY
H. & B.
Brierley Jc.
MOORTHORPE S.Jc.
BROCKHOLES
MELTHAM
THONGS BRIDGE
Thurstonland Tun.
STOCKSMOOR
HAIGH
DARTON
ROYSTON & NOTTON
CUDWORTH (Goods)
SHAFTON Jc.
MOORTHORPE & SOUTH KIRKBY
MOORHOUSE & STH. ELMSALL
SOUTH ELMSALL
SKELMANTHORPE
Shelley Woodhouse Tun.
CLAYTON WEST
Silkstone Jc.
STAINCROSS
Goods Jc.
North Jc.
South Jc.
Frickley Col.
FRICKLEY
HOLMFIRTH
SHEPLEY & SHELLEY
Cumberworth Tun.
DENBY DALE & CUMBERWORTH
BARNSLEY
Monk Bretton Jc.
MONK BRETTON
Gds.
CUDWORTH
GREAT HOUGHTON HALL
Hickleton S.Jc.
HICKLETON & THURNSCOE
Hick. Mn. Gds.

E

SILKSTONE
SUMMER LANE
COURT HOUSE
L.Y.
Ardsley Tun.
STAIRFOOT
D.V.
WELLHOUSE Tun.
Penistone Via.
SILKSTONE
DODWORTH
DOVECLIFFE
DARFIELD
BOLTON-ON-DEARNE
HAZELHEAD BRIDGE
DUNFORD BRIDGE
PENISTONE
MOOR END (Gds)
THURGOLAND (Goods)
WORSBRO' (Gds.)
WOMBWELL
Wath Curve Jnt. Comm. (G.C., MID. & N.E.)
Woodhead Tun.
Thurgoland Tun.
BIRDWELL
PILLEY (Gds.)
BIRDWELL & HOYLAND COMMON
WOMBWELL
WATH
WATH-ON-DEARNE
Wath Rd. Jc.
WORTLEY
WESTWOOD
ELSECAR & HOYLAND
Dearne Jc.
Wath Rd. Jc.

F

CROWDEN
WOODHEAD
G.C.
DEEPCAR
WENTWORTH & HOYLAND COMMON
Tankersley Tun.
CHAPELTOWN
G.C.
ELSECAR (Goods)
PARKGATE & RAWMARSH
PARKGATE & ALDWARKE
MID. SWINTON G.C.
KILNHURST
MID.
Thrybergh Jc.
Roundwood Jc.
MID.
ECCLESFIELD
GRANGE LANE
G.C.
MEADOW HALL & WINCOBANK
ROTHERHAM (MASBRO')
ROTHERHAM ROAD
G.C. & MID. Jnt.

G

OUGHTY BRIDGE
WADSLEY BRIDGE
WINCOBANK & MEADOW HALL
BRIGHTSIDE
ATTERCLIFFE RD.
VICKER (Gds.)
HOLMES
ROTHERHAM (WESTGATE)
SHEFFIELD
NEEPSEND
Tunnel Jc.
VICTORIA
PARK (Goods)
CITY (Goods)
(L.N.W.)
Tinsley Jcs.
TINSLEY
BROUGHTON LANE
ATTERCLIFFE
CATCLIFFE
Treeton Jc.
TREETON
NUNNERY (Goods) (L.N.W.)
QUEENS ROAD (Goods)
POND STREET
DARNALL
WOODHOUSE JUNC.
WOODHOUSE MILL

WEST RIDING

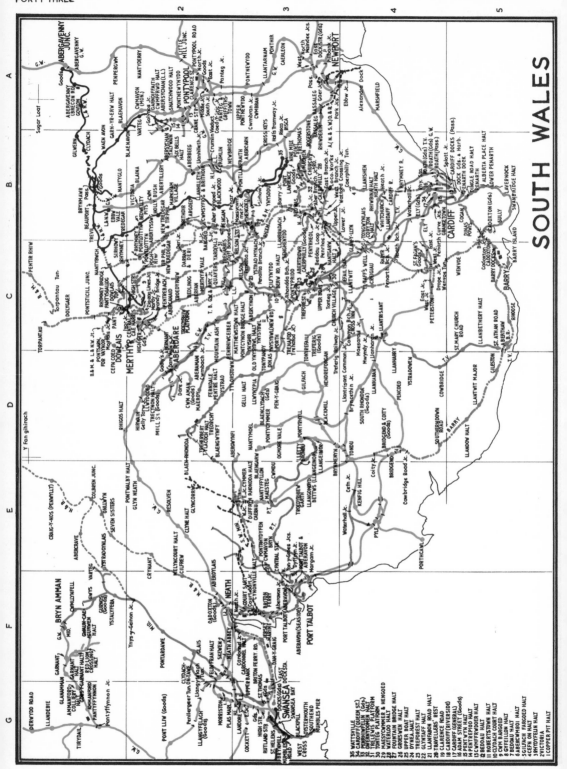

SOUTH WALES

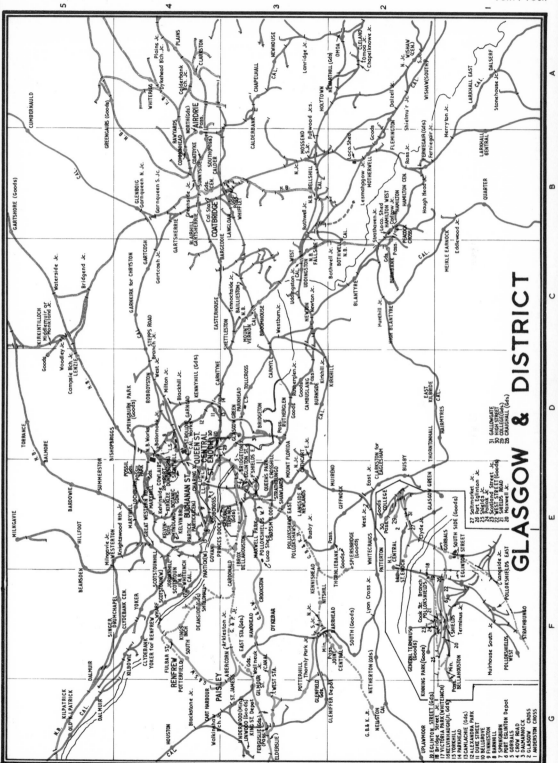

GLASGOW & DISTRICT

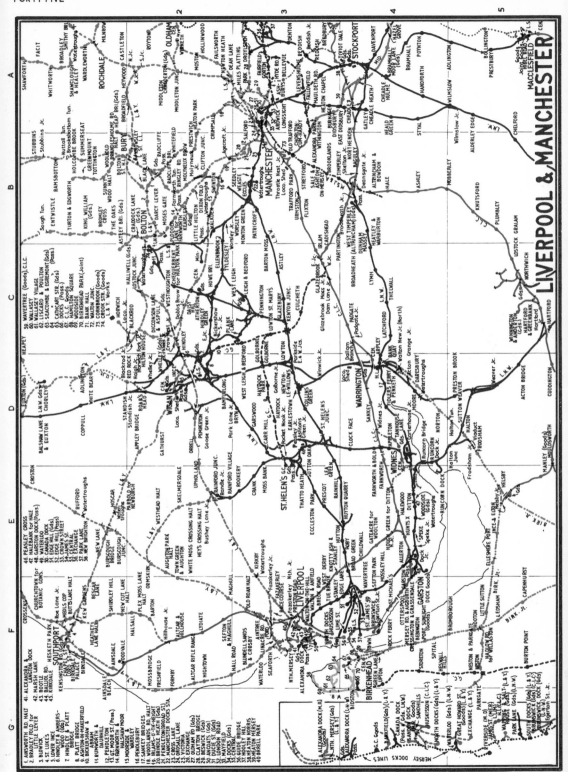

GAZETTEER

This Gazetteer to the Atlas is divided into six parts, in the following order:—

1. List of abbreviations used to represent the various companies owning and/or using the various stations, meeting at junctions, etc.

2. Index to tunnels named on the maps.

3. Index to water troughs which appear on the maps.

4. Index to principal summits named on the maps.

5. Index to principal viaducts marked on the maps.

6. Index to Stations, Junctions, etc.

Stations with Dual Titles

Dual titles are only used for stations having the word " & " in such title: they are not cross-indexed and only appear under the first name, e.g., Dunkeld & Birnam only appears under the letter " D ". In the case of dual titles joined by the word " for ", only the first name is shown.

Stations Sub-titled

When the sub-title is characteristic, it is indexed in its own right, in addition to the main title, e.g., Norwich is indexed generally under " N " and also under " T " as Thorpe (Norwich). Similar entries include the various " Victorias ", Paragon (Hull), Warrior Square (St. Leonards), etc. Non-characteristic titles like " Central ", " Exchange ", " North ", " New ", etc., are not directly entered as such, if at all, but when shown, they follow the name of the place, e.g. Barnsley (Exchange), Leeds (New).

Plurality of Stations at a Single Place.

Where two companies each have their own station(s) at any given place, the companies' initials are separated by " & ", thus: Bedford, LNW. & Mid., Tunbridge Wells, LBSC. & SEC. When three or more companies have stations in a place, a comma (,) separates the first two or more, e.g. Cymmer, GW., RSB. & SWM.

Joint Stations are shown with the initials of the owning partners or of the Joint undertaking if it has a specific name, e.g. Cosham, LBSC&LSWJt.; Ludlow, S&H.

Ownership and User of Stations

Stations used by more than one company, in so far as passenger traffic is concerned, are shown with the owning company or companies in bolder type, followed by other users shown within brackets, as under: the ramifications of goods workings are too complex to be included.

    Aberdeen (Pass.), **Cal&GNSJt** (NB).
    Branksome, **LSW**(SD).
    Crewe, **LNW**(GW/NS).

In some instances, " foreign " user has been shown as a matter of interest even though such user may have ceased slightly earlier than 1922. It has also been shown in those cases where an absorbed company appears in its own right on the maps, e.g. Bridgend, **GW**(BRY), the Barry Railway having been absorbed by the G.W.R. prior to the general grouping.

Joint stations used by other companies in addition to the Joint owning partners are shown thus, the joint partners not being individually shown.

    Ackworth, **SK**(GN/GC).
    Carlisle, **CJC**(G&SW/M&C/Mid/NB/NE).
    Knutsford, **CLC**(LNW).

Details of the component partners of all Joint undertakings will be found against the appropriate title in the list of abbreviations.

Joint services using junction or other stations which are purely the property of one or other of the joint partners (the joint line having terminated at some point short thereof) are not shown against such stations unless the Joint Company actually runs its own trains, e.g.:—

SD *is* shown against Bath, Broadstone, etc., since the Somerset & Dorset Joint did work trains through between Bath and Bournemouth.

QYM *is not* shown against Quaker's Yard or Merthyr since the Quaker's Yard & Merthyr Joint had no rolling stock or locomotives and was merely a section of G.W. and Rhymney joint property lying between Quaker's Yard and Merthyr GW.

CKP *is* shown against Penrith since the Cockermouth, Keswick & Penrith Company's trains, although worked by the L. & N.W. nevertheless arrived and departed Penrith in their own right, and were not, in any sense, " Joint ".

An exception to this method has been made in the case of the Birkenhead Joint which, although owning neither rolling stock nor locomotives and whose line terminated at Walton Jc. (Warrington), has been shown against certain L. & N.W. stations between Warrington and Manchester Exchange by virtue of the joint service operated between Chester and Manchester, worked variously by L. & N.W. and G.W. trains.

Line Junctions are shown in italics. Those situated on individual companies' lines which can readily be identified by an adjoining or nearby station of the same name are not generally indexed but those which form a meeting point of two or more companies are shown thus,

Acton Wells Jc., NSW/GW/LNW/Mid.

Bopeep Jc., LBSC/SEC.

WHERE IS IT ON THE MAP?

Example from Index: Abermule, Cam., 14, B2. Answer: On Map 14, in the square found by following section B across until it meets the vertical column No. 2.

The assistance of the B.T.C. Archivist, Mr. L. C. Johnson, and his staff, in making available Timetables and other documents of the period is gratefully acknowledged.

1. LIST OF ABBREVIATIONS

(In the case of Joint or Subsidiary Lines with individual titles, the owning or leasing partners or Companies are indicated in brackets immediately after the title.)

AD   —Alexandra (Newport & South Wales) Docks & Railway
AJ   —Axholme Joint (L&Y and NE).
AN   —Ashby & Nuneaton Joint (L&NW and Midland).

BAC   —Bere Alston & Calstock Light. (PDSW)
BC   —Bishop's Castle
BJ   —Birkenhead Joint (GW and L&NW)
BL   —Brackenhill Light
BM   —Brecon & Merthyr
BPGV   —Burry Port & Gwendraeth Valley
BRY   —Barry
BWHA   —Bideford, Westward Ho ! & Appledore

Cal.   —Caledonian.
Cam.   —Cambrian
Car.   —Cardiff
CE   —Clifton Extension (GW and Midland)
CJC   —(Carlisle) Citadel Station Joint Committee (Cal. and L&NW)
CKP   —Cockermouth, Keswick & Penrith
CLC   —Cheshire Lines Committee (GC, GN and Midland)
CM   —Campbeltown & Machrihanish Light
CMDP   —Cleobury Mortimer & Ditton Priors Light
CO   —Croydon & Oxted Joint (LB&SC and SE&C)
CVH   —Colne Valley & Halstead
CWJ   —Cleator & Workington Junction

Dist.   —Metropolitan District.
D&A   —Dundee & Arbroath Joint (Cal. and NB)
D&B   —Dumbarton & Balloch Joint (Cal. and NB)
DJ   —(Carlisle) Dentonholme Joint Committee (G&SW, Midland and NB)
DV   —Dearne Valley
DVL   —Derwent Valley Light

Eas.   —Easingwold
ECH   —Easton & Church Hope (GW and L&SW)
EK   —East Kent
EL   —East London (GE, LB&SC, Met., Met.Dist., and SE&C)
EWY   —East & West Yorkshire Union

Fest.   —Festiniog
Fur.   —Furness
FB   —Forth Bridge Railway Co. (GN, Midland, NB and NE)
FYN   —Freshwater, Yarmouth and Newport

GBK   —Glasgow, Barrhead & Kilmarnock Joint (Cal. and G&SW)
GC   —Great Central
GE   —Great Eastern
GN   —Great Northern
GNS   —Great North of Scotland
G&P   —Glasgow & Paisley Joint (Cal. and G&SW)
G&SW   —Glasgow & South Western
GTC   —(Carlise) Goods Traffic Committee (Cal., G&SW, L&NW and Midland)
GV   —Gwendraeth Valley
GVT   —Glyn Valley Tramway
GW   —Great Western

HB   —Hull & Barnsley
H&C   —Hammersmith & City (GW and Met.)
HHL   —Halifax High Level (GN and L&Y)
HJ   —Halesowen Joint (GW and Midland)
H&O   —Halifax & Ovenden Joint (GN and L&Y)
HR   —Highland

IMR   —Isle of Man Railway
IW   —Isle of Wight Railway
IWC   —Isle of Wight Central Railway

K&B   —Kilsyth & Bonnybridge Joint (Cal. and NB)
KE   —Knott End
KES   —Kent & East Sussex

LB   —Lynton & Barnstaple
LBSC   —London, Brighton & South Coast
LC   —Liskeard & Caradon (GW)
LE   —London Electric
LL   —Liskeard and Looe (GW)
LM   —Llanelly & Mynydd Mawr
LNW   —London & North Western
LOR   —Liverpool Overhead
LSW   —London & South Western
LTS   —London Tilbury & Southend
LU   —Lancashire & Yorkshire & Lancashire Union Joint (L&NW and L&Y)
LY   —Lancashire & Yorkshire

Mawd. —Mawddwy Light (Cambrian)
M&C   —Maryport & Carlisle
MDHB   —Mersey Docks & Harbour Board
Mer.   —Mersey
Met.   —Metropolitan
ME   —Manx Electric
MGN   —Midland & Great Northern Joint (GN and Midland)
Mid.   —Midland
MJ   —Methley Joint (GN, L&Y and NE)
MSJA   —Manchester South Junction & Altrincham (GC and L&NW)
MSL   —Mid-Suffolk Light
MSW   —Midland & South Western Junction
Mum.   —Swansea & Mumbles

N&B   —Neath & Brecon
NB   —North British
NE   —North Eastern
NL   —North London
NS   —North Staffordshire
NSJ   —Norfolk & Suffolk Joint (GE and M&GNJt.)
NSL   —North Sunderland Light
NSW   —North & South Western Junction (L&NW, Midland and NL)
NU   —North Union Joint (L&NW and L&Y)
NV   —Nidd Valley
NWNG   —North Wales Narrow Gauge

OAGB   —Oldham, Ashton-under-Lyne & Guide Bridge (GC and L&NW)
OAT   —Oxford & Aylesbury Tramroad (Met&GCJt.)
O&I   —Otley & Ilkley Joint (Midland and NE)

QYM   —Quaker's Yard & Merthyr Joint (GW and Rhymney)

PCB   —Portmadoc, Croesor & Beddgelert
PDJ   —Princes Dock Joint (Cal, G&SW & NB)
PDSW   —Plymouth, Devonport & South Western Junction
PL   —Preston & Longridge Joint (L&NW and L&Y)
PLA   —Port of London Authority
PT   —Port Talbot Railway and Docks
P&W   —Portpatrick & Wigtownshire Joint (Cal., G&SW, L&NW and Midland)
PWY   —Preston & Wyre (L&NW and L&Y)

RCT   —Rye & Camber Tramway
Rhy.   —Rhymney
RKF   —Rowrah & Kelton Fell
RSB   —Rhondda & Swansea Bay

SBH   —Snailbeach District Railways
SD   —Somerset & Dorset Joint Committee (L&SW and Midland)
SEC   —South Eastern & Chatham
S&H   —Shrewsbury & Hereford Joint (GW and L&NW)
SHD   —Sheffield District Railway (GC and Midland)
SK   —Swinton & Knottingley (Midland and NE)
SL   —Selsey Light
S&M   —Shropshire & Montgomeryshire Light
SMJ   —Stratford-on-Avon & Midland Junction
SMR   —Snowdon Mountain Railway
SSM   —South Shields, Marsden & Whitburn Colliery
SVW   —Severn & Wye Joint (GW and Midland)
SWD   —Southwold
SWM   —South Wales Mineral
SWN   —Shrewsbury & Wellington Joint (GW and L&NW)
SWP   —Shrewsbury & Welshpool Joint (GW and L&NW)
SYJ   —South Yorkshire Joint (GC, GN, L&Y, Midland and NE)

Tal   —Talyllyn
Tan.   —Tanat Valley Light (Cambrian)
TBJ   —Taff Bargoed Joint (GW and Rhymney)
TFG   —Tottenham & Forest Gate (LTS and Midland)
THJ   —Tottenham & Hampstead Junction (GE and Midland)
TV   —Taff Vale

Van.   —Van Light (Cambrian)
VR   —Vale of Rheidol (Cambrian)
VT   —Vale of Towy Joint (GW and L&NW)

WB   —Whitechapel & Bow Joint (LTS and Met.District)
WCE   —Whitehaven, Cleator & Egremont Joint (Furness and L&NW)
WCJ   —Wath Curve Joint Committee (GC, Midland and NE)
WCP   —Weston, Clevedon & Portishead
Wir.   —Wirral
W&L   —Welshpool & Llanfair Light (Cambrian)
WL   —West London Joint (GW and L&NW)
WLE   —West London Extension Joint (GW, L&NW, LB&SC and L&SW)
WM   —Wrexham & Minera Joint (GW and L&NW)
WP   —Weymouth & Portland Joint (GW and L&SW)
WRG   —West Riding & Grimsby Joint (GC and GN)
WSC   —Woodside & South Croydon (LB&SC and SE&C)
WT   —Wantage Tramway
WUT   —Wisbech & Upwell Tramway.

2. INDEX TO TUNNELS

(*See also page 84*)

51

Buriton, LSW., 4, D2.
Butternab LY., 45, D2.

Caerphilly, Rhy., 43, B4.
Campden, GW., 9, C5.
Castle Hill, LY., 21, E1.
Catesby, GC., 10, B4.
Charlton, SEC., 6, D2.
Chee Tor, Mid., 15, A5.
Chelsfield, SEC., 5, C4.
Chilcompton, SD., 3, B3; 8, E1.
Chislehurst, SEC., 40, F2.
Christleton, LNW., 20, D3.
Clarborough, GC., 16, A2.
Clay Cross, Mid., 41, D2.
Clayton, LBSC., 5, F3.
Combe Down, SD., 3, B3; 8, D1.
Copenhagen, GN., 40, B5.
Corby, Mid., 16, G1.
Cowburn, Mid., 15, A5.
Cressbrook, Mid., 15, A5.
Crick, LNW., 10, A3.
Crimple, NE., 21, C3.
Crigglestone, Mid., 21, E3; 42, D2.
Cumberworth, LY., 21, F2; 42, D3.

Dainton, GW., 2, D3.
Darnall, GC., 41, A3; 42, G1.
Devonshire, SD., 3, B3; 8, D1.
Dinmore. S&H., 9, B1.
Disley, Mid. !5. A4.
Dove Holes, Mid., 15, A4.

Festiniog, LNW., 19, E3.
Fisherton, LSW., 4, C5.
Fort Pitt, SEC., 6, B5.

Elland, LY., 42, C5.

Gas Works (Kings Cross), GN., 40, B5.
Gillingham (Kent), SEC., 6, B5.
Gisburn, LY., 24, C1.
Glaston, Mid., 16, F1.
Glenfield, Mid., 16, F4.
Greet, GW., 9, D4.
Grimston, Mid., 16, E3.
Grove, SEC., 5, D5.
Guston, SEC., 6, D2.

Haddon, Mid., 15, B5.
Halton, BJ., 45, D5.
Hampstead, GC., 39, B5.
Haverstock Hill, Mid., 39, B5.
Haywards Heath, LBSC., 5, E3.
Headstone, Mid., 15, B5.
Healey House, LY., 42, D5.
Helm, Mid., 27, F2.
High Tor, Mid., 16, B5; 41, D1.
Honiton, LSW., 2, A1.
Honley, LY., 42, D5.
Horsfall, LY., 21, E1.
Hunsbury Hill, LNW., 10, B2.
Hunting Butts, GW., 9, D4.

Kensal Green, LNW., 39, C4.
Kilsby, LNW., 10, A4.
Kirton, GC., 22, F4.
Kitsonwood, LY., 20, A1; 21, E1.
Knighton, Mid., 16, F3.
Knights Hill, LBSC., 40, E5.

Lea Bank, H&O., 42, B5.
Lea Wood, Mid., 16, B5; 41, E1.
Leigham, LBSC., 40, F5.
Lightcliffe, LY., 42, B5.
Linslade, LNW., 10, D1.
Litchfield, LSW., 4, B3.
Litton, Mid., 15, A5.
Llandegai, LNW., 19, D2.
Llangyfelach, GW., 43, G2.
Lord's, GC., 39, C5.
Lydden, SEC., 6, D2.

Manton, Mid., 16, F2.
Marley, GW., 2, D4.

Martello, SEC., 6, D2.
Merstham, LBSC. & SEC., 5, C3.
Mickleham, LBSC., 5, C2.
Middle Hill, GW., 3, A4.
Milford (Derbys.), Mid., 16, C5; 41, F2.
Millwood, LY., 21, E1.
Moncrieff, Cal., 33, F5.
Moorcock, Mid., 27, G2; 24, A1.
Morley, LNW., 21, E3. 42, B3.
Mossdale Head, Mid., 24, A1; 27, G3.
Mountfield, SEC., 6, E5.
Mount Pleasant, SEC., 6, F5.

Netherton, LY., 42, D5.
New Furnace, LY., 42, B4.
Northchurch, LNW., 10, E1.
North Stoke, LBSC., 5, F1.
Nuttal, LY., 45, B1.

Old Lane, H&O., 42, B5.

Patcham, LBSC., 5, F3.
Peascliffe, GN., 16, D1.
Penge, SEC., 40, F4.
Penllergaer, GW., 43, G2.
Penmaenrhos, LNW., 19, D4.
Polhill, SEC., 5, C4.
Ponsbourne, GN., 11, F2.
Popham, LSW., 4, C3.
Preston Hall, SEC., 6, C5.
Primrose Hill, LNW., 39, B5.
Priory, SEC., 6, D2.

Queensbury, GN., 42, B5.

Redhill, LBSC., 5, C3.
Rise Hill, Mid., 24, A1; 27, G2.
Robin Hood, LY., 21, E2; 42, D5.
Royal George, LNW., 21, F1.

St. Anne's Wood, GW., 3, A3; 8, C1.
St. John's Wood, GC., 39, B5.
Salterhebble, LY., 42, C5.
Saltwood, SEC., 6, D2.
Sapperton, GW., 9, F4.
Saxelby, Mid., 16, E3.
Scout, LNW., 21, F1.
Seaton, Mid., 16, F1.
Sevenoaks, SEC., 5, C4.
Severn, GW., 8, C2; 9, F1/G1.
Shakespeare, SEC., 6, D2.
Sharnbrook, Mid., 10, B1.
Shelley Woodhouse, LY., 42, D4.
Shillamill, LSW., 1, C5.
Shillingham, GW., 1, D5.
Shotlock Hill, Mid., 27, G2.
Shugborough, LNW., 15, E4.
Sodbury, GW., 9, G3.
Somerhill, SEC., 5, D5.
Sough, LY., 20, A2; 24, F1; 45, B1.
Spittal, GW., 13, G1.
Springwood (Derbys.), GC., 41, C3.
Springwood (Yorks.), LNW&LYJt., 42, C5.
Standedge, LNW., 21, F1.
Stockingford, Mid., 16, F5.
Stoke, GN., 16, D1.
Stowe Hill, LNW., 10, B3.
Strawberry Hill, SEC., 5, D5.
Streatham, LBSC., 40, F5.
Summit (Littleborough), LY., 21, E1.
Sydenham, SEC., 40, F4.

Taitlands, Mid., 24, B1.
Tankersley, Mid., 21, F3; 42, F2.
Thackley, Mid., 42, A4.
Thurgoland, GC., 21, F3; 42, F3.
Thurstonland, LY., 21, F2; 42, D4.
Torpantau, B&M., 8, A5., 43, C1.
Totley, Mid., 16, A5; 41, B1.
Treverrin, GW., 1, D3.
Twerton, GW., 3, B3; 8, D1.

Wadhurst, SEC., 5, E5.
Waller's Ash, LSW., 4, C3.

Waste Bank, Mid., 27, E1.
Watford (Herts.), LNW., 11, G1.
Watford (Northants.), LNW., 10, A3.
Weasel Hall, LY., 21, E1.
Wellhouse, LY., 21, F3; 42, E3.
Wells, SEC., 5, D5.
Wenvoe, BRY., 43, C4.
Wheatley, HHL., 42, B5.
Whiteball, GW., 8, G5.

Whitehouse Farm, GW&GCJt., 5, A1; 10, F2.
Wickwar, Mid., 8, B1; 9, F2.
Willersley, Mid., 16, B5; 41, D1.
Wing, Mid., 16, F2.
Wingfield, Mid., 16, C5; 41, E2.
Winsor Hill, SD., 3, C2; 8, E1.
Winterbutlee, LY., 21, E1.
Woodhead, GC., 21, F2; 42, E5.
Wyke, LY., 21, E2; 42, B4.

3. INDEX TO WATERTROUGHS

Aber, LNW., 19, D3.
Aldermaston, GW., 4, A3.
Aynho, GW., 10, C4.

Brock, LNW., 24, D3.
Bushey, LNW., 5, A2.

Castlethorpe, LNW., 10, C2.
Charlbury, GW., 10, D5.
Charwelton, GC., 10, B4.
Chester, LNW., 20, D4.
Chipping Sodbury, GW., 9, G2.
Creech (Durston), GW., 8, F3.

Denham, GW., 5, A1; 10, G1.
Diggle, LNW., 21, F1.
Dillicar, LNW., 27, F1.

Eccles, LNW., 45, B3.
Eckington, GC., 16, A4; 41, B2.
Exminster, GW., 2, B3.

Fairwood (Westbury), GW., 3, B4.
Ferryside (Carmarthen), GW., 7, A2.
Flint, LNW., 20, D5.

Garsdale, Mid., 24, A1; 27, G2.
Goring, GW., 4, A2; 10, G3.

Halebank, LNW., 45, E4.
Hademore, LNW., 15, E5.
Haselour, Mid., 15, F5.
Hest Bank, LNW., 24, B3.
Holbrook Park (Rugby), LNW., 10, A4.
Hoscar, LY., 20, B3; 24, F3; 45, E1.

Ipswich, GE., 12, D3.

Keynsham, GW., 3, A3; 8, D1.
Kirkby, LY., 20, B4; 24, F3; 45, E3.

Langley (Knebworth), GN., 11, E2.
Lapworth, GW., 9, A5.
Lea Road (Salwick), PWY., 24, D3.
Lostock Jc., LY., 20, B2; 24, F2; •J, C2.
Loughborough, Mid., 16, E4.
Lucker, NE., 31, E4.
Luddendenfoot, LY., 21, E1.
Ludlow, S&H., 9, A1.

Magor, GW., 8, B2.
Melton Mowbray, Mid., 16, E2.
Moore, LNW., 15, A1; 20, C3; 45, D4.
Muskham (Newark), GN., 16, B2.

Newbold (Rugby), LNW., 10, A4.
New Cumnock, G&SW., 29, F5.

Oakley, Mid., 10, B1; 11, C1.

Prestatyn, LNW., 19, C5.

Rufford, LY., 20, A3; 24, E3; 45, E1.

Scrooby, GN., 21, G5.
Smithy Bridge, LY., 21, E1; 45, A1.
Sowerby Bridge, LY., 21, E1.

Tivetshall, GE., 12, A3; 18, G3.

Wakefield, LY., 21, E3; 42, C2.
Walkden, LY., 20, B2; 24, F1; 45, B2.
Werrington, GN., 17, F2.
Whitmore, LNW., 15, C3; 20, F1.
Wiske Moor (Northallerton), NE., 28, G5.

4. INDEX TO SUMMITS

Aisgill, Mid., 27, G2.
Beattock, Cal., 30, F4.
Corriemuillie, HR., 35, C4.
County March, HR., 38, D4.
Dainton, GW., 2, D3.
Dava, HR., 36, E3.
Desborough, Mid., 10, A2; 16 G2.
Druimuachdair, HR., 33, B2.
Dutchlands, Met&GCJt., 10, E2.
Corrour, NB., 32, C1.
Falahill, NB., 30, C1.
Glenoglehead, Cal., 33, E2.
Hewish, LSW., 3, E1.
Honiton, LSW., 2, A2.
Ingrave, GE., 5, A5.
Lickey Incline, Mid., 9, A4.
Luib, HR., 35, D3.

Masbury, SD., 3, B2; 8, E1.
Peak Forest, Mid., 15, A4.
Penmanshiel, NB., 31, C2.
Raven's Rock, HR., 35, D5.
Sapperton, GW., 9, F4.
Shap, LNW., 27, F1.
Sharnbrook, Mid., 10, B1.
Slochd, HR., 36, F4.
Stainmore, NE., 27, F3.
Stoke, GN., 16, D1.
Talerddig, Cam., 14, B4.
Tring, LNW., 10, E1.
Tyndrum, Cal. & NB., 32, E1.
Whistlefield, NB., 29, A3.
Whiteball, GW., 8, G5.
Whitrope, NB., 31, G1.
Wrangton, GW., 2, D5.

5. INDEX TO VIADUCTS

Barmouth, Cam., 13, A5.
Belah, NE., 27, F3.
Britannia Tubular Bridge, LNW., 19, D2.
Chearsley, GW&GCJt., 10, E3.
Chirk, GW., 20, F4.
Crumlin, GW., 8, B4; 43, B2.
Dee, GW., 20, F4.
Dinting, GC., 21, F1.
Forth Bridge, FB., 30, B3.
Halton, BJ., 20, D3; 45, D5.
Hawarden Swing Bridge, GC., 20, D4.
Hewenden, GN., 42, A5.
King Edward Bridge (Newcastle-on-Tyne), NE., 28, Inset.

King's Ferry Bridge, SEC., 6, B4.
Mottram, GC., 21, G1.
Ouse, LBSC., 5, E3.
Penistone, LY., 42, E3.
Royal Albert Bridge (Saltash), GW., 1, D5.
Royal Border Bridge, NE., 31, C3.
Runcorn, LNW., 45, D4.
Severn, SVW., 8, A1; 9, E2.
Solway, Cal., 26, B2.
Stonehouse, GW., 9, E3.
Southborough, SEC., 5, D5.
Tay Bridge, NB., 34, E4.
Welland, Mid., 16, F1.
Welwyn, GN., 11, F2.

53

6. INDEX TO STATIONS, JUNCTIONS, ETC.

(See also page 84)

Arrochar & Tarbet, NB., 32, G1.
Arthington, NE., 21, D3.
Arthog, Cam., 13, A5.
Arundel, LBSC., 5, F1.
Ascot & Sunninghill, LSW., 4, A1; 5, B1.
Ascott - under - Wychwood, GW., 10, D5.
Asfordby, Mid., 16, E3.
Ash, SEC(LSW), 4, B1; 5, C1.
Ashbourne, LNW&NSJt., 15, C5.
Ashburton, GW., 2, C4.
Ashburton Grove Gds., GN., 40, B5.
Ashburton Jc., GW., 2, D4.
Ashbury, LSW., 1, B5.
Ashburys, GC., 20, B1; 45, A3.
Ashby - de - la - Zouch, Mid(LNW), 16, E5.
Ashby Magna, GC., 16, G4.
Ashchurch, Mid., 9, D3.
Ashcott, SD., 3, C1; 8, E2.
Ashdon Halt, GE., 11, D4.
Ashendon Jc., GW&GCJt/GC., 10, E3.
Ashey, IWC., 4, F3.
Ashford (Kent), SEC., 6, D4.
Ashford (Middx.), LSW., 5, B2
Ash Green, LSW., 4, B1; 5, C1
Ashington, NE., 27, A5.
Ash Jc., SEC/LSW., 4, B1; 5,C1
Ashley (Ches.), CLC., 20, C1; 45, B4.
Ashley & Weston (Northants), LNW., 16, F2.
Ashley Hill, GW., 8, C1.
Ashperton, GW., 9, C2.
Ashtead, LSW&LBSCJt., 5,C2
Ashton (Devon), GW., 2, C3.
Ashton (Lancs.), OAGB., LY., GC., & LNW., 21, F1 and Inset A2; *see also* Dukinfield.
Ashton Jc. (Bristol), GW., 3, Inset.
Ashton-in-Makerfield, GC., 45, D3.
Ashton Moss Jcs., LNW. & LY/GC., 21, Inset.
Ashton-under-Hill, Mid., 9,C4
Ashton's Green Jc., LNW., 45, D3.
Ash Town, EK., 6, C2.
Ashurst, LBSC., 5, D4.
Ashwater, LSW., 1, B5.
Ashwell (Rutland), Mid., 16, E2.
Ashwell & Morden (Cambs.), GN., 11, D2.
Ashwellthorpe, GE., 12, A3; 18, F3.
Askam, Fur., 24, B5.
Askern, LY(GN), 21, E5.
Askern Jc., GN/LY., 21, F5.
Askrigg, NE., 21, A1; 27, G3.
Aslockton, GN., 16, C2.
Aspall & Thorndon, MSL., 12, C3.
Aspatria, M&C., 26, D3.
Aspley Guise Halt, LNW., 10, C1.
Astley, LNW(BJ), 20, B2; 24, G2; 45, C3.
Astley Bridge (Goods), LY., 20, B2; 24, F1; 45, C1.
Aston (Warwicks.), LNW., 13, B4; 15, G5.
Aston-by-Stone, NS., 15, D3; 20, F1.
Aston Rowant, GW., 10, F3.
Aswarby & Sedringham, GN., 17, D1.
Athelney, GW., 3, D1; 8, F3.
Atherstone, LNW., 16, F5.
Atherton, LY. & LNW., 20, B2; 24, F2; 45, C2.
Attadale, HR., 35, E2.
Attenborough, Mid., 16, D4; 41, G4.
Attercliffe, GC., 42, G2.
Attercliffe Rd., Mid., 42, G2.

Attleborough, GE., '12, A4; 18, F4.
Attlebridge, MGN., 18, E3.
Auchendinny, NB., 30, C2.
Auchengray, Cal., 30, D4.
Auchenheath, Cal., 30, D5.
Auchenmade, Cal., 29, D3.
Auchincruive, G&SW., 29, F3.
Auchindachy, GNS., 37, D1.
Auchinleck, G&SW., 29, F5.
Auchmacoy, GNS., 37, E4.
Auchnagatt, GNS., 37, D4.
Auchterarder, Cal., 33, F4.
Auchterhouse, Cal., 34, E5.
Auchterless, GNS., 37, D3.
Auchtermuchty, NB., 34, F5.
Auchtertool (Goods), NB., 30, A2.
Audenshaw Jc., OAGB., 21, Inset A2.
Audlem, GW., 15, C2; 20, F2.
Audley, NS., 15, C3; 20, E1.
Audley End, GE., 11, E4.
Aughton Park Halt, LY., 20, B4; 24, F3; 45, E2.
Auldbar Rd., Cal., 34, D3.
Auldearn, HR., 36, D3.
Auldgirth, G&SW., 26, A4.
Aultmore, HR., 37, D1.
Aumbry, HR., 37, D1.
Authorpe, GN., 17, A3.
Aviemore, HR., 36, F3.
Avoch, HR., 36, D5.
Avoncliff Halt, GW., 3, B4.
Avonbridge, NB., 30, B4.
Avonmouth, GW. & CE., 3, A2; 8, C2; 9, G1.
Avonside Wharf (Goods), Mid., 3, Inset.
Avonwick, GW., 2, D4.
Awre, GW., 8, A1; 9, E2.
Awsworth, GN., 16, C4; 41, F3.
Axbridge, GW., 3, B1; 8, E3.
Axminster, LSW., 2, B1.
Aycliffe, NE., 28, E5.
Aylesbury, GW&GCJt/Met&GCJt. 10, E2; LNW., 10, E2.
Aylesford, SEC., 6, C5
Aylsham, GE. & MGN., 18, D3.
Aynho, GW., 10, D4.
Aynho Park Plat., GW., 10, D4.
Ayot, GN., 11, F2.
Ayr, G&SW., 29, F3.
Aysgarth, NE., 21, A1; 27, G4
Ayton, NB., 31, C3.

B

Backworth, NE., 28, B5.
Bacton, GW., 14, F1.
Bacup, LY., 20, A1.
Badminton, GW., 9, G3.
Baggrow, M&C., 26, D2.
Baghill (Pontefract), SK(GC/GN), 21, E4; 42, C1.
Bagillt, LNW., 20, D5.
Bagshot, LSW., 4, A1; 5, C1.
Bagthorpe Jc., GC/GN., 41, F4
Baguley, CLC., 20, C1; 45, B4
Bagworth & Ellistown, Mid., 16, E4.
Baildon, Mid., 21, D2; 42, A4.
Bailey Gate, SD., 3, E4.
Bailiff Bridge, LY., 21, E2; 42, B4.
Baillieston, Cal., 44, C3.
Bainton, NE., 22, C4.
Baker St., Met(Dist/GW/H&C), 39, C5.
Bakewell, Mid., 15, B5.
Bala, GW., 19, F4.
Bala Jc., GW., 19, F4.
Balado, NB., 30, A3; 33, G5.
Balby Jc., GN/GC., 21, F5 and Inset, F2.
Balcombe, LBSC., 5, E3.
Baldersby, NE., 21, A3.
Balderton, GW., 20, E4.
Baldock, GN., 11, E2.
Baldovan, Cal., 34, E4.
Baldragon, Cal., 34, E4.

Balerno, Cal., 30, C3.
Balfron, NB., 29, A4.
Balgowan, Cal., 33, F4.
Balham, LBSC(LNW), 5, B3; 39, E5.
Ballabeg, IMR., 23, C2.
Ballachulish, Cal., 32, D3.
Ballachulish Ferry, Cal., 32, D3.
Ballasalla, IMR., 23, C2.
Ballater, GNS., 34, A5.
Ballathie (Goods), Cal., 33, E5.
Ballaugh, IMR., 23, A2.
Ballindalloch, GNS., 36, E2.
Ballingham, GW., 9, D1,
Ballinluig, HR., 33, D4.
Balliol Rd. LNW., 45 F3, *See also* Bootle (Lancs.).
Balloch, D&B., 29, B3.
Balloch Pier, D&B., 29, B3.
Balmano Jc., NB., 33, F5.
Balmore, NB., 29, B5; 44, E5.
Balnacoul, HR., 36, C1.
Balne, NE., 21; E5.
Balne Moor (Goods), HB., 21, E5.
Balornock Jc., Cal., 44, D4.
Balquhidder, Cal., 33, F2.
Balshaw Lane & Euxton, LNW., 20, A3; 24, E2; 45, D1, *see also* Euxton.
Bamber Bridge, LY., 20, A3; 24, E2.
Bamford, Mid., 15, A5.
Bamfurlong, LNW., 20, B2; 24, F2; 45, D2.
Bampton (Devon), GW., 7, G5; 8, G5.
Bampton (Oxon)., GW., 10, E5
Banavie, NB., 32, C3.
Banavie Pier, NB., 32, C3.
Banbury, GW(GC), & LNW(SMJ), 10, C4.
Banchory, GNS., 34, A3.
Banff, GNS., 37, C2.
Banff Bridge, GNS., 37, C2.
Bangor, LNW., 19, D2.
Bangor-on-Dee, Cam., 20, F4.
Bankfield (L'pool) Goods, LY., 45, Inset.
Bankfoot, Cal., 33, E5.
Bank Hall, LY., 45, F3.
Bankhead (Aberdeen), GNS., 37, F4.
Bankhead (Lanark), Cal., 30, D4.
Banknock, K&B., 30, B5.
Bank Quay (Warrington), LNW(BJ) & LNW., 45, D4.
Banks, LY., 20, A4; 24, E3.
Bank Top (Burnley), LY, 24, D1.
Bank Top (Darlington), NE., 28 F5.
Bannockburn, Cal., 30, A5.
Banstead, LBSC., 5, C3.
Barassie, G&SW., 29, E3.
Barber's Bridge, GW., 9, D2.
Barbon, LNW., 24, A2.
Barcombe, LBSC., 5, F4.
Barcombe Mills, LBSC., 5, F4.
Bardney, GN., 17, B1.
Bardon Hill, Mid., 16, E4.
Bardon Mill, NE., 27, B2.
Bardowie, NB., 29, B5; 44, E5
Bardsey, NE., 21, D3.
Bare Lane, LNW., 24, B3.
Bargeddie, NB., 29, C5; 44, C4
Bargoed, Rhy(BM), 8, B4; 43, B2.
Bargoed & Aberbargoed, BM., 8, B4; 43, B2.
Barham, SEC., 6, C2.
Barking, LTS(Dist/Mid), 5, A4; 40, B1.
Barkingside, GE., 40, A1.
Barkston, GN., 16, C1.
Barlaston & Tittenson NS., 15, D3; 20, F1.
Barlby Jc., NE., 21, D5.
Barlow, NE., 21, D5.
Barmby, HB., 21, E5.
Barming, SEC., 6, C5.

Barmouth, Cam., 13, A5.
Barmouth Jc., Cam., 13, A5.
Barnack, GN., 17, F1.
Barnard Castle, NE., 27, E4.
Barnby Dun, GC(NE), 21, F5.
Barnby Moor & Sutton, GN., 16, A3.
Barnehurst, SEC., 5, B4.
Barnes, LNW., 5, B3; 39, E4.
Barnes Bridge, LSW., 39, D3.
Barnetby, GC., 22, F3.
Barnham, GE., 12, B5.
Barnham Jc., LBSC., 5, F1.
Barnhill (Dundee), Cal., 34, E4.
Barnhill (Glasgow),NB., 44, D4
Barnoldswick, Mid., 21, Inset.
Barnsley, 21, F3; 42, E2.
    Goods: GC., Mid. & LY.
    Pass:
        Court House, Mid(GC).
        Low Town, LY(GC).
Barnstaple, GW., 7, F3.
Barnstaple Jc., LSW(GW), 7, F3.
Barnstaple Town, LSW(GW), & LB., 7, F3.
Barnstone, GN&LNWJt., 16, D2.
Barnt Green, Mid., 9, A4.
Barnton, Cal., 30, B3.
Barnwell (Cambs.), GE., 11,C3
Barnwell (Northants), LNW., 11, B1; 17, G1.
Barons Court, Dist., 39, D4.
Barras, NE., 27, F3.
Barrasford, NB., 27, B3.
Barrhead, GBK., Cal. & G&SW., 29, C4; 44, F2.
Barrhead, South (Goods), Cal., 29, C4; 44, F2.
Barrhill, G&SW., 25, A3.
Barrmill, GBK. & Cal., 29, D3.
Barrow (Ches.), CLC., 20, D3.
Barrow Haven, GC., 22, E3.
Barrow Hill & Staveley, Works Mid., 16, A4; 41, B3. *See also* Staveley Works.
Barrow-in-Furness, Fur., 24, B5.
Barrow-on-Soar & Quorn, Mid., 16, E3.
    See also Quorn, GC.
Barr Rd. Jc., GN., 16, D1.
Barr's Court (Hereford), S&H(Mid), 9, C1.
Barr's Court Jcs. (Hereford), S&H/GW., 9, C1.
Barry, BRY., 8, D4; 43, C5.
Barry Docks, BRY., 8, D4; 43, C5.
Barry Island, BRY., 8, D4; 43, C5.
Barry Jc., BM/BRY., 8, B4; 43, B3.
Barry Links, D&A., 34, E3.
Bartlow, GE., 11, D4.
Barton (Goods) (Hereford), GW., 9, C1.
Barton (Lancs.), LY., 20, B4; 24, F4; 45, F2.
Barton (Lincs.), GC., 22, E4.
Barton (Goods) (Yorks.), NE., 27, F5.
Barton & Broughton. LNW., 24, D3.
Barton & Walton, Mid(LNW), 15, E5.
Barton Hill, NE., 22,B5.
Barton-le-street, NE., 22, B5.
Barton Moss, LNW., 20, B2; 24, F1; 45, B3.
Baschurch, GW., 20, G4.
Basford (Notts.), Mid., 16, C4; 41, F4.
Basford & Bulwell, GN., 41, F4.
Basingstoke, LSW(GW), & GW., 4, B2.
Bason Bridge, SD., 3, C1; 8, E3.
Bassaleg, GW(LNW) & BM., 8, B3/4; 43, A3.

Bassenthwaite Lake, CKP., 26, E2.
Bat & Ball (Sevenoaks), SEC., 5, C4.
Bath, GW. & Mid(SD), 3, A3; 8, D1.
Bathampton, GW., 3, A3.
Bathgate, NB., 30, C4.
Batley, LNW. & GN., 21, E3; 42, B3.
Batley Carr, GN., 42, C3. *See also* Staincliffe.
Battersby, NE., 28, F4.
Battersea, WLE., 5, B3; 39, E5 *and* Inset E3.
Battersea Park, LBSC., 39, D5 *and* Inset E4.
Battle, SEC., 6, F5.
Battlesbridge, GE., 6, A5.
Battyeford, LNW., 42, C4.
Bawtry, GN., 21, G5.
Baxenden, LY., 20, A1; 24, E1.
Bay Horse, LNW., 24, C3.
Baynards, LBSC., 5, D2.
Bayswater, Met(Dist), 39, C5. A1; 10, F1.
Beaconsfield, GW&GCJt., 5, A1; 10, F1.
Beal, NE., 31, D4.
Bealings, GE., 12, D3.
Beamish, NE., 27, C5.
Beanacre Halt, GW., 3, A4.
Bearley, GW., 9, B5.
Bearsden, NB., 29, B4; 44, E5.
Bearstead & Thurnham, SEC., 6, C5.
Beasdale, NB., 32, B5.
Beattock, Cal., 30, G3.
Beauchief, Mid., 16 A5; 41, A2
Beaufort, LNW., 8, A4; 43, B1
Beaulieu Road, LSW., 4, E4.
Beauly, HR., 35, D5.
Beaumont's Halt, Mid., 11, F1.
Bebington & New Ferry, BJ., 20, C4; 45, F4.
Bebside, NE., 27, A5.
Beccles, GE., 12, A2; 18, G2.
Beckenham Hill, SEC., 40, F3.
Beckenham Jc., SEC., 40, F3.
Beckermet, WCE., 26, F3.
Beckfoot, RE., 26, F2.
Beckford, Mid., 9, C4.
Beckhole, NE., 28, F2.
Beckingham, GN&GEJt., 22, G5.
Beckton, GE., 5, B4; 40, C1.
Bedale, NE., 21, A3; 27, G5.
Beddau Halt, Rhy., 43, B3.
Beddau Halt, TV., 43, C4.
Beddgelert, NWNG., 19, E2.
Beddington Lane Halt, LBSC., 40, G5.
Bedford (Beds.), Mid. & LNW., 10, C1; 11, D1.
Bedhampton Halt, LBSC., 4, E2.
Bedlington, NE., 27, A5.
Bedlinog, TBJ., 8, B5; 43, C2.
Bedminster, GW., 3, Inset.
Bedwas, BM., 8, B4; 43, B3.
Bedworth, LNW., 16, G5.
Bedwyn, GW., 4, A5.
Beechburn, NE., 27, D5.
Beeston (Notts.), Mid., 16, D4; 41, G4.
Beeston (Yorks.), GN(GC), 21, D3; 42, B3.
Beeston Castle & Tarporley, LNW., 15, B1; 20, E3.
Beeston Tor, NS., 15, C5.
Beighton, GC., 16, A4; 41, A3
Beith, G&SW. & GBK., 29, D3
Bekesbourne, SEC., 6, C2.
Belford, NE., 31, E4.
Belgrave & Birstall, GC., 16, E3.
Bellahouston, G&SW., 44, E3 *and* Inset G1.
Bell Busk, Mid., 21, C1.
Belle Vue, GC&MidJt., 20, C1; 45, A3.
Bellfield Jc., G&SW., 29, E4.

Bell Green, LNW., 10, A5.
Bellgrove, NB., 44, D4.
Bellingham (Kent), SEC., 40, F3.
Bellingham (Northumb.), NB., 27, A3.
Bellshill, Cal. & NB., 30, C5; 44, B3.
Bellwater Jc., GN., 17, C3.
Belmont (Surrey), LBSC., 5, C3.
Belper, Mid., 16, C5; 41, F2.
Belses, NB., 31, E1.
Belston Jc., G&SW., 29, F4.
Belton (Lincs.), AJ., 22, F5.
Belton (Norfolk), GE., 18, F1.
Beluncle Halt, SEC., 6, B5.
Belvedere, SEC., 5, B4.
Belvoir Jc., GN., 16, D2.
Bembridge, IW., 4, F2.
Bempton, NE., 22, B3.
Benderloch, Cal., 32, E4.
Benfleet, LTS., 6, A5.
Bengeworth, Mid., 9, C4.
Beningborough, NE., 21, C4.
Ben Rhydding, O&I., 21, C2.
Bensham, NE., 27, C5.
Bentham, Mid., 24, B2.
Bentley (Hants.), LSW., 4, C1.
Bentley (Suffolk), GE., 12, D4.
Bentley Jc., GC., 21, F5 *and* Inset, F2.
Benton, NE., 27, B5.
Bents, NB., 30, C4.
Bentworth & Lasham, LSW., 4, C2.
Benwick Goods, GE., 11, A3; 17, G3.
Bere Alston, LSW/BAC., 1, D5.
Bere Ferrers, LSW., 1, D5.
Berkeley, SVW., 8, B1; 9, F2.
Berkeley Rd., Mid. & SVW., 8, B1; 9, F2.
Berkhamsted, LNW., 10, E1.
Berkswell, LNW., 9, A5.
Berney Arms, GE., 18, F1.
Berrington, GW., 15, F1.
Berrington & Eye, S&H., 9, B1
Berry Brow, LY., 21, E2; 42, D5.
Bervie, NB., 34, B2.
Berwick (Sussex), LBSC., 5, F4
Berwick-on-Tweed, NE&NBJt., 31, C3.
Berwig Halt, GW., 20, E5.
Berw Rd. Halt, TV., 43, C3.
Berwyn, GW., 20, F5.
Bescar Lane, LY., 20, A4; 24, E3; 45, F1.
Bescot, LNW., 13, A3; 15, F4.
Bessacarr Jc., SYJ/DV., 21, F5 *and* Inset D1.
Bestwood Colliery, GN., 16, C4; 41, F4.
Betchworth, SEC., 5, C2.
Bethesda, LNW., 19, D2.
Bethnal Green, GE., 40, C4.
Betley Road, LNW., 15, C2; 20, E2.
Bettisfield, Cam., 20, F3.
Bettws (Llangeinor), PT., 7, B5; 43, D3. *See also* Llangeinor.
Bettws Garmon, NWNG., 19, E2.
Bettws-y-Coed, LNW., 19, E4.
Beverley, NE., 22, D3.
Beverley Rd. (Hull), HB., 22, Inset.
Bewdley, GW., 9, A3.
Bexhill, LBSC. & SEC., 6, F5.
Bexley, SEC., 5, B4.
Bexleyheath, SEC., 5, B4.
Bicester, GW. & LNW., 10, D3.
Bickershaw & Abram, GC., 45, C2.
Bickershaw Jcs., LNW., 45, C2
Bickleigh, GW., 2, D5.
Bickley, SEC., 40, G2.
Biddenden, KES., 6, D4.
Biddulph, NS., 15, B3; 20, E1.

Bideford, LSW., & BWHA., 7, F2.
Bidford-on-Avon, SMJ., 9, B5.
Bidston (Goods), GC. & Wir., 20, C4; 45, F4.
Bidston (Pass.), Wir(GC), 20, C4; 45, F4.
Bieldside, GNS., 37, G4.
Biggar, Cal., 30, E3.
Biggleswade, GN., 11, D2.
Biglis Jc., BRY/TV., 8, D4; 43, B5.
Bilbster, HR., 38, D2.
Billacombe, GW., 2, D5.
Billericay, GE., 5, A5; 11, G5.
Billing, LNW., 10, B2.
Billingboro' & Horbling, GN., 17, D1.
Billinge Green Halt, LNW., 15, B2; 20, D2.
Billingham-on-Tees, NE., 28, E4.
Billingshurst, LBSC., 5, E2.
Bilson (Goods), GW. & SVW., 8, A1; 9, E2.
Bilson Jc., GW/SVW., 8, A1; 9,E2.
Bilston, GW., 15, F4; 13, A1 *see also* Ettingshall Road.
Bilton Road Jc., NE., 21, C3.
Binegar, SD., 3, B2; 8, E1.
Bingham, GN.,16, C3.
Bingham Road (Notts.), GN&LNWJt., 16, D3.
Bingley, Mid., 21, D2; 42, A5.
Binton, SMJ., 9, B5.
Birchfield Plat., GNS., 36, D1
Birchills, LNW., 15, F4.
Birchington-on-Sea, SEC., 6, B2.
Birch Vale, GC&MidJt., 15, A4; 21, G1.
Birdbrook, CVH., 11, D5.
Birdingbury, LNW.. 10, A4.
Birdwell & Hoyland Common, GC., 21, F3; 42, E2.
Birdwell & Pilley (Goods), Mid., 21, F3; 42, E2.
Birkdale, LY(LNW), 20, A4; 24, E4; 45, F1.
Birkdale Palace, CLC., 20, A4; 24, E4; 45, F1.
Birkenhead, BJ., CLC., GC., GW., LNW., Mer., Wir., 20, C4; 24, G4; 45, F4.
Birkenshaw & Tong, GN., 21, D2; 42, B4.
Birmingham (Goods), GW., LNW., & Mid., 13, — and 15, —.
Birmingham (Pass.), GW. & LNW&MidJt., 13, — and 15, —.
Birnie Rd., NB., 34, C2.
Birstall (Yorks.), LNW., 21, E2; 42, B4.
Birstwith, NE., 21, C3.
Birtley, NE., 27, C5.
Bishop Auckland, NE., 27, E5.
Bishopbriggs, NB., 29, C5; 44, D4.
Bishopsbourne, SEC., 6, C2.
Bishops Castle, BC., 14, C1.
Bishop's Cleeve, GW., 9, D4.
Bishopsgate, GE., 40, C4.
Bishop's Lydeard, GW., 8, F4.
Bishop's Nympton & Molland, GW., 7, F5.
Bishops Rd., GW&MetJt., 39, C5 *and* Inset, C2.
Bishop's Stortford, GE., 11, E3
Bishopstone, LBSC., 5, G4.
Bishop's Waltham, LSW., 4, D3.
Bishopton, Cal., 29, C4.
Bisley, GW., 5, C1.
Bispham, PWY., 24, D4.
Bittaford Platform, GW., 2, D5
Bitterley, S&H., 9, A1.
Bitterne, LSW., 4, E4.
Bitton, Mid., 3, A3; 8, D1.
Blaby, LNW., 16, F4.
Black Bank, GE., 11, B4; 17, G4.

Black Bull, NS., 15, C3; 20, E1.
Blackburn, LY(LNW/Mid), 24, D2.
Black Carr Jc., GN/GN&GEJt., 21, Inset G2.
Black Carr East Jc., DV/LY&GNJt., 21, Inset G2.
Black Carr West Jc., DV/LY., 21, Inset, G2.
Black Dyke, NB., 26, C3.
Blackford, Cal., 33, F4.
Blackford Hill, NB., 30, Inset.
Blackfriars, Dist(Met), 40, C5.
Blackhall Rocks, NE., 28, D4.
Blackhall Jc., NB., 30, C4.
Blackheath (London), SEC., 5, B4; 40, E4.
Blackheath Hill, SEC., 40, D3
Blackhill, NE., 27, C4.
Blackhill Jc. (Glasgow), Cal., 44, D4.
Blackhorse Rd., TFG., 40, A3.
Blackhouse Jc., G&SW., 29, F3
Black Lane (Radcliffe), LY., 20, B1; 24, F1; 45, B2.
Blackmill, GW., 7, B5; 43, D3.
Blackmoor, LB., 7, E4.
Blackpill, Mum., 43, G3.
Blackpool, PWY., 24, D4.
Blackrod, LY., 20, B2; 24, F2; 45, C2.
Blacksboat, GNS., 36, E2.
Blackstone, NB., 30 B4.
Blackstone Jc., Cal., 44, G4.
Blackthorn, GW., 10, E3.
Blackwall (Goods), GN., 40, C3; *and* Inset D1.
Blackwall (Pass.), GE., 5, B4; 40, C2.
Blackwater & Camberley, SEC., 4, B1; *see also* Camberley & York Town.
Blackwater (I. of W.), IWC., 4, F3.
Blackwell (Worcs.), Mid., 9,A4
Blackwood (Lanark), Cal., 30, D5.
Blackwood (Mon.), LNW., 8, B4; 43, B2.
Blacon, GC., 20, D4.
Blaenau Festiniog, LNW., GW. & Fest., 19, F3.
Blaenavon, GW. & LNW(GW) 8, A4; 43, A1.
Blaenclydach (Goods), GW., 8, B5; 43, D3.
Blaengarw, GW(PT), 7, B5; 43, D3.
Blaengwynfi, RSB., 7, B5; 43, D2.
Blaenplwyf Halt, GW., 13, E5.
Blaenrhondda, RSB., 7, B5; 43, D2.
Blagdon, GW., 3, B2; 8, D2.
Blaina, GW., 8, A4; 43, B2.
Blairadam, NB., 30, A3.
Blair Atholl, HR., 33, B5.
Blairgowrie, Cal., 33, D5.
Blairhill & Gartsherrie, NB., 29, C5; 44, B4. *See also* Gartsherrie.
Blake Hall, GE., 11, G4.
Blakeney (Goods), GW., 8, A1; 9, E2.
Blakesley, SMJ., 10, C3.
Blake Street, LNW., 15, F5.
Blakey Jc., NE., 28, F3.
Blandford, SD., 3, E4.
Blanefield, NB., 29, B4.
Blankney & Metheringham, GN&GEJt., 16, B1; 17, B1
Blantyre, Cal., 29, C5; 44, C2.
Blaydon, NE(NB), 27, B5.
Bleadon & Uphill, GW., 3, B1; 8, D3.
Blean & Tyler Hill Halt, SEC., 6, C3.
Bleasby, Mid., 16, C3.
Bledlow, GW., 10, F2.
Bledlow Bridge Halt, GW., 10, F2.
Blencow, CKP., 26, E1.

Blenheim & Woodstock, GW., 10, E4.
Bletchington, GW., 10, E4.
Bletchley, LNW., 10, D2.
Blidworth & Rainworth, Mid., 16, B3; 41, D5.
Blisworth, LNW. & SMJ., 10, B3.
Blockley, GW., 9, C5.
Blodwell Jc., Cam., 14, A2; 20, G5.
Blowick, LY., 20, A4; 24, E4; 45, F1.
Bloxham, GW., 10, C4.
Bloxwich, LNW., 15, F4.
Blue Anchor, GW., 8, E5.
Blundellsands & Crosby, LY(LNW), 20, B4; 24, F4; 45, F3.
Blunham, LNW., 11, D1.
Blunsdon, MSW., 9, F5.
Bluntisham, GE., 11, B3.
Blyth, NE., 28. A5.
Blythe Bridge, NS., 15, C4.
Blythburgh, Southwold, 12, B2.
Blyton, GC., 22, G5.
Boarhills, NB., 34, F3.
Boar's Head, LNW. & LU., 20, B3; 24, F2; 45, D2.
Boat of Garten, HR(GNS), 36, F3.
Boddam, GNS., 37, D5.
Bodfari, LNW., 19, D5.
Bodiam, KES., 6, E5.
Bodmin, GW. & LSW., 1, D3.
Bodmin Road, GW., 1, D3.
Bodorgan, LNW., 19, D1.
Bognor, LBSC., 5, G1.
Bogside (Fife), NB., 30, A4.
Bogside (Renfrew), Cal. & G&SW., 29, E3.
Bogston, Cal., 29, B3.
Boldon (Goods), NE., 28, C5.
Bollington, GC&NSJt., 15, A4; 45, A5.
Bollo Lane Jc., LSW/NSW., 39, D3.
Bolsover, GC. & Mid., 16, B4; 41, C3.
Bolton, LY(Mid), LY & LNW. 20, B2; 24, F1; 45, B2.
Bolton Abbey, Mid., 21, C1.
Bolton-le-Sands, LNW., 24, B3
Bolton-on-Dearne, SK(GC), 21, F4; 42, E1.
Bolton Percy, NE(LY/GN), 21, D4.
Bonar Bridge, HR., 36, B5.
Boncath, GW., 13, F3.
Bo'ness, NB., 30, B4.
Bonnington, Cal. & NB., 30, Inset.
Bonnybridge, Cal., K&B. & NB., 30, B5.
Bonnyrigg, NB., 30, C2.
Bonnywater Jc., Cal/K&B., 30, B5.
Bontnewydd, GW., 14, A5.
Bookham, LSW., 5, C2.
Boosbeck, NE., 28, E3.
Boot, RE., 26, F2.
Bootham Jc., NE., 21, C5 and Inset, A4.
Bootle (Cumb.), Fur., 24, A5; 26, G3.
Bootle (Lancs.), LY., 45, F3. See also Balliol Rd.
Bopeep Jc., SEC/LBSC., 6, F5.
Bordesley, GW.,13, C4; 15, G5
Bordon, LSW., 4, C1.
Boroughbridge, NE., 21, B4.
Borough Market Jc., SEC., 40, C4.
Borrobol Plat., HR., 38, F5.
Borrowash, Mid., 16, D4; 41, G2.
Borth, Cam., 13, C5.
Borwick, Fur&MidJt., 24, B3.
Boscarne Jc., LSW/GW., 1, D3
Boscombe, LSW., 3, F5.
Bosham, LBSC., 4. E1.
Bosley, NS., 15, B3; 20, D1.

Boston, GN., 17, C3.
Botanic Gardens (Glasgow), Cal., 44, E4.
Botanic Gardens (Hull), NE., 22, Inset.
Bothwell, Cal. & NB., 29, C5; 44, C2.
Botley, LSW., 4, E3.
Bottesford, GN., 16, D2.
Botteslow Jc., NS., 15, C3.
Bottisham & Lode, GE., 11, C4
Boughton & Llyswen, Cam., 14, F3.
Boughton, GC., 16, B3.
Boultham Jc., GN&GEJt., 16, B1.
Bourne, GN(Mid/MGN), 17, E1.
Bourne End, GW., 5, A1; 10, G2.
Bournemouth
  Central: LSW., 3, F5.
  West: LSW(SD), 3, F5.
Bournville, Mid., 9, A4.
Bourton-on-the-Water, GW., 9, D5.
Bovey, GW., 2, C4.
Bow (Devon), LSW., 2, B4.
Bow (London), NL. & LNW., 40, C5.
Bow Brickhill Halt, LNW., 10, D2.
Bowbridge Crossing Halt, GW., 9, E3.
Bower, HR., 38, C3.
Bowes, NE., 27, F4.
Bowhouse, NB., 30, B4.
Bowland, NB., 30, D1.
Bowling, Cal. & NB., 29, B4.
Bowling Jc., LY., 42, B4.
Bowness, Cal., 26, C2.
Bow Road, WB. & GE., 40, C3
Bow Street, Cam., 13, C5.
Box, GW., 3, A4.
Boxford, GW., 4, A4.
Box Hill, SEC., 5, C2.
Box Hill & Burford Bridge, LBSC., 5, C2.
Boxmoor & Hemel Hempsted, LNW., 10, E1; 11, F1; see also Hemel Hempsted.
Boyce's Bridge, WUT., 17, F4.
Braceborough Spa, GN., 17, E1.
Bracebridge (Gds.), GN., 16, B1.
Brackenhill Jc. (Ayrshire), G&SW., 29, E4.
Brackenhill Jc. (Yorks.), SK/BL., 21, E4; 42, C1.
Brackenhills, Cal., 29, D3.
Brackley, GC. & LNW., 10, C3.
Bracknell, LSW., 4, A1.
Bradbury, NE., 28, E5.
Bradfield, GE., 12, E4.
Bradford (Goods), GN., LY & Mid., 21, D2; 42, A4.
Bradford(Pass.), 21, D2; 42, A4
  Exchange, LY(GN).
  Market St., Mid(NE).
Bradford-on-Avon, GW., 3, B4
Brading Jc., IW., 4, F3.
Bradley (Yorks.), LNW(LY), 42, C4.
Bradley Fold, LY., 20, B2; 24, F1; 45, B2.
Bradley Wood Jc., LY., 21, E2; 42, C4.
Bradnop, NS., 15, C4.
Bradwell, LNW., 10, C2.
Brafferton, NE., 21, B4.
Braidwood, Cal., 30, D5.
Braintree & Bocking, GE., 11. E5.
Braithwaite, CKP., 26, E2.
Braithwell Jc., HB&GCJt/ GCMid&HBJt., 21, G4.
Bramber, LBSC., 5, F2.
Brambledown Halt, SEC., 6, B4.
Bramford, GE., 12, D4.
Bramhall, LNW(NS), 15, A3; 20, C1; 45, A4.

Bramhall Moor Lane (Goods), Mid., 45, A4.
Bramley (Hants.), GW., 4, B2.
Bramley (Yorks.) GN(LY)., 21, D3; 42, A3.
Bramley & Wonersh, LBSC., 5, D1.
Brampford Speke, GW., 2, B3.
Brampton Gds. (Chesterfield) Mid., 16, B5; 41, C2.
Brampton (Suffolk), GE., 12, B2.
Brampton Jc. (Cumb.), NE., 27, C1.
Brampton Town (Cumb.), NE., 27, C1.
Bramwith (Goods), WRG., 21, F5.
Brancepeth, NE., 27, D5.
Brancliffe Jc., GC/GC&MidJt., 16, A4; 41, A4.
Brandlesholme Rd. Halt, LY., 45, B1.
Brandon (Durham), NE., 27, D5.
Brandon (Norfolk), GE., 11, A5; 17, G5.
Brandon & Wolston. LNW., 10, A5.
Brandy Bridge Jc., TV/GW&TVJt., 43, C2.
Branksome, LSW(SD), 3, F5.
Bransford Road, GW., 9, B3.
Branston (Staffs.), Mid., 15, E5.
Branston & Heighington, GN&GEJt., 16, B1; 17, B1.
Bransty (Whitehaven), Fur&LNWJt., 26, E4.
Branthwaite, WCE., 26, E3.
Brasted, SEC., 5, C4.
Bratton Fleming, LB., 7, E3.
Braughing, GE., 11, E3.
Braunston, LNW., 10, B4.
Braunston & Willoughby, GC., 10, B4.
Braunton, LSW(GW), 7, F3.
Brayton, M&C(Cal.), 26, D2.
Brayton Jc., NE., 21, D5.
Breadsall (Gds.), GN., 16, D5; 41, G2
Breakwater Jc., Cal., 30, Inset.
Breamore, LSW., 4, D5.
Brechin, Cal., 34, C3.
Breck Rd., LNW., 20, C4; 24, G4; 45, F3.
Brecon, BM(Cam/Mid/N&B), 14, F3.
Brecon Curve Jc. (Hereford) GW/Mid., 9, C1.
Brecon Rd. (Abergavenny), LNW., 43, A1.
Bredbury, GC&MidJt., 21, G1; 45, A3.
Bredon (Worcs.), Mid., 9, C3.
Breich, Cal., 30, C4.
Brent (Devon), GW., 2, D4.
Brentford, LSW. & GW., 5, B2; 39, D2.
Brentford Jc., LSW., 39, D3
Brentham, GW., 39, C2.
Brent Jc. (Cricklewood), Mid., 39, B4.
Brent Jc. (Willesden), LNW., 39, C3.
Brent Knoll, GW., 3, B1; 8, E3.
Brentor, LSW., 1, C5.
Brentwood & Warley, GE., 5, A5.
Bretby, Mid., 16, E5.
Brettell Lane, GW., 15, G3.
Breydon Jc., GE., 18, F1.
Bricket Wood, LNW., 11, G1.
Bricklayers Arms Goods, SEC., 40, D4.
Bricklayers Arms Jc., LBSC., 40, D4.
Bridestowe, LSW., 2, B5.
Bridge, SEC., 6, C3.
Bridgend, GW(BRY), 7, C5; 43, D4.
Bridgend & Coity (Goods), BRY., 43, D4.

Bridgend Jc., NB., 29, B5; 44, C5.
Bridgefoot, WCE., 26, E3.
Bridgeness, NB., 30, B4.
Bridge of Allan, Cal., 30, A5.
Bridge of Dee, G&SW., 26, C5.
Bridge of Dun, Cal., 34, C3.
Bridge of Earn, NB., 33, F5.
Bridge of Orchy, NB., 32, E1.
Bridge of Weir, G&SW., 29, C3.
Bridge St. (Northampton), LNW., 10, B2.
Bridge St. (Shipley), GN., 42, A5.
Bridge St. Jc., (Glasgow), Cal/G&P., 44, Inset F2.
Bridgeton, Cal., 44, D3.
Bridgeton Cross, Cal. & NB(G&SW), 44, D3.
Bridgnorth, GW., 15, F2.
Bridgwater, GW. & SD., 3, C1; 8, F3.
Bridlington, NE., 22, B3.
Bridport, GW., 3, F1.
Brierfield, LY., 24, D1.
Brierley Hill, GW., 15, G3.
Brierley Jc., HB/DV., 21, F4; 42, D1.
Brigg, GC., 22, F4.
Brigham, LNW and M&C Jt., 26, E3.
Brighouse, LY., 21, E2; 42, C4. See also Clifton Rd.
Brightlingsea, GE., 12, F4.
Brighton, LBSC., 5, F3.
Brighton Rd. (Birmingham), Mid., 13, D4.
Brightside, Mid., 21, G3 and 42, G2.
Brill, OAT., 10, E3.
Brill & Ludgershall, GW., 10, E3.
Brimscombe, GW., 9, F3.
Brimscombe Bridge Halt., GW., 9, F3.
Brimsdown, GE., 5, A3; 11, G3.
Brindle Heath (Goods), LY., 45, B3.
Brinkburn, NB., 31, G4.
Brinklow, LNW., 10, A4.
Brinkworth, GW., 9, G4.
Brinnington Jc., GC&MidJt., 21, G1.
Brinscall, LU., 20, A2; 24, E2.
Brislington, GW., 3, A2; 8, D1.
Bristol, GW/Mid., GW. & Mid., 3, A2 and Inset; 8, C1/2.
Bristol Rd., WCP., 3, A1; 8, D3.
Britannia, LY., 20, A1.
Brithdir, Rhy., 8, B4; 43, B2. See also Cwmsyfiog.
Briton Ferry, RW., RSB. & SWM., 7, B4; 43, F3.
Briton Ferry Road, GW., 43, F3.
Brixham, GW., 2, D3.
Brixton, SEC., 5, B3; 40, E5.
Brixton Coal Depot., Mid, 40, E5.
Brixton Road (Devon), GW., 2, E5.
Brixworth, LNW., 10, A2.
Broad Clyst, LSW., 2, B3.
Broadfield, LY., 20, B1; 24, F1; 45, A2.
Broad Green, LNW., 20, C4; 45, E4.
Broadheath, LNW., 20, C2; 45, B4.
Broadheath Jc., LNW/CLC., 45, B4.
Broadley, LY., 20, A1; 45, A1.
Broadstairs, SEC., 6, B1.
Broadstone, LSW(SD), 3, F5.
Broad St. (London), NL. & LNW., 5, A3; 40, C4.
Broad St. (Pendleton), LY., 45, B3.

Broadway, GW., 9, C4.
Brock, LNW., 24, D3.
Brockenhurst, LSW., 4, E4.
Brocketsbrae, Cal., 30, D5.
Brockford & Wetheringsett. MSL., 12, C4.
Brockholes, LY., 21, F2; 42, D5.
Brocklesby, GC., 22, E3.
Brockley, LBSC., 40, E3.
Brockley Lane, SEC. 40 E3.
Brockley Whins, NE., 28, C5.
Brodie, HR., 36 D3.
Bromborough, BJ., 20, C4; 45, F5.
Bromfield (Cumb.),Cal., 26, D2
Bromfield (Salop,), S&H., 9, A1.
Bromford Bridge, Mid., 15, G5
Bromham & Rowde, GW., 3, B5.
Bromley (London), LTS(Dist), 40, C3.
Bromley Cross, LY., 20, A2; 24, F1; 45, B1.
Bromley Jc. (Norwood), LBSC/SEC., 40, F4.
Bromley North (Kent), SEC., 5, B4; 40, F2.
Bromley South (Kent), SEC., 5, B4; 40, G2.
Brompton (Yorks.), NE.,28,G5
Brompton & Fulham Goods, LNW., 39, D4.
Bromsgrove, Mid., 9, A4.
Bromshall (Goods), NS., 15, D4.
Bromyard, GW., 9, B2.
Brondesbury, LNW(NL), 39, B4. *See also* Kilburn, Met.
Brondesbury Park, LNW(NL), 39, B4.
Bronwydd Arms, GW., 13, G4.
Brookland, SEC., 6, E4.
Brooklands, MSJA(CLC). 20, C1; 45, B3.
Brooksby, Mid., 16, E3.
Brookwood, LSW., 5, C1.
Brookwood Cemetery (London Necropolis Co.) LSW., 5, C1
Broom (Jc.), Mid(SMJ), 9, B4.
Broome, LNW., 14, C1.
Broomfield Jc., Cal/NB., 34, C2.
Broomfleet, NE(GC). 22, E4.
Broomhill (Inverness), HR., 36, F3.
Broomhill (Northumb.), NE., 31, G5.
Broomhouse, NB., 29, C5; 44, C3.
Broomieknowe, NB., 30, C2.
Broomielaw, (Durham), NE., 27, E4.
Broomlee, NB., 30, D3.
Brora, HR., 36, A4; 38, G5.
Brotton, NE., 28, E3.
Brough, NE(GC/LNW) 22, E4
Broughton (Peebles), Cal., 30, E3.
Broughton & Bretton, LNW., 20, D4.
Broughton Astley, Mid., 16,G4
BroughtonCross,LNW., 26, E3
Broughton Gifford Halt, GW., 3, B4.
Broughton-in-Furness, Fur., 24, A5.
Broughton Lane, GC., 42, G2.
Broughty Ferry, D&A., 34, Inset E1.
Browndown Halt, LSW., 4, E3.
Brownhill Jc., G&SW., 29, D3.
Brownhills, LNW. & Mid., 15, F4.
Broxbourne & Hoddesdon, GE., 11, F3.
Broxton, LNW., 15, C1; 20, E3.
Bruce Grove, GE., 40, A4.
Brucklay, GNS., 37, D4.
Brundall, GE., 18, F2.

Brunswick (L'pool) Goods, CLC., 20, C4; 45, F4 *and* Inset.
Brunswick Dock (L'pool) Goods, LNW., 45, F4 *and* Inset.
Bruton, GW,. 3, C3; 8, F1.
Brymbo, GW(LNW), & GC. 20, E4.
Brymbo West Crossing Halt, GW., 20, E4.
Bryn (Glam.), PT., 7, B5; 43, E3.
Bryn (Lancs.), LNW., 20, B3; 24, F2; 45, D3.
Brynamman, GW. & Mid., 7, A4; 43, F1.
Brynglas, Tal., 13, B5.
Bryngwyn (Carnarvon), NWNG., 19, E2.
Bryngwyn Halt (Montgomery), Cam., 14, A2.
Brynkir, LNW., 19, F2.
Brynmawr, LNW(GW), 8, A4; 43, B1.
Brynmenyn, GW., 7, C5; 43,D3
Brynmill, Mum., 43, G3.
Bryn Teify, GW., 13, F4.
Bubwith, NE., 21, D5.
Buccleuch Dock Jc., Fur., 24 B5.
Buchanan St. (Glasgow), Cal., 29, C5; 44, E4.
Buchlyvie, NB., 29, A4.
Buckden, Mid., 11, C2. *See also* Offord.
Buckenham, GE., 18, F2.
Buckfastleigh, GW., 2, D4.
Buckhaven, NB., 30, A2; 34,G5
Buckhurst Hill, GE., 5, A4.
Buckie, GNS. & HR., 37, C1.
Buckingham, LNW., 10, D3.
Buckingham West Jc., Cal., 34, Inset E2.
Buckland Jc., SEC., 6, D2.
Buckley, GC., 20, D5. *See also* Padeswood.
Buckley Jc., GC., 20, D4.
Bucknall & Northwood, NS., 15, C3.
Bucknell, LNW., 14, D1.
Buckpool, GNS., 37, C1.
Bucksburn, GNS., 37, F4.
Buddon, D&A., 34, E4.
Bude, LSW., 1, A4.
Budleigh Salterton, LSW., 2, C2.
Bugle, GW., 1, D2.
Bugsworth, Mid., 15, A4.
Buildwas, GW., 15, F2.
Builth Road, Cam. & LNW., 14, E3.
Builth Wells, Cam., 14, E3.
Bulford, LSW., 4, C5.
Bulford Camp, LSW., 4, C5.
Bulkington, LNW., 16, G5.
Bullers o' Buchan Plat., GNS., 37, E5.
Bullgill, M&C., 26, D3.
Bullo Pill, GW., 8, A1; 9, E2.
Bulwell, Mid., 16, C4; 41, F4. *See also* Basford.
Bulwell Common, GC., 16, C4; 41, F4.
Bulwell Forest, GN., 16, C4; 41, F4.
Bunchrew, HR., 36, D5.
Bungalow Town Halt, LBSC., 5, F2.
Bungay, GE., 12, A2; 18, G2
Buntingford, GE., 11, E3.
Burbage (Goods), GW., 4, A5.
Burdale, NE., 22, B5.
Burdett Rd., GE(LTS), 40, C3.
Bures, GE., 12, E5.
Burgess Hill, LBSC., 5, E3.
Burgh (Cumb.), NB., 26, C1.
Burgh (Lincs.), GN., 17, B4.
Burghclere, GW., 4, B3.
Burghead, HR., 36, C2.
Burlescombe, GW., 8, G5.

Burley, O&I., 21, C2.
Burleigh St. (Goods) (Hull), HB., 22, Inset.
Burlington Rd. Halt, PWY., 24, D4.
Burnage, LNW., 45, A3.
Burnbank, NB., 44, C2.
Burneside, LNW., 27, G1.
Burngullow, GW., 1, D2.
Burnham (Som.), SD., 3, B1; 8, E3.
Burnham Beeches, GW., 5, B1.
Burnham Market, GE., 18, D5.
Burnham - on - Crouch, GE., 6, A4; 12, G5.
Burn Hill, NE., 27, D4.
Burnley, LY., 24, D1.
Burnmouth, NB., 31, C3.
Burn Naze Halt, PWY., 24, D4
Burnside, Cal., 29, C5; 44, D3.
Burnt House (Goods), GE., 11, A3; 17, G3.
Burntisland, NB., 30, A2.
Burnt Mill, GE., 11, F3.
Burrington, GW., 3, B2; 8, D2.
Burry Port, BPGV., 7, B2. *see also* Pembrey, GW.
Burscough Bridge, LY., 20, A4; 24, F3; 45, E1.
Burscough Jc., LY., 20, B4; 24, F3; 45, E1.
Bursledon, GW., 4, E3.
Burslem, NS., 15, C3; 20, E1.
Burston, GE., 12, B3.
Burton Agnes, NE., 22, B3.
Burton & Holme, LNW., 24, B3
Burton Joyce, Mid., 16, C3; 41, F5.
Burton Lane Jc., NE., 21, C5 and Inset A4.
Burton-on-Trent (Goods), Mid., GN. & LNW., 15, Inset D5.
Burton - on - Trent (Pass.), Mid(GN/LNW/NS), 15, D5 and Inset.
Burton Point, GC., 20, D4; 45, F5.
Burton Salmon, NE(GN), 21, E4; 42, B1.
Burwarton, CMDP., 15, G2.
Burwell, GE., 11, C4.
Bury (Lancs.), LY., 20, B1; 24, F1; 45, B1/2.
Bury St. Edmunds, GE., 12, C5
Busby, Cal., 29, C5; 44, E2.
Busby Jc., Cal./GBK., 44, E3.
Bushbury (Goods), LNW., 15, F3.
Bushbury Jc., LNW/GW., 15, F3.
Bushey and Oxhey, LNW., 5, A2; 11, G1.
Bushey Lane Jc., LY., 20, B3; 45, E2.
Bush Hill Park, GE., 5, A3; 11, G3.
Butler's Hill, GN., 16, C4; 41, E4.
Butterknowle, NE., 27, E4.
Butterley, Mid., 16, C5; 41, E4.
Butterton, NS., 15, B5.
Buttington, Cam. & SWP., 14, A2.
Butts Jc., LSW., 4, C2.
Butts Lane Halt, LY., 20, A4; 24, E4; 45, F1.
Buxted, LBSC., 5, E4.
Buxton, LNW. & Mid., 15, A4.
Buxton Lamas, GE., 18, E3.
Byers Green, NE., 27, D5.
Byfield, SMJ., 10, B4.
Byfleet & Woodham, LSW., 5, C1.
Byker, NE., 28, Inset.
Bynea (Carmar.), GW., 7, B3.

C

Cadbury Rd., WCP., 3, A1; 8, C2.

Cadeleigh, GW., 2, A3.
Cadishead, CLC., 20, C2; 24, G1; 45, C3.
Cadoxton, BRY(TV), 8, D4; 43, B5.
Cadoxton Goods (Neath), N&B., 43, F2.
Cadzow Jc., Cal., 44, B2.
Cae Harris, TBJ., 43, C2.
Caerau, GW., 7, B5; 43, E3.
Caergwrle Castle, GC., 20, E4.
Caerleon, GW., 8, B3; 43, A3.
Caerphilly, Rhy(AD), 8, C4; 43, B3.
Caersws, Cam., 14, C3.
Caerwys, LNW., 20, D5.
Cairnbulg, GNS., 37, C5.
Cairneyhill, NB., 30, A3.
Cairnie Jc., GNS., 37, D1.
Cairn Valley Jc., G&SW., 26, B4.
Caister-on-Sea, MGN., 18, E1.
Calbourne & Shalfleet, FYN., 4, F4.
Calcots, GNS., 36, C1.
Caldarvan, NB., 29, B4.
Calder, Cal., 44, B4.
Calderbank, Cal., 30, C5; 44, A3.
Calderbank Branch Jc., NB., 44, A4.
Caldercruix, NB., 30, C5.
Caldon Low Halt, NS., 15, C4.
Caldwell, GBK., 29, D4.
Caldy, BJ., 20, C5.
Caledonian Rd. & Barnsbury, NL(LNW), 40, B5.
Callander, Cal., 33, G2.
Callerton, NE., 27, B5.
Callington, BAC., 1, C5.
Callowland, LNW., 11, G1.
Calne, GW., 3, A5.
Calstock, BAC., 1, C5.
Calthwaite, LNW., 27, D1.
Calveley, LNW., 15, B1; 20, E3.
Calverley & Rodley, Mid., 21, D2; 42, A4.
Calvert, GC., 10, D3.
Cam, Mid., 8, B1; 9, F2.
Camber, RCT., 6, E4.
Camberley & York Town, LSW., 4, B1. *See also* Blackwater, SEC.
Camberwell, SEC., 40, D5.
Camborne, GW., 1, Inset E5.
Cambria Rd. Jc., LBSC/SEC., 40, E4.
Cambridge (Goods), GE., GN., LNW. & Mid., 11, C3.
Cambridge (Pass.), GE(GN/LNW/Mid), 11, C3.
Cambridge Heath, GE., 40, C4.
Cambus, NB., 30, A5.
Cambusavie Plat., HR., 36, A4
Cambuslang, Cal., 29, C5; 44, D3.
Cambus o'May, GNS., 34, A4.
Camden Goods, LNW., 40, C5 *and* Inset A1.
Camden Town, NL(LNW), 40, B5.
Camelford, LSW., 1, B3.
Camelon, NB(Cal.), 30, B5.
Camelon (Goods), NB. & Cal., 30, B5.
Cameron Bridge, NB., 30, A2; 34, G5.
Camerton (Cumb.), LNW., 26, E3.
Camerton (Som.), GW., 3, B3; 8, D1.
Camlachie (Goods), NB., 44, D4.
Campbell Rd. Jc., LTS/WB., 40, C3.
Campbeltown, CM., 29, Inset.
Campden, GW., 9, C5.
Camperdown East Jc., NB/D&A., 34, Inset E2.
Camp Hill, Mid., 13, C4.
Campsie Branch Jc., NB., 29, B5; 44, D5.

Churston, GW., 2, D3.
Churwell, LNW., 21, D3; 42, B3.
Chwilog, LNW., 19, F1.
Cilfrew, N&B., 7, B4; 43, F2.
Cilfynydd, TV., 8, B5; 43, C3.
Ciliau-Aeron, GW., 13, E4.
Cilmery, LNW., 14, E3.
Cinderford, GW. & SVW., 8, A1; 9, E2.
Cirencester, GW. & MSW., 9, F4.
City Basin Jc., (Exeter), GW., 2, B3
City Rd. Goods (Bradford), GN., 42, A4.
Clackmannan, NB., 30, A4.
Clacton-on-Sea & Southcliff, GE., 12, F3.
Clandon, LSW., 5, C1.
Clapham (London), SEC(LBSC), 40, E5.
Clapham (Yorks.), Mid., 24, B1.
Clapham Jc. (London), LSW., LBSC(LNW), & WLE., 5, B3; 39, E5 and Inset F3.
Clapton, GE., 40, B4.
Clapton Rd., WCP., 3, A1; 8, C2.
Clarbeston Road, GW., 13, G1
Clarboro' Jc., GC., 16, A2.
Clare, GE., 11, D5.
Clarence Road (Cardiff), GW(BRY/TV), 43, B4.
Clarence St. (Pontypool), G.W.,'43, A2.
Clarence Yard Gds., GN., 40, B5.
Clarkston (Lanark), NB., 30, C5; 44, A4.
Clarkston (Renfrew), Cal., 29, C5; 44, E2.
Clatford, LSW(MSW), 4, C4.
Claverdon, GW., 9, B5.
Claxby & Usselby, GC., 22, G3.
Clay Cross, Mid., 16, B5; 41, C2, D2.
Claydon (Bucks.), LNW., 10, D3.
Claydon (Suffolk), GE., 12, D4
Claygate & Claremont, LSW., 5, C2.
Claypole, GN., 16, C2.
Clayton, GN., 21, D2; 42, B5.
Clayton Bridge, LY., 45, A3.
Clayton West, LY., 21, F3; 42, D3.
Cleator Moor, WCE. & CWJ., 26, E3.
Cleckheaton, LY. & LNW., 21, E2; 42, B4.
Cledford Bridge Halt, LNW., 15, B2; 20, D2.
Clee Hill, S&H., 9, A1.
Cleethorpes, GC., 22, F2.
Cleeve, Mid., 9, D3.
Clegg St. (Oldham) OAGB(LY)., 21, Inset D1; 45, A2.
Cleghorn, Cal., 30, D4.
Clenchwarton, MGN., 17, E4.
Cleobury Mortimer, GW. & CMDP., 9, A2.
Cleobury Town, CMDP., 9, A2.
Clevedon, GW. & WCP., 3, A1; 8, D3.
Clevedon East, WCP., 3, A1; 8, D3.
Cliburn, NE., 27, E1.
Cliddesden, LSW., 4, B2.
Cliff Common, NE. & DVL., 21, D5.
Cliffe, SEC., 6, B5.
Clifford, GW., 14, E2.
Clifton (Derbys.), NS., 15, C5.
Clifton (Westmorland), NE., 27, E1.
Clifton & Lowther, LNW., 27, E1.
Clifton Bridge, GW., 3, A2.

Clifton Down, CE., 3, Inset; 3, A2; 8, C2.
Clifton Jc. (Lancs.), LY., 20, B1; 24, F1; 45, B2.
Clifton Maybank (Goods), GW., 3, E2; 8, G2.
Clifton Mill, LNW., 10, A4.
Clifton-on-Trent, GC., 16, B2.
Clifton Rd. (Brighouse), LY., 21, E2; 42, C4.
Clipstone & Oxendon, LNW., 10, A2; 16, G2.
Clipstone (Goods), GC., 16, B3; 41, C5.
Clitheroe, LY(Mid), 24, D1.
Clock Face, LNW., 20, C3; 24, G3; 45, D4.
Clock House, SEC., 40, F4.
Clocksbriggs, Cal., 34, D4.
Closeburn, G&SW., 26, A4.
Clough Fold, LY., 20, A1; 24, E1.
Cloughton, NE., 28, G1.
Clovenfords, NB., 30, E1.
Clown, GC. & Mid., 16, A4; 41, B4.
Clunes, HR., 35, D5.
Clutton, GW., 3, B3; 8, D1.
Clydach (Brecknock), LNW., 8, A4; 43, B1.
Clydach Court Halt, TV., 43, C3.
Clydach-on-Tawe, Mid. & GW., 7, B4; 43, F2.
Clydebank, Cal. & NB., 29, C4; 44, F4.
Clyde Jc., G&SW., 44, Inset E2.
Clynderwen, GW., 13, G2.
Clyne Halt, GW., 43, E2.
Coalbrookdale, GW., 15, F2.
Coalburn, Cal., 30, E5.
Coaley Jc., Mid., 8, B1; 9, F2.
Coalpit Heath, GW., 8, C1; 9, G2.
Coalport, GW. & LNW., 15, F2.
Coalville, Mid. & LNW., 16, E4.
Coanwood, NE., 27, C2.
Coatbridge, Cal. & NB., 30, C5; 44, B4.
Coatdyke, NB., 44, B4.
Coates (Glos.), GW., 9, F4.
Cobbinshaw, Cai., 30, C4.
Cobham & Stoke d'Abernon, LSW., 5, C2.
Coborn Rd., GE., 40, C3.
Cobridge, NS., 15, C3; 20, E1.
Cockburnspath, NB., 31, B2.
Cockerham Cross Halt, KE., 24, C3.
Cockermouth, LNW&CKPJt (M&C)., 26, E3.
Cockett, GW., 7, B3; 43, G3.
Cockfield (Suffolk), GE., 12, C5.
Cockfield (Durham), NE., 27, E4.
Cocking, LBSC., 4, D1.
Cockley Brake Jc., LNW/SMJ., 10, C4.
Codford, GW., 3, C5.
Codnor Park, GN., 16, C4; 41, E3.
Codnor Park Jc., Mid/GN., 41, E3.
Codnor Park & Ironville, Mid., 16, C4; 41, E3.
Codsall, GW., 15, F3.
Coed Poeth, GW., 20, E5.
Coed Talon, LNW., 20, E5.
Coed-y-gric Jc., GW., 8, B3; 43, A2.
Cogan, BRY., 8, C4; 43, B5.
Cogie Hill Halt, KE., 24, C3.
Cogload Jc., GW., 8, F3.
Coity Jc., GW/BRY., 7, C5; 43, D4.
Colbren Jc., N&B(Mid), 7, A5; 43, E1.
Colby, IMR., 23, C2.
Colchester, GE., 12, E4.
Coldham, GE., 17, F3.

Coldham Lane Jc., GE., 11, C3.
Cold Norton, GE., 12, G5.
Coldstream, NE., 31, D3.
Cole, SD., 3, C3; 8, F1.
Coleburn, GNS., 36, D1.
Coleford, SVW. & GW., 8, A1; 9, E1.
Coleford Jc., LSW., 2, B4.
Cole Green, GN., 11, F2.
Colehouse Lane, WCP., 3, A1; 8, D3.
Coleorton Tramway, 16, E5.
Coleshill, Mid., 15, G5.
Colfin, P&W., 25, C2.
Colinton, Cal., 30, C2.
College Goods (Glasgow) G&SW., 44, D4 and Inset E2
Collessie, NB., 34, F5.
Collingbourne, MSW., 4, B5.
Collingham, Mid., 16, B2.
Collingham Bridge, NE., 21, C4.
Collins Green, LNW., 20, C3; 24, G2; 45, D3.
Colliston, Cal., 34, D3.
Colnbrook, GW., 5, B1.
Colne, LY&MidJt., 21, Inset.
Coltfield Plat., HR., 36, C2.
Coltishall, GE., 18, E3.
Colwall, GW., 9, C2.
Colwich, LNW&NSJt., 15, E4.
Colwyn Bay, LNW., 19, D4.
Colyford, LSW., 2, B1.
Colyton, LSW., 2, B1.
Colzium, K&B., 30, B5.
Combe Hay Halt, GW., 3, B3; 8, D1.
Combpyne, LSW., 2, B1.
Commercial Rd. Goods, LTS., 40, C4.
Common Branch Jc., TV., 43, C4.
Commondale, NE., 28, F3.
Commondyke, G&SW., 29, F5
Commonhead, NB., 44, B4.
Compton, GW., 10, G4.
Comrie, Cal., 33, F3.
Conder Green, LNW., 24, C3.
Condover, S&H., 14, B1; 15, F1.
Congleton, NS(LNW), 15, B3; 20, D1.
Congresbury, GW., 3, A1; 8, D3.
Coningsby, GN., 17, C2.
Conisbrough, GC(Mid), 21, F4.
Coniston, Fur., 26, G1.
Connah's Quay, LNW., 20, D4
Connah's Quay & Shotton, GC., 20, D4.
Connaught Rd., PLA(GE)., 40, C2.
Connel Ferry, Cal., 32, E4.
Conon, HR., 35, D5.
Cononley, Mid., 21, C1.
Consall, NS., 15, C4.
Consett, NE., 27, C4.
Constable Burton, NE., 21, A2; 27, G5.
Conway, LNW., 19, D3.
Conwil, GW., 13, G4.
Cookham, GW., 5, A1; 10, G2.
Cooksbridge, LBSC., 5, F4.
Cook St. Branch, G&SW., 44, Inset, E2.
Coombe, LL., 1, D4.
Coombe Lane, WSC., 5, C3.
Cooper Bridge, LY., 21, E2; 42, C4.
Copenhagen Jc., GN., 40, B5.
Copgrove, NE., 21, B3.
Cop Lane Halt, LY., 20, A3; 24, E3.
Copley, LY., 21, E2; 42, C5.
Copley Hill, LNW., 21, Inset C2; 42, A3.
Copmanthorpe, NE(GN), 21, C5.
Copperas Hill, CWJ., 26, E3.
Copper Mill Jc., GE., 40, A4.
Copper Pit Halt, GW., 43, G2
Copplestone, LSW., 2, A4.

Coppull, LNW., 20, A3; 24, E2; 45, D1.
Copyhold Jc., LBSC., 5, E3.
Corbet's Lane Jc., LBSC/SEC., 40, D4.
Corbridge, NE(NB), 27, C4.
Corby (Lincs.), GN., 16, D1; 17, E1.
Cordio Jc., NE., 21, A3; 28, G5.
Corfe Castle, LSW., 3, G5.
Corfe Mullen Jc., SD., 3, F5.
Corkickle (Whitehaven), Fur., 26, E4.
Cornbrook Goods, CLC., 45, B3.
Cornhill, GNS., 37, C2.
Cornholme, LY., 20, A1; 21, E1.
Cornwood, GW., 2, D5.
Corpach, NB., 32, C3.
Corpusty & Saxthorpe, MGN., 18, D4.
Corris, Corris, 14, B5.
Corrour, NB., 32, C1.
Corsham, GW., 3, A4.
Corstorphine, NB., 30, B3.
Corton, NSJ., 12, A1; 18, F1.
Corwen, GW(LNW), 19, F5.
Coryates, GW., 3, F3.
Coryton (Devon), GW., 1, C5.
Coryton Halt (Glam.), Car., 43, B4.
Cosham, LSW&LBSCJt., 4, E2
Cossington, SD., 3, C1; 8, E3.
Cotehill, Mid., 27, C1.
Cotham, GN., 16, C2.
Cotherstone, NE., 27, E4.
Coton Hill (Goods), GW., 15, E1.
Cottam, GC., 16, A2.
Cottesmore, Mid., 16, E1.
Cottingham, NE., 22, D3.
Cottingwith, DVL., 21, D5.
Coughton, Mid., 9, B4.
Coulsdon & Cane Hill, SEC., 5, C3.
Coulsdon & Smitham Downs, LBSC., 5, C3.
Coulter, Cal., 30, E4.
Coundon, NE., 27, E5.
Coundon Road, LNW., 10, A5.
Counter Drain, MGN., 17, E2.
Countesthorpe, Mid., 16, F3.
County Boundary Jc., Cal/G&SW., 29, E5.
County School, GE., 18, E4.
Coupar Angus, Cal., 34, D5.
Court House (Barnsley), Mid(GC), 42, E2.
Court Sart, RSB., 7, B4; 43, F3.
Cove Bay, Cal., 34, A1; 37, G4.
Coventry, LNW., 10, A5.
Cowbit, GN&GEJt., 17, E2.
Cowbridge, TV., 8, C5; 43, D4.
Cowbridge Rd. Jc., BRY/GW., 43, D4.
Cowden, LBSC., 5, D4.
Cowdenbeath, NB., 30, A3.
Cowes, IWC., 4, F3.
Cowlairs, NB., 44, D4.
Cow Lane Jc., LBSC/SEC., 40, D4.
Cowley, GW., 5, A2; 10, G1.
Cowley Bridge Jc., GW/LSW., 2, B3.
Cowton, NE., 28, F5.
Coxbench, Mid., 16, C5; 41, F2.
Cox Green, NE., 28, C5.
Coxhoe (Goods), NE., 28, D5.
Coxhoe Bridge, NE., 28, D5.
Coxlodge, NE., 27, B5.
Coxwold, NE., 21, A4.
Craddock Lane (Bolton) Goods, LY., 45, B2.
Cradley Heath, GW., 15, G2.
Cradoc, N&B(Mid), 14, F4.
Craigellachie, GNS., 36, D1.
Craigendoran, NB., 29, B3.

62

Finchley Rd. & Frognal, LNW(NL), 39, B5.
Findochty, GNS., 37, C1.
Finedon, Mid., 10, A2.
Fingask Plat., GNS., 37, E3.
Finghall Lane, NE., 21, A2; 27, G5.
Finmere, GC., 10, D3.
Finnieston, NB., 44, E4.
Finningham, GE., 12, C4.
Finningley, GN&GEJt., 21, F5
Finsbury Park, GN(NL), 5, A3; 40, B5.
Firsby, GN., 17, B3.
Fishbourne Halt, LBSC., 4, E1.
Fisherrow (Goods), NB.,'30, B2
Fishersgate Halt, LBSC., 5, F3.
Fishguard & Goodwick, GW., 13, F1.
Fishguard Harbour, GW., 13, F1.
Fish Ponds, Mid., 3, A3; 8, C1.
Fiskerton, Mid., 16, C3.
Fittleworth, LBSC., 5, E1.
Five Mile House, GN., 17, B1.
Five Ways (Staffs.), LNW., 15, E4.
Five Ways (Warwicks.), Mid., 13, C3; 15, E4.
Fladbury, GW., 9, C4.
Flamborough. NE., 22, B3.
Flax Bourton, GW., 3, A2; 8, D2.
Flaxton, NE., 21, B5.
Flecknoe, LNW., 10, B4.
Fledborough, GC., 16, B2.
Fleet (Hants.), LSW., 4, B1.
Fleet (Lincs.), MGN., 17, E3.
Fleet Jc., GE., 12, A2; 18, F1.
Fleetwood, PWY. & LY., 24, C4.
Flemington, Cal., 30, C5; 44, A2
Fletton (Goods), GN., 11, A2; 17, F2.
Flimby, LNW., 26, D3.
Flint, LNW., 20, D5.
Flitwick, Mid., 10, D1; 11, E1
Flixton, CLC., 20, C2; 45, B3.
Flordon, GE., 12, C3; 18, F3.
Floriston, Cal., 26, B1.
Flushdyke, GN., 21, E3; 42, C3.
Fochabers Town, HR., 36, C1.
Fochriw, BM., 8, A5; 43, C2.
Fockerby, AJ., 22, E5.
Fodderty Jc., HR., 35, D5.
Foggathorpe, NE., 22, D5.
Foleshill, LNW., 10, A5.
Folkestone, SEC.,
  Central, 6, D2.
  Harbour, 6, D2.
  Junction, 6, D2.
Fontburn, NB., 27, A4; 31, G4
Forcett Depot, NE., 27, F5.
Ford (Devon), LSW. & GW., 1, D5 *and* Inset.
Ford (Lancs.), LY., 20, B4; 24, G4; 45, F3.
Ford & Crossgates (Salop), S&M., 14, A1.
Ford Bridge, S&H., 9, B1.
Forden, Cam., 14, B2.
Ford Green, NS., 15, C3; 20, E1.
Fordham, GE., 11, B4.
Fordingbridge, LSW., 4, E5.
Ford Jc. (Sussex), LBSC., 5, F1.
Fordoun, Cal., 34, B2.
Foregate St. (Worcester), GW., 9, B3.
Forest Gate, GE., 40, B2.
Forest Gate Jc., GE/LTS., 40, B2.
Forest Hall, NE., 27, B5.
Forest Hill, LBSC., 40, E4.
Forest Mill, NB., 30, A4.
Forest Row, LBSC., 5, D4.
Forfar, Cal., 34, D4.
Forgandenny, Cal., 33, F5.
Forge Mills, Mid., 15, F5.
Forge Valley, NE., 22, A4.
Formby, LY(LNW), 20, B4; 24, F4; 45, G2.

Forncett, GE., 12, A3; 18, G3.
Forres, HR., 36, D3.
Forrestfield, NB., 30, C5.
Forsinard, HR., 38, E5.
Fort Augustus, NB., 32, A1; 35, G4.
Fort Brockhurst, LSW., 4, E3.
Forteviot, Cal., 33, F4.
Fort George, HR., 36, D4.
Fort Gomer Halt, LSW., 4, E3.
Fort Matilda, Cal., 29, B3.
Fortrose, HR., 36, D5.
Forty Hill, GE., 11, G3.
Foryd Pier, LNW., 19, C5.
Foss Cross, MSW., 9, E4.
Foss Islands (Goods), NE., 21, Inset A4.
Fotherby Halt, GN., 17, A3; 22, G2.
Foulis, HR., 36, C5.
Foulridge, Mid., 21, Inset.
Foulsham, GE., 18, E4.
Fountain Bridge Halt, BM(Rhy), 43, B3.
Fountainhall Jc., NB., 30, D1.
Four Ashes, LNW., 15, E3.
Four Crosses, Cam., 14, A2.
Four Oaks, LNW., 15, F5.
Fourstones, NE., 27, B3.
Fowey, GW., 1, D3.
Foxdale, IMR., 23, B2.
Foxfield, Fur., 24, A5.
Foxhall Jc., GW., 10, F4.
Foxton, GE(GN), 11, D3.
Framlingham, GE., 12, C3.
Frankton, Cam., 20, F4.
Fransham, GE., 18, E5.
Frant, SEC., 5, D5.
Fraserburgh, GNS., 37, C4.
Fratton, LSW&LBSCJt., 4, E2.
Fremington, LSW., 7, F3.
French Drove, GN&GEJt., 17, F3.
Freshfield, LY(LNW), 20, B4; 24, F4; 45, G2.
Freshford, GW., 3, B3.
Freshwater, FYN., 4, F4.
Friargate (Derby), GN., 16, D5; 41, G2.
Friary (Plymouth), LSW., 1, Inset.
Friary Jc., GW/LSW., 1, Inset.
Frickley, SK(GC), 21, F4; 42, D1.
Friden (Goods), LNW., 15, B5
Friezland, LNW., 21, F1:
Frimley, LSW., 4, B1.
Frinton-on-Sea, GE., 12, E3.
Friockheim, Cal., 34, D3.
Frisby, Mid., 16, E3.
Frittenden Rd., KES., 6, D5.
Fritwell & Somerton, GW., 10, D4.
Frizinghall, Mid., 21, D2; 42, A5.
Frizington, WCE., 26, F3.
Frocester, Mid., 9, E3.
Frodingham & Scunthorpe, GC., 22, F4. *See also* Scunthorpe.
Frodsham, BJ., 20, D3; 45, D5.
Frome, GW., 3, C3.
Frongoch, GW., 19, F4.
Frosterley, NE., 27, D4.
Fryston (Goods), NE., 21, E4; 42, B1.
Fulbar St. (Renfrew), G&SW., 44, F4.
Fulbourne, GE., 11, C4.
Fullerton, LSW(MSW), 4, C4.
Fulwell (Middx.), LSW., 5, B2; 39, F1.
Fulwell & Westbury (Bucks.), LNW, 10, D3.
Fullwood Jcs., Cal., 44, B3.
Furness Abbey, Fur., 24, B5.
Furness Vale, LNW., 15, A4.
Fushiebridge, NB., 30, C2.
Fyling Hall, NE., 28, F1.
Fyvie, GNS., 37, E3.

G

Gadlys Jc., GW/TV., 8, A5; 43, D2.
Gaer Jc., GW., 43, A3.
Gaerwen, LNW., 19, D2.
Gailes, G&SW., 29, E3.
Gailey, LNW., 15, E3.
Gainford, NE., 27, E5.
Gainsborough, GC. & GN&GEJt., 16, A2; 22, G5.
Gairlochy, NB., 32, B2.
Gaisgill, NE., 27, F2.
Galashiels, NB., 30, E1.
Galgate, LNW., 24, C3.
Gallions, PLA(GE), 40, C1.
Gallowgate, G&SW., 44, Inset E2.
Galston, G&SW., 29, E4.
Gamlingay, LNW., 11, D2.
Ganton, NE., 22, A4.
Gara Bridge. GW., 2, D4.
Garelochhead, NB., 29, A3.
Garforth, NE., 21, D4; 42, A1.
Gargrave, Mid., 21, C1.
Gargunnock, NB., 29, A5.
Garlieston, P&W., 25, D4.
Garmouth, GNS., 36, C1.
Garnant, GW., 7, A4; 43, F1.
Garnant Halt, GW., 43, F1.
Garndiffaith, LNW., 43, A2.
Garneddwen, Corris, 14, A5.
Garngad, NB., 44, D4.
Garnkirk, Cal., 29, C5; 44, C4.
Garnqueen S. Jc., Cal/NB., 44, B4.
Garn-yr-erw, LNW(GW), 43, B1.
Garrochburn (Goods), G&SW., 29, E4.
Garstang & Catterall, LNW(KE), 24, D3.
Garstang Town, KE., 24, D3.
Garston, CLC. & LNW., 20, C4; 45, E4.
Garston Dock, LNW., 20, C4; 45, E4.
Garswood, LNW., 20, B3; 24, F2; 45, D3.
Gartcosh, Cal., 44, C4.
Garth, LNW., 14, E4.
Garth Rd., Van., 14, C4.
Gartly, GNS., 37, E1.
Gartmore, NB. 29, A4.
Gartness, NB., 29, B4.
Garton, NE., 22, C4.
Gartsherrie, Cal., 44, B4. *See also* Blairhill.
Gartshore (Goods), NB., 29, B5; 44, B5.
Garve, HR., 35, C4.
Gascoigne Wood Junction, NE., 21, D4.
Gask Jc., NB., 30, A3.
Gateacre, CLC., 20, C4; 45. E4
Gatehead, G&SW., 29, E4.
Gatehouse-of-Fleet, P&W., 25, C5.
Gateshead. NE., 28, Inset.
Gateside, NB., 33, F5.
Gatewen Halt. GW., 20, E4.
Gathurst, LY., 20, B2; 24, F3; 45, D2.
Gatley, LNW., 20, C1; 45, A4.
Gatwick Racecourse, LBSC., 5, D3.
Gayton Road, MGN., 17, E5.
Geddington, Mid., 16, G2.
Gedling, GN., 16, C3; 41, F5.
Gedney, MGN., 17, E3.
Geldard Jc., NE&GNJt., 21, Inset B2.
Geldeston, GE., 12, A2; 18, G2
Gelli Halt, TV., 43, D3.
Gelly Tarw Jc., GW., 8, A5; 43 D2.
General Terminus Goods (Glasgow), Cal., 44, E3 *and* Inset F2.
George Lane, GE., 5, A4; 40, A2.
Georgemas, HR., 38, C3.
Gerrards Cross. GW&GCJt., 5, A1; 10, F1.

Gidea Park, GE., 5, A4;
Giffen, Cal., 29, D3.
Giffnock, Cal., 44, E2.
Gifford, NB., 31, C1.
Giggleswick, Mid., 24, B1.
Gildersome, GN. & LNW., 21, D3; 42, B3.
Gileston, BRY., 8, D5; 43, D5.
Gilfach, GW., 8, B5; 43, D3.
Gilfach Fargoed Halt, Rhy., 43, B2.
Gillett's Crossing Halt, PWY., 24, D4.
Gillfoot (Goods), WCE., 26, F3.
Gilling, NE., 21, A5.
Gillingham (Dorset), LSW., 3, D4.
Gillingham (Kent), SEC., 6, B5.
Gilmerton, NB., 30, C2.
Gilmour Street (Paisley), G&P., 44, G3.
Gilnockie, NB., 26, B1.
Gilsland, NE., 27, B1.
Gilwern, LNW., 8, A4; 43, B1.
Gipsy Hill, LBSC(LNW), 40, F4.
Girvan, G&SW., 29, G2.
Gisburn, LY., 24, B1.
Glais, Mid., 7, B4; 43, F2.
Glaisdale, NE., 28, F2.
Glamis, Cal., 34, D5.
Glanamman, GW., 7, A4; 43, F1.
Glan Conway, LNW., 19, D4.
Glandyfi, Cam., 14, B5.
Glanrafon, VR., 13, C5.
Glanrhyd, VT., 14, G5.
Glanton, NE., 31, F4.
Glan-y-llyn, Car., 43, C4.
Glanyrafon, Tan., 14, A2; 20, G5.
Glapwell, Mid., 16, B4; 41, C3.
Glasbury-on-Wye, Mid., 14, F2.
Glasgow (Goods), Cal., GBK., G&P., G&SW., & NB., 29, —; 44, —.
Glasgow (Pass.), Cal., G&SW. & NB., 29, —; 44, —.
Glasgow Cross, Cal., 44, D4. *and* Inset E2.
Glasgow Green, Cal., 44, D3 *and* Inset E2.
Glassel, GNS., 34 A3; 37, G2.
Glassford, Cal., 29, D5.
Glassaugh, GNS., 37, C2.
Glasson Dock, LNW., 24. C3.
Glasson Plat., LNW., 26, C2.
Glasterlaw, Cal., 34, D3.
Glastonbury & Street, SD., 3, C2; 8, E2.
Glazebrook, CLC., 20, C2; 45, C3.
Glazebrook Moss Jc., CLC/GC., 20, C2; 45, C3.
Glazebury, LNW(BJ), 20, B2; 24, G2; 45, C3.
Glemsford, GE., 12, D5.
Glenbarry, GNS., 37, D1.
Glenboig, Cal., 30, C5; 44, B4.
Glenbuck, Cal., 30, E5.
Glenburnie Jc., NB., 34, F5.
Glencarron Plat., HR., 35, D2.
Glencarse, Cal., 33, F5.
Glencorse, NB., 30, C2.
Glencrutten Crossing, Cal., 32, E4.
Glendon & Rushton, Mid., 10, A2; 16, G2.
Gleneagles, Cal., 33, F4.
Glenfarg, NB., 33, F5.
Glenfield (Leicester), Mid,, 16, F4.
Glenfield Goods (Paisley), Cal., 44, G3.
Glenfinnan, NB., 32, B4.
Glengarnock, G&SW. & Cal., 29, D3.
Gleniffer (Goods), G&SW., 44, G2.
Glenluce, P&W., 25, C3.

Hamilton, Cal. & NB., 30, D5; 44, B2.
Hamilton Sq. (Birkenhead), Mer., 45, F4.
Ham Lane, WCP., 3, A1; 8, D3.
Ham Mill Crossing Halt, GW., 9, F3.
Hammersmith Broadway, Dist. & H&C., 39, D4.
Hammersmith & Chiswick, NSW., 39, D3.
Hammerton, NE., 21, C4
Hammerwich, LNW., 15, F4.
Hampden Park, LBSC., 5, F5.
Hampole, WRG., 21, F4.
Hampstead Heath, LNW(NL), 39, B5; 40, Inset., C1.
Hampstead Norris, GW., 4, A3; 10, G4.
Hampsthwaite, NE., 21, C3.
Hampton, LSW., 5, B2; 39, F1.
Hampton Court, LSW., 5, B2; 39, G2.
Hampton-in-Arden, LNW. & Mid., 9, A5; 15, G5.
Hampton Loade, GW., 15, G2.
Hampton Wick, LSW., 39, F2.
Ham Street & Orlestone, SEC., 6, D4.
Hamworthy (Goods), LSW., 3, F5.
Hamworthy Jc., LSW., 3, F5.
Handborough, GW., 10, E4.
Handforth, LNW., 15, A3; 20, C1; 45, A4.
Handsworth & Smethwick, GW., 13, B3.
Handsworth Wood, LNW., 13, B3.
Hanley, NS., 15, C3; 20, E1.
Hannington, GW., 9, F5.
Hanwell & Elthorne, GW., 5, B2; 39, C2.
Hanwood, SWP., 14, A1; 15, E1.
Hapton, LY., 24, D1.
Harborne, LNW., 13, C3; 15, G4.
Harburn, Cal., 30, C3.
Harby & Stathern, GN&LNWJt., 16, D2.
Hardengreen Jc., NB., 30, C2.
Hardham Jc., LBSC., 5, F1.
Hardingham, GE., 18, F4.
Hardwick Road (Goods), MGN., 17, E5.
Harecastle, NS., 15, C3; 20, E1.
Hare Park & Crofton, WRG., 21, E3; 42, C2. See also Crofton.
Haresfield, Mid., 9, E3.
Harker, NB., 26, C1.
Harlech, Cam., 19, F2.
Harlesden, LNW(LE) & Mid., 39, B3.
Harleston, GE., 12, B3; 18, G3.
Harling Road, GE., 12, A4; 18, G4.
Harlington (Beds.), Mid., 10, D1; 11, E1.
Harlington (Yorks.), DV., 21, F4.
Harlow, GE., 11, F3.
Harmston, GN., 16, B1.
Harold Wood, GE., 5, A5.
Harpenden, Mid. & GN., 11, F1.
Harperley, NE., 27, D4.
Harpur Hill, LNW., 15, B4.
Harrietsham, SEC., 6, C4.
Harringay, GN(NL)., 40, A5.
Harringay Park, THJ(LTS)., 40, A5.
Harrington, LNW., 26, E3.
Harringworth, Mid., 16, F1.
Harrogate, NE(Mid/GN), 21, C3.
Harrow & Wealdstone, LNW(LE), 5, A2; 39, A2.
Harrow - on - the - Hill, Met&GCJt., 5, A2; 39, A2.
Harston, GE(GN), 11, D3.
Hart, NE., 28, D4.

Hartfield, LBSC., 5, D4.
Hartford, LNW., 15, B2; 20, D2; 45, C5.
Hartford & Greenbank, CLC(LNW), 15, B2; 20, D2; 45, C5.
Hartington, LNW., 15, B5.
Hartlebury, GW., 9, A3.
Hartlepool, NE., 28, D4.
Hartley, NE., 28, B5.
Harton Road, GW., 15, G1.
Harts Hill, GW., 15, G3.
Hartwood, Cal., 30, C5.
Harty Rd. Halt, SEC., 6, B3.
Harvington, Mid., 9, C4.
Harwich, GE., 12, E3.
Hasland (Goods), Mid., 16, B5; 41, C2.
Haslemere, LSW., 4, C1; 5, E1.
Haslingden, LY., 20, A1; 24, E1
Hassall Green, NS., 15, B3; 20, E1.
Hassendean, NB., 31, F1.
Hassocks, LBSC., 5, F3.
Hassop, Mid., 15, B5.
Hastings, SEC(LBSC), 6, F5.
Haswell, NE., 28, D5.
Hatch, GW., 3, D1; 8, G3.
Hatch End, LNW(LE), 5, A2.
Hatfield (Herts.), GN., 11, F2.
Hatfield Moor Depot, AJ., 22, F5.
Hatfield Peverel, GE., 11, F5.
Hatherley Curve Jc., GW., 9, D3.
Hathern, Mid., 16, D4.
Hathersage, Mid., 15, A5.
Hatton (Aberdeen), GNS., 37, E5.
Hawthornden, NB., 30, C2.
Hatton (Warwicks.), GW., 9, B5.
Haugh Head Jc., Cal., 44, B2.
Haughley, GE. & MSL., 12, C4.
Haughton, LNW., 15, E3; 20, G1.
Havant, LBSC(LSW), 4, E2.
Havenhouse, GN., 17, B4.
Haven Street, IWC., 4, F3.
Haverfordwest, GW., 7, C2.
Haverhill, GE. & CVH., 11, D5.
Haverthwaite, Fur., 24, A4.
Haverton Hill, NE., 28, E4.
Hawarden, GC., 20, D4.
Hawes, Mid&NEJt., 27, G3.
Hawes Jc. & Garsdale, Mid(NE), 24, A1; 27, G2.
Hawick, NB., 31, F1.
Hawkesbury Lane, LNW., 16, G5.
Hawkhead, G&SW., 44, F3.
Hawkhill Jc., G&SW., 29, F3.
Hawkhurst, SEC., 6, E5.
Haworth, Mid., 21, D1.
Hawsker, NE., 28, F2.
Hawthornden, NB., 30, C2.
Haxby, NE., 21, C5.
Haxey & Epworth, GN&GEJt., 22, F5.
Haxey Jc., AJ., 22, F5.
Haxey Town, AJ., 22, F5.
Hay, Mid(GW), 14, F2.
Hayburn Wyke, NE., 28, G1.
Haydock, GC., 20, B3; 24, G2; 45, D3.
Haydock Park, GC., 45, D3.
Haydon Bridge, NE., 27, B3.
Haydon Sq. Goods, LNW., 40, C4.
Haydons Rd., LBSC&LSWJt., 39, F5.
Hayes (Kent), SEC., 5, C4; 40, G2.
Hayes & Harlington (Middx) GW., 5, B2.
Hayfield, GC&MidJt., 15, A4; 21, G1.
Hayle, GW., 1, Inset E4.
Hayling Island, LBSC., 4, E2.
Haymarket (Edinburgh), NB., 30, Inset.
Haywards Heath, LBSC., 5, E3.
Haywood, Cal., 30, C4.

Hazel Grove, LNW. & Mid., 15, A4; 20, C1; 21, G1; 45, A4.
Hazelwell, Mid., 9, A4.
Hazelwood, Mid., 16, C5; 41, F1.
Hazlehead Bridge, GC., 21, F2; 42, E4.
Heacham, GE., 17, D5.
Headcorn, SEC,. & KES. 6, D5.
Headingley, NE., 21, D3; 42, A3.
Heads Nook, NE., 27, C1.
Heads of Ayr, G&SW., 29, F3.
Healu Green, LNW., 15, A3; 45, A4.
Healey House, LY., 21, F2; 42, D5.
Healing, GC., 22, F2.
Heanor, Mid. & GN., 16, C4; 41, F3.
Heap Bridge (Goods), LY., 20, B1; 24, F1; 45, A1.
Heapey, LU., 20, A2; 24, E2; 45, D1.
Heath (Derbys.), GC., 16, B4; 41, C3.
Heather & Ibstock, AN., 16, E5.
Heathey Lane Halt, LY., 20, A4; 24, E4; 45, F1.
Heathfield (Devon), GW., 2, C4
Heathfield (Sussex), LBSC., 5, E5.
Heath Halt (Glam.), Car., 43, B4.
Heath Jc., Rhy/Car., 8, C4; 43, B4.
Heath Park Halt. Mid., 10, E1; 11, F1.
Heath Town Jc., LNW/Mid., 15, Inset E3.
Heatley & Warburton, LNW., 20, C2; 45, C4.
Heaton, NE., 28, Inset.
Heaton Chapel(LNW., 45, A3.
Heaton Lodge Jc., LY/LNW., 42, C4.
Heaton Mersey, Mid., 20, C1; 45, A4.
Heaton Norris, LNW., 45, A3.
Heaton Park, LY., 20, B1; 24, F1; 45, A2.
Hebburn, NE., 28, B5.
Hebden Bridge, LY., 21, E1.
Heck, NE., 21, E5.
Heckington, GN., 17, C2.
Heckmondwike, LY. & LNW., 21, E2; 42, C4.
Heddon - on - the - Wall, NE., 27, B5.
Hedgeley, NE., 31, F4.
Hednesford, LNW., 15, E4.
Hedon, NE., 22, E3.
Heeley, Mid., 16, A5; 21, G3; 41, A2.
Heighington (Durham), NE., 27, E5.
Hele & Bradninch, GW., 2, A3.
Helensburgh, NB., 29, B3.
Helensburgh Upper, NB., 29, B3.
Hellaby (Goods), GCMid&HBJt., 21, G4.
Hellesdon MGN., 18, F3.
Hellifield, Mid(LY) & Mid., 24, C1.
Hellingly, LBSC., 5, F5.
Helmdon, GC. & SMJ., 10, C3.
Helmsdale, HR., 38, F4.
Helmshore, LY., 20, A1; 24, E1
Helmsley, NE., 21, A5.
Helpringham, GN&GEJt., 17, D1.
Helpston, Mid., 17, F1.
Helsby, BJ. & CLC., 20, D3; 45, E5.
Helston, GW., 1, Inset F5.
Hemel Hempsted, Mid., 10, E1; 11, F1. See also Boxmoor.
Hemingborough, NE,, 21, D5.
Hemsby, MGN, 18, E1.

Hemsworth, WRG., 21, E4; 42, D1.
Hemsworth & South Kirkby, HB., 21, E4; 42, D1.
Hemyock, GW., 2, A2; 8, G4.
Henbury, GW., 8, C2; 9, G1.
Hendon, Mid., 5, A3; 39, A4.
Hendreforgan, GW., 8, B5; 43, D3.
Henfield, LBSC., 5, F2.
Hengoed, GW. & Rhy., 8, B4; 43, B3. See also Maesycwmmer.
Henham Halt, GE., 11, E4.
Heniarth, W&L., 14, B3.
Henley-in-Arden, GW., 9, B5.
Henley-on-Thames, GW., 10, G2.
Henllan, GW., 13, F4.
Henlow, Mid., 11, E1.
Hensall, LY., 21, E5.
Henstridge, SD., 3, D3; 8, G1.
Henwick (Worcs.), GW., 9, B3.
Hepscott, NE., 27, A5.
Hereford (Goods), S&H., GW. & Mid., 9, C1.
Hereford (Pass.), S&H(Mid), 9, C1.
Heriot, NB., 30, C1.
Hermitage, GW., 4, A3.
Herne Bay, SEC., 6, B2.
Herne Hill, SEC., 5, B3; 40, E5.
Herriard, LSW., 4, C2.
Hertford, GN. & GE., 11, F2.
Hertingfordbury, GN., 11, F2.
Hesketh Bank & Tarleton, LY., 20, A3; 24, E3.
Hesketh Park, LY., 20, A4; 24, E4; 45, F1.
Hesleden, NE., 28, D5.
Heslerton, NE., 22, A4.
Hessay, NE., 21, C4.
Hessle, NE(GC), 22, E4.
Hest Bank, LNW., 24, B3.
Heswall, BJ., 20, C5.
Heswall Hills, GC., 20, C4; 45, F4.
Hethersett, GE., 18, F3.
Hetton, NE., 28, D5.
Hever, LBSC., 5, D4.
Heversham, Fur., 24, A3.
Hexham, NE(NB), 27, B3.
Hexthorpe Jc., GC., 21, Inset G2.
Heyford, GW., 10, D4.
Heys Crossing Halt, LY(LNW), 20, B3; 24, F3; 45, E2.
Heysham Harb., Mid., 24, C3.
Heytesbury, GW., 3, C4.
Heywood, LY., 20, B1; 24, F1; 45, A1.
Hibel Road (Macclesfield), LNW(NS), 15, A3; 45, A5.
Hickleton & Thurnscoe, HB., 21, F4; 42, E1.
Hickleton South Jc., SK/DV., 21, F4; 42, E1.
Higham (Kent), SEC., 6, B5.
Higham (Suffolk), GE., 11, C5.
Higham Ferrers, Mid., 10, A1.
Higham - on - the - Hill, AN., 16, F5.
Highams Park, GE., 5, A4.
High Barnet, GN(NL), 5, A3.
High Blaithwaite, M&C., 26, D2.
High Blantyre, Cal., 29, C5; 44, C2.
Highbridge, GW. & SD., 3, B1; 8, E3.
Highbury & Islington, NL(LNW), 40, B5.
Highbury Vale Gds., GN., 40, B5.
Highclere, GW., 4, B3.
Higher Buxton, LNW., 15, A4.
High Field, NE., 22, D5.
Highgate, GN(NL), 5, A3; 39, A5.
Highgate Rd., Mid(LTS), & THJ., 40, B5.
High Halden Rd., KES., 6, D4.

Llangyfelach (Goods), GW., 7, B4; 43, G2.
Llangynog, Tan., 19, G5.
Llanharan, GW., 8, C5; 43, D4.
Llanharry, TV., 8, C5; 43, C4.
Llanhilleth, GW., 8, B4; 43, B2
Llanidloes, Cam., 14, C4.
Llanilar, GW., 13, D5.
Llanishen, Rhy., 8, C4; 43, B4.
Llanmorlais, LNW., 7, B3.
Llanpumpsaint, GW., 13, F4.
Llanrhaiadr, LNW., 19, E5.
Llanrhaiadr Mochnant, Tan., 20, G5.
Llanrhystyd Road, GW., 13, C5
Llanrwst & Trefriw, LNW., 19, E4.
Llansamlet, GW., 7, B4.
Llansantffraid, Cam., 14, A2.
Llansilin Road, Tan., 20, G5.
Llantarnam, GW., 8, B3; 43, A3.
Llantrisant, GW(TV), & TV., 8, C5; 43, C4.
Llantrisant Common Jc., TV/GW., 43, C4.
Llantwit, TV., 8, C5; 43, C4.
Llantwit Major, BRY., 8, D5; 43, D5.
L nuwchllyn, GW., 19, G4.
Llanvihangel (Mon.), GW., 14, G1.
Llanwern, GW., 8, B3.
Llanwnda, LNW., 19, E2.
Llanwrda, VT., 14, F5.
Llanwrtyd Wells, LNW., 14, E4.
Llanyblodwell, Tan., 20, G5.
Llanybyther, GW., 13, E5.
Llan-y-Cefn, GW., 13, G2.
Llanymynech, Cam. & S&M., 14, A2; 20, G4.
Lletty Brongu, PT., 7, B5; 43, D3.
Llong, LNW., 20, E5.
Llwydcoed, GW., 8, A5; 43, D2.
Llwyn Gwern, Corris, 14, B5.
Llwyngwril, Cam., 13, A5.
Llwynypia, TV., 8, B5; 43, D3.
Llynclys, Cam., 14, A2; 20, G4
Llysfaen, LNW., 19, D4.
Loanhead, NB., 30, C2.
Lochailort, NB., 32, B5.
Lochanhead, G&SW., 26, B4.
Locharbriggs, Cal., 26, A3.
Loch Awe, Cal., 32, F2.
Lochburn, NB., 44, E4.
Lochearnhead, Cal., 33, F2.
Lochee, Cal., 34, E4.
Lochee West, Cal., 34, E4.
Locheilside, NB., 32, B3.
Lochend Jcs., NB., 30, Inset.
Lochgelly, NB., 30, A3.
Lochgorm Works, HR., 36, E5.
Lochgreen Jc., G&SW., 29, E3.
Loch Leven (Goods), NB., 30, A3; 33, G5.
Lochluichart, HR., 35, C4.
Lochmaben, Cal., 26, A3.
Lochmill (Goods), NB., 30, B4.
Lochside, G&SW., 29, C3.
Loch Tay, Cal., 33, E2.
Lochty Goods, NB., 34, F4.
Lochwinnoch, G&SW., 29, C3.
Lockerbie, Cal., 26, A3.
Lockington, NE., 22, C4.
Lockwood, LY., 21, E2; 42, D5.
Loddington, Mid., 10, A2.
Loddiswell, GW., 2, E4.
Lodge Hill, GW., 3, B2; 8, E2.
Lofthouse & Outwood, GN(GC), & MJ., 21, E3; 42, B2.
Lofthouse-in-Nidderdale, NV., 21, B2.
Loftus, NE., 28, E3.
Logan Jc., G&SW., 29, F5.
Logierieve, GNS., 37, E4.
Login, GW., 13, G2.
Londesborough, NE., 22, D5.
London: 5, —; 39, —; 40, —.
London Bridge, LBSC. & SEC., 5, B3; 40, D4.

London Road (Brighton), LBSC., 5, F3.
London Rd. (Guildford), LSW., 5, C1.
London Rd. (Manchester), LNW(NS), GC., & MSJA., 20, B1; 45, A3.
London Rd. (Nottingham), GN(LNW), 41, G5.
Long Buckby, LNW., 10, B3.
Long Clawson & Hose, GN&LNWJt., 16, D2.
Longcliffe (Goods), LNW., 15, C5.
Longdon Rd., GW., 9, C5.
Longdown, GW., 2, B3.
Long Eaton, Mid., 16, D4; 41, G3.
Longford & Exhall, LNW., 10, A5; 16, G5.
Longforgan, Cal., 34, E5.
Longhaven, GNS., 37, D5.
Longhedge Jc., WLE/SEC., 39, Inset E3.
Longhirst, NE., 27, A5.
Longhope, GW., 8, A1; 9, E2.
Longhoughton, NE., 31, F5.
Long Marston, GW., 9, C5.
Long Marton, Mid., 27, E2.
Long Melford, GE., 12, D5.
Longmorn, GNS., 36, D2.
Longniddry, NB., 30, B1.
Longparish, LSW., 4, C4.
Longport, NS., 15, C3; 20, F1.
Long Preston, Mid., 24, C1.
Longridge, PL., 24, D2.
Longriggend, NB., 30, C5.
Longside, GNS., 37, D5.
Longsight, LNW., 24, G1; 45, A3.
Long Stanton, GE(Mid), 11, C3
Long Stow (Goods), Mid., 11, B1.
Long Sutton (Lincs.), MGN., 17, E3.
Long Sutton & Pitney (Som.), GW., 3, D1; 8, F2.
Longton, NS., 15, C3; 20, F1.
Longton Bridge, LY., 20, A3; 24, E3.
Longtown, NB., 26, B1.
Longville, GW., 15, F1.
Longville Jc., LNW/GN., 11, A1; 17, F2.
Long Witton, NB., 27, A4.
Longwood & Milnsbridge, LNW., 21, E2; 42, D5.
Lonmay, GNS., 37, C4.
Looe, LL., 1, D4.
Lord's Bridge, LNW., 11, C3.
Lordship Lane, SEC., 40, E4.
Lord Street (Southport) CLC., 20, A4; 24, E3; 45, F1.
Lossiemouth, GNS., 36, C1.
Lostock Gralam, CLC., 15, A2; 20, D2; 45, C5.
Lostock Hall, LY., 20, A3; 24, E3.
Lostock Jc., LY., 20, B2; 24, F2; 45, C2.
Lostwithiel, GW., 1, D3.
Loth, HR., 38, G4.
Lothian Rd. (Goods), Cal., 30, Inset F2.
Loudounhill, G&SW., 29, E5.
Loudwater, GW., 5, A1; 10, F2.
Loughborough, Mid., GC., & LNW., 16, E4.
Loughborough Jc., SEC., 40, E5.
Loughor, GW., 7, B3.
Loughton, GE., 5, A4; 11, G3.
Loughton Jc., GE., 40, B3.
Louth, GN., 17, A3; 22, G2.
Loversall Carr Jc., GN/DV., 21, F5 and Inset G2.
Low Bentham (Goods), Mid., 24, B2.
Lowca, CWJ., 26, E3.
Lowdham, Mid., 16, C3.
Low Ellers Jc., SY., 21, F2 and Inset F2.

Lower Darwen, LY., 20, A2; 24, E2.
Lower Edmonton, GE., 5, A3.
Lower Ince, GC., 45, D2. *See also* Ince (Lancs.).
Lower Penarth, TV., 8, D4; 43, B5.
Lower Sydenham, SEC., 40, F3.
Lowesby, GN., 16, F2.
Lowestoft, GE(MGN), 12, A1; 18, G1.
Lowestoft North, NSJ., 12, A1; 18, F1.
Low Fell, NE., 27, C5.
Low Gill, LNW., 27, G1.
Low Moor, LY(GN), LY. & GN., 21, E2; 42, B4.
Low Row, NE., 27, C1.
Low Street, LTS., 5, B5.
Lowthorpe, NE., 22, C3.
Lowton, LNW., 20, C2; 24, G2; 45, D3.
Lowton St. Mary's, GC., 45, C3.
Low Town (Barnsley), LY(GC). 42, E.2.
Lowtown (Pudsey), GN., 21, D2; 42, A4.
Lubenham, LNW., 16, G3.
Lucker, NE., 31, E4.
Luckett, BAC., 1, C5.
Ludborough, GN., 22, G2.
Luddenfoot, LY., 21, E1.
Luddington, AJ., 22, E5.
Ludgate Jc., LSW., 39, Inset E3.
Ludgershall (Wilts.), MSW., 4, B5.
Ludlow, S&H., 9, A1.
Luffenham, Mid(LNW) 16, F1.
Lugar, G&SW., 29, F5.
Lugton, Cal. & GBK., 29, D4.
Luib, Cal., 33, E1.
Lumphanan, GNS., 37, G2.
Lunan Bay, NB., 34, D3.
Luncarty, Cal(HR), 33, E5.
Lundin Links, NB., 34, G4.
Lustleigh, GW., 2, C4.
Luthrie, NB., 34, F5.
Luton, Mid. & GN(LNW), 11, E1.
Luton Hoo, GN., 11, F1.
Lutterworth, GC., 10, A4; 16, G4. *See also* Ullesthorpe
Luxulyan, GW., 1, D3.
Lybster, HR., 38, E2.
Lydbrook Jc., GW. & SVW., 8, A2; 9, E1.
Lydd, SEC., 6, E3.
Lydford, LSW. & GW., 1, C5.
Lydham Heath, BC., 14, C1.
Lydiate, CLC., 20, B4; 24, F4; 45, F2.
Lydney, GW., 8, B1; 9, F2.
Lydney Jc., SVW., 8, A1; 9, E2.
Lydney Town, SVW., 8, A1; 9, E2.
Lydstep, GW., 7, D2.
Lye, GW., 15, G3.
Lyghe Halt, SEC., 5, D5.
Lyme Regis, LSW., 3, F1.
Lyminge, SEC., 6, D3.
Lymington Pier, LSW., 4, F4.
Lymington Town, LSW., 4, F4.
Lymm, LNW., 20, C2; 45, C4.
Lympstone, LSW., 2, C3.
Lyndhurst Rd., LSW., 4, E4.
Lyne, Cal., 30, D2.
Lynedoch, G&SW., 29, B3.
Lyneside, NB., 26, B1.
Lynton, LB., 7, E4.
Lyon Cross Jc., Cal., 44, F2.
Lyonshall, GW., 14, E1.
Lytham, PWY., 24, E4.

M

Mablethorpe, GN., 17, A4.
Macbie Hill, NB., 30, D3.
Macclesfield Central, NS., 15, A3; 20, D1; 45, A5.

Macclesfield (Goods), LNW&NSJt. & GC&NSJt., 15, A3; 20, D1; 45, A5.
Macclesfield, Hibel Road, LNW(NS), 15, A3; 20, D1; 45, A5.
Macduff, GNS., 37, C2.
Machen, BM(Rhy), 8, B4; 43, B3.
Machrihanish, CM., 29, Inset.
Machrihanish Farm Halt., CM., 29, Inset.
Machynlleth, Cam. & Corris, 14, B5.
Macmerry, NB., 30, B1.
Madderty, Cal., 33, F4.
Madeley (Salop.), GW., 15, F2.
Madeley (Staffs.), LNW., 15, C3; 20, F1.
Madeley Market, LNW.,15, F2
Madeley Road, NS., 15, C3; 20, F1.
Maenclochog, GW., 13, F2.
Maentwrog Rd., GW., 19, F3.
Maerdy, TV., 8, B5; 43, D2.
Maesaraul Jc., TV/GW., 43, C4.
Maesteg, GW. & PT., 7, B5, 43, E3.
Maesycrugiau, GW., 13, F4.
Maesycwmmer & Hengoed, BM., 43, B3. *See also* Hengoed.
Maesycwmmer Jc., BM/GW., 43, B3.
Magdalen Green (Dundee), Cal., 34, Inset E2.
Magdalen Road, GE., 17, F4.
Maghull, LY., 20, B4; 24, F4; 45, F2. *See also* Sefton.
Magor, GW., 8, C3.
Maidenhead, GW., 5, B1; 10, G2.
Maiden Lane (Goods), LNW., 40, B5.
Maiden Lane, (Pass.), NL., 40, B5.
Maiden Newton, GW., 3, F2.
Maidens, G&SW., 29, G3.
Maidstone, SEC., 6, C5.
Maindee Jcs., GW., 8, B3; 43, A3.
Malden, LSW., 5, B3; 39, F3.
Maldon East & Heybridge, GE., 12, F5.
Maldon West, GE., 12, F5.
Malins Lee, LNW., 15, E2.
Mallaig, NB., 32, A5.
Mallaig Jc., NB., 32, C3.
Malling, SEC., 5, C5; 6, C5.
Mallwyd, Mawd., 14, A4.
Malmesbury, GW., 9, F3.
Malpas, LNW., 15, C1; 20, E3.
Maltby, SYJ., 21, F4.
Malton, NE., 22, B5.
Malvern Link, GW., 9, C3.
Malvern Rd. (Cheltenham), GW., 9, D4.
Malvern Wells, GW. & Mid., 9, C3.
Manchester (Goods), CLC., GC., GN., LNW., LY. & Mid., 20, —; 24, —; 45, —.
Manchester (Pass.), 20, —; 24, —; 45, —.
  Central: CLC.
  Exchange: LNW(BJ).
  London Rd.: LNW(NS), GC. & MSJA.
  Victoria: LY(LNW/Mid).
Manchester Docks, LY., 45, B3.
Manchester Rd. (Burnley), LY., 24, D1.
Manea, GE., 11, A3; 17, G4.
Mangotsfield, Mid., 3, A3; 8, C1.
Manley Goods, CLC., 45, E5.
Manningham, Mid(NE), 21, D2; 42, A4.
Manningtree, GE., 12, E4.

Manod, GW., 19, F3.
Manorbier, GW., 7, D2.
Manor Park, GE., 40, B2.
Manors, NE., 28, Inset.
Manor Way, PLA(GE), 40, C1.
Mansfield, Mid(GC), & GC., 16, B4; 41, D4.
Mansfield Woodhouse, Mid(GC), 16, B4; 41, D4.
Mansion House, Dist(Met), 40, C5.
Manton, Mid., 16, F2.
Manuel, NB., 30, B4.
Marazion, GW., 1, Inset, F4.
March, GE., 11, A3; 17, F3.
Marchington, NS(GN), 15, D5
Marchmont, NB., 31, D2.
Marchwiel, Cam., 20, E4.
Marden, SEC., 6, D5.
Mardock, GE., 11, F3.
Mardy Jc., GW/GW&TVJt., 43, C2.
Marefield Jcs.
 GN&LNWJt/GN., 16, F2.
Marfleet, NE., 22, D3.
Margam Jc., GW/PT., 7, B4; 43, F3.
Margate, SEC., 6, B1.
Marishes Road, NE., 22, A5.
Market Bosworth, AN., 16, F5.
Market Drayton, GW(NS), 15, D2; 20 F2.
Market Drayton Jc. (Nantwich), LNW/GW., 15, C2. 20, E2.
Market Drayton Jc. (Wellington), SWN/GW., 15, C2.
Market Harborough, LNW. & Mid., 16, G2.
Market Place (Chesterfield), GC., 16, B5; 41, C2.
Market Rasen, GC., 17, A1; 22, G3.
Market St. (Bradford), Mid(NE), 42, A4.
Market Weighton, NE., 22, D4
Markham Village, LNW., 43, B2.
Markinch, NB., 30, A2; 34, G5
Mark Lane, Dist&MetJt., 40, C4.
Mark's Tey. GE., 12, E5.
Marlborough, GW. & MSW., 4, A5.
Marlborough Road, Met., 39, B5.
Marlesford, GE., 12, C2.
Marlow, GW., 10, G2.
Marlpool, GN., 16, C4; 41, F3.
Marple, GC&MidJt., 21, G1.
 See also Rose Hill.
Marron Jc., LNW/WCE., 26, E3.
Marsden (Durham), SSM., 28, B5.
Marsden (Yorks.), LNW., 21, F1.
Marsden Cottage, SSM., 28, B5.
Marsh Brook, S&H., 14, C1; 15, G1.
Marsh Farm Jc., S&H/GW., 14, C1; 15, G1.
Marshfield, GW., 8, C3; 43, A4.
Marsh Gate (Goods), GC., 21, Inset G2.
Marsh Gibbon & Poundon, LNW., 10, D3.
Marsh Jc., GE., 12, A1; 18, F1
Marshland Jc., NE/AJ., 22, E5.
Marsh Lane (Lancs.), LY., 45, F3.
Marsh Lane (Yorks.), NE., 21, D3; 42, A2.
Marsh Mills, GW., 2, D5.
Marske, NE., 28, E3.
Marston Gate, LNW., 10, E2.
Marston Green, LNW., 15, G5.
Marston Magna, GW., 3, D2; 8, G1.
Marston Moor, NE., 21, C4.
Martham, MGN., 18, E1.
Martin Mill, SEC., 6, D1.

Martock, GW., 3, D1; 8, G2.
Marton, LNW., 10, A5.
Maryfield (Dundee), Cal., 34, E4.
Maryhill, Cal. & NB., 29, C5; 44, E4.
Marykirk, Cal., 34, C3.
Maryland Point, GE., 40, B2.
Marylebone, GC., 5, A3; 39, C5.
Maryport, M&C(LNW), 26, D3.
Marytavy & Blackdown, GW., 1, C5.
Masbury, SD., 3, C2; 8, E1.
Masham, NE., 21, A3.
Massingham, MGN., 18, E5.
Maxton, NB., 31, E1.
Matlock, Mid., 16, B5; 41, D1.
Matlock Bath, Mid., 16, B5; 41, D1.
Mauchline, G&SW., 29, E4.
Maud Jc., GNS., 37, D4.
Maud's Bridge (Goods), GC., 22, F5.
Mauldeth Rd., LNW., 45, A3.
Mawcarse, Cal., 33, G5.
Maxton, NB., 31, E1.
Maxwell Jc., Cal., 44, Inset.
Maxwell Park, Cal., 44, E3.
Maxwelltown, G&SW., 26, B4.
Maybole, G&SW., 29, F3.
Mayfield (Manchester), LNW., 45, A3.
Mayfield (Sussex), LBSC., 5, E5.
May Hill (Monmouth), GW., 8, A2; 9, E1.
Maze Hill, SEC., 40, D3.
Meadow Hall & Wincobank, GC., 42, F2.
 See also Wincobank.
Mealsgate, M&C., 26, D2.
Measham, AN., 16, E5.
Medge Hall, GC., 22, F5.
Medina Wharf, IWC., 4, F3.
Medstead, LSW., 4, C2.
Meigle, Cal., 34, D5.
Meikle Earnock, Cal., 29, D5; 44, B1.
Meir, NS., 15, C4.
Melangoose Mill, GW., 1, D2.
Melbourne, Mid., 16, D5.
Melcombe Regis, WP., 3, G3.
Meldon, NB., 27, A5.
Meldon Jc., LSW., 2, B5.
Meldreth & Melbourn, GN., 11, D3.
Meledor Mill, GW., 1, D2.
Meliden, LNW., 19, C5.
Melksham, GW., 3, A4.
Melling, Fur&MidJt., 24, B2.
Mellis, GE., 12, B4.
Mells Road, GW., 3, B3; 8, E1.
Melmerby, NE., 21, A3.
Melrose, NB., 31, E1.
Meltham, LY., 21, F2; 42, D5.
Melton, GE., 12, D3.
Melton Constable, MGN., 18, D4.
Melton Mowbray, Mid(MGN) & GN&LNWJt., 16, E2.
Melverley, S&M., 14, A1.
Melyncourt Halt, GW., 43, E2.
Menai Bridge, LNW., 19, D2.
Mendlesham, MSL., 12, C4.
Menheniot, GW., 1, D4.
Menston, Mid(NE), 21, D2.
Menstrie, NB., 30, A5.
Menthorpe Gate, NE., 21, D5.
Meole Brace, S&M., 15, E1.
Meols, Wir., 20, C5.
Meols Cop, LY., 20, A4; 24, E4; 45, F1.
Meopham, SEC., 5, B5.
Merchiston, Cal., 30, Inset.
Merrybent Jc., NE., 27, E5.
Merryton Jc., Cal., 44, B1.
Mersey Rd. & Aigburth, CLC., 45, F4.
Merstham, SEC., 5, C3.
Merstone, IWC., 4, F3.

Merthyr, GW(BM LNW RLY TV), & TV., 8. A5; 43, C2.
Merthyr Vale, TV., 8, B5; 43, C2.
Merton Abbey, LSBC&LSWJt 39, F5.
Merton Park, LBSC&LSWJt., 39, F4.
Methil, NB., 30, A2; 34, G4.
Methley, Mid(LY), LY., & MJ., 21, E4; 42, B1.
Methven, Cal., 33, E4.
Methven Jc., Cal., 33, E4.
Metropolitan Jc., SEC., 40, C5.
Mexborough, GC(Mid), 21, F4.
Micheldever, LSW., 4, C3.
Micklam, CWJ., 26, E3.
Micklefield, NE., 21, D4; 42, A1.
Micklehurst (Goods), LNW., 21, F1.
Mickleover, GN., 16, D5; 41, G1.
Mickleton, NE., 27, E4.
Mickle Trafford, BJ. & CLC., 20, D3.
Midcalder, Cal., 30, C3.
Mid Clyth, HR., 38, E2.
Middle Drove, GE., 17, F4.
Middlemuir Jc., NB., 44, C5.
Middlesbrough, NE., 28, E4.
Middle Stoke Halt, SEC., 6, B5.
Middlestown, Mid., 42, C3.
Middleton (Lancs.), LY., 20, B1; 45, A2.
Middleton (Norfolk), GE., 17, E5.
Middleton (Northumb.), NE., 27, A4.
Middleton (Salop.), S&H., 9, A1.
Middleton (Westmorland), LNW., 24, A2; 27, G1.
Middleton-in-Teesdale, NE., 27, E3.
Middleton Jc., LY., 20, B1; 45, A2.
Middleton-on-the-Wolds, NE., 22, C4.
Middleton Rd. (Heysham) Goods, Mid., 24, C3.
Middletown, S&W., 14, A2.
Middlewich, LNW., 15, B2; 20, D2.
Middlewood, LNW. & GC&NSJt., 15, A4.
Midford, SD., 3, B3; 8, D1.
Midford Halt, GW., 3, B3; 8, D1.
Midge Hall, LY., 20, A3; 24, E3.
Midgham, GW., 4, A3.
Midhurst, LBSC., 5, E1.
Midhurst, LSW., 4, D1; 5, E1
Midsomer, Norton & Welton, GW. & SD., 3, B3; 8, E1.
Midville, GN., 17, C3.
Milborne Port, LSW., 3, D3; 8, G1.
Milcote, GW., 9, B5.
Mildenhall, GE., 11, B5.
Mildmay Park, NL., 40, B4.
Mile End, WB., 40, C3.
Miles Platting, LY., 20, B1; 45, A3.
Milford (Surrey), LSW., 5, D1.
Milford & Brocton, LNW., 15, E4.
Milford Haven, GW., 7, D1.
Milford Jc. (Wilts.), LSW., 4, D5.
Milford Jc. (Yorks.), NE., 21, D4.
Milkwall, SVW., 8, A2; 9, E1.
Millbay (Plymouth), GW., 1, D5 and Inset.
Millbrook (Beds.), LNW., 10, C1; 11, D1.
Millbrook (Hants.), LSW(MSW), 4, E4.
Millerhill, NB., 30, B1.
Miller's Dale, Mid., 15, A5.

Millfield, NE., 28, C5.
Mill Hill (I. of W.), IWC., 4, F3.
Mill Hill (Lancs.), LY(LNW), 20, A2; 24, E2.
Mill Hill (Middx.), Mid. & GN., 5, A3.
Millhouses & Ecclesall, Mid., 16, A5; 41, A2.
Milliken Park, G&SW., 29, C4.
Millisle, P&W., 25, D4.
Millom, Fur., 24, A5.
Mill St. (Aberdare) Goods, GW., 8, A5; 43, D2.
Milltimber, GNS., 37, G3.
Millwall Docks, GE., 40, D3.
Millwall Jc., GE., 40, C3 and Inset D1.
Millwood Jc., Fur., 24, B5.
Milnathort, NB., 33, G5.
Milner Royd Jc., LY., 21, E1; 42, C5.
Milner Wood Jc., Mid/O&I., 21, C2.
Milngavie, NB., 29, B4; 44, E5.
Milnrow, LY., 20, B1; 21, E1; 45, A1.
Milnthorpe, LNW., 24, A3.
Milton (Staffs.), NS., 15, C3. 20, E1.
Milton of Campsie, NB., 29, B5
Milton Halt, GW., 10, C4.
Milton Jc. (Glasgow), Cal., 44, D4.
Milton Rd., WCP., 3, A1; 8, D3.
Milverton (Som.). GW., 8, F4.
Milverton (Warwick), LNW., 10, B5.
Mindrum, NE., 31, E3.
Minehead, GW., 8, E5.
Minety & Ashton Keynes, GW., 9, F4.
Minffordd, Cam. & Fest., 19, F2.
Minions, LC., 1, C4.
Minories Jc., Met/Dist., 40, C4.
Minshull Vernon, LNW., 15, B2; 20, E2.
Minster (Thanet), SEC., 6, C2.
Minster-on-Sea, (Sheppey), SEC., 6, B4.
Minsterley, SWP., 14, B1.
Mintlaw, GNS., 37, D4.
Mint St. Goods, GN. & Mid., 40, C4.
Mirehouse Jc., Fur., 26, F3.
Mirfield, LY(LNW), 21, E2; 42, C4.
Mislingford (Goods), LSW., 4, E1.
Misson (Goods), GN., 21, G5.
Misterton, GN&GEJt., 22, G5.
Mistley, GE., 12, E4.
Mitcham, LBSC., 5, B3; 39, G5.
Mitcham Jc., LBSC., 5, B3; 39, G5.
Mitcheldean Road, GW., 9, D2.
Mitchell & Newlyn Halt, GW., 1, D1.
Mithian Halt, GW., 1, D1.
Mitre Bridge Goods, LNW., 39, C4.
Moat Lane Jc., Cam., 14, C3.
Mobberley, CLC., 20, C1; 45, B5.
Mochdre & Pabo, LNW., 19, D4.
Moffat, Cal., 30, G3.
Moira, Mid., 16, E5.
Mold, LNW., 20, E5.
Mold Jc., LNW., 20, D4.
Mollington, BJ., 20, D4.
Molyneux Brow, LY., 45, B2.
Molyneux Jc., LY/LNW., 45, B2.
Moniaive, G&SW., 26, A5.
Monifieth, D&A., 34, E4.
Monikie, Cal., 34, D4.
Monk Bretton, Mid., 21, F3; 42, E2.

71

Padiham, LY., 24, D1.
Padstow, LSW., 1, C2.
Paignton, GW., 2, D3.
Paisley, G&P., Cal., & G&SW., 29, C4; 44 F3.
Palace Gates, GE., 5, A3; 40, A5.
Pallion, NE., 28, C5.
Palmers Green, GN(NL), 5, A3.
Palnure, P&W., 25, B4.
Palterton & Sutton, Mid., 16, B4; 41, C3.
Pampisford, GE., 11, D4.
Pandy, GW., 14, G1.
Pangbourne, GW., 4, A2.
Pannal, NE., 21, C3.
Pant (Glam.), BM., 8, A5; 43, C1.
Pant (Salop), Cam., 14, A2; 20, G4.
Panteg & Griffithstown, GW., 8, B3; 43, A2.
Pant Glas, LNW., 19, E1.
Pantydwr, Cam., 14, D4.
Pantyffynnon, GW(LNW), 7, A3; 43, G1.
Pantysgallog, BM., 43, C1.
Papcastle, M&C., 26, D3.
Par, GW., 1, D3.
Paragon (Hull), NE(GC/LNW/LY), 22, E3.
Parbold, LY., 20, B3; 24, F3; 45, E1.
Parham, GE., 12, C2.
Park (Aberdeen), GNS, 37, G3.
Park (Barrow) (Goods), Fur., 24, B5.
Park (Birkenhead), Wir&MerJt., 45, F4.
Park (Kincard.), GNS., 37, G3.
Park (Manchester), LY., 45, A3.
Park (Sheffield) (Goods), GC., 41, A2; 42, G2.
Park Bridge, OAGB., 21, F1.
Park Drain, GN&GEJt., 22, F5.
Parkend, SVW., 8, A1; 9, E2.
Parkeston Quay, GE., 12, E3.
Parkgate (Ches.), BJ., 20, D4; 45, F5. See also Neston.
Parkgate (Yorks.) & Rawmarsh, Mid., 21, G4; 42, F1.
Parkgate (Yorks.) & Aldwarke, GC., 21, G4; 42, F1.
Parkhead (Glasgow), Cal. & NB., 44, D3.
Parkhead (Goods), NE., 27, D4
Parkhill, GNS., 37, F4.
Park Jcs., (Newport, Mon.), GW., 43, A3.
Park Lane (L'pool) Goods, LNW., 45, F4 and Inset.
Park Lane Jc., (Gateshead), NE., 28, Inset.
Park Lane Jc. (Lancs.), LNW., 45, D3.
Park Parade (Ashton), GC., 21, Inset A2.
Park Royal, GW., 39, C3.
Park Royal & Twyford Abbey, Dist., 39, C3.
Parkside Jcs., LNW., 45, D3.
Parkstone, LSW(SD), 3, F5.
Park Street & Frogmore LNW., 11, G1.
Parracombe, LB., 7, E4.
Parsley Hay, LNW., 15, B5.
Partick, Cal. & NB., 44, E4.
Partick West, Cal., 44, E4.
Partington, CLC., 20, C2; 24, G1; 45, B3.
Parton (Cumb.), LNW., 26, E4.
Parton (Kirkcud.), G&SW., 26, B5.
Partridge Green, LBSC., 5, E2.
Paston & Knapton, NSJ., 18, D2.
Patchway, GW., 8, C1; 9, G1.
Pateley Bridge, NE. & NV., 21, B2.
Patna, G&SW., 29, F4.

Patney & Chirton, GW., 3, B5.
Patricroft, LNW(BJ), 20, B2; 24, F1; 45, B3.
Patrington, NE., 22, E2.
Patterton, Cal., 29, C4; 44, E2.
Paulton Halt, GW., 3, B3; 8, D1.
Peacock Cross, NB., 44, B2.
Peak Forest, Mid., 15, A5.
Peakirk, GN., 17, F2.
Pear Tree & Normanton, Mid., 16, D5; 41, G2.
Peasley Cross, LNW., 45, D3.
Peasmarsh Jc., LSW/LBSC., 5, D1.
Peckham Rye, LBSC(SEC), 40, D4.
Peckham Rye Coal Depot, LNW&MidJt., 40, D4.
Pedair Ffordd, Tan., 19, G5.
Peebles, NB. & Cal., 30, D2.
Peel, IMR., 23, B2.
Peel Road, IMR., 23, B2.
Pegswood, NE., 27, A5
Pelaw, NE., 28, C5.
Pellon, HHL., 21, E2; 42, B5.
Pelsall, LNW., 15, F4.
Pelton, NE., 27, C5.
Pemberton, LY., 20, B3; 24, F2; 45, D2.
Pembrey, BPGV., 7, B2.
Pembrey & Burry Port, GW., 7, B2.
Pembridge, GW., 14, E1.
Pembroke, GW., 7, D2.
Penallta Jc., GW/Rhy., 43, C3.
Penallta Branch Jc., Rhy., 43, B3.
Penally, GW., 7, D3.
Penar Jc., GW., 43, B3.
Penarth, TV., 8, D4; 43, B5.
Penarth Branch Jc., TV., 43, C4.
Penarth Dock, TV., 8, C4; 43, B5.
Pencader, GW., 13, F4.
Pencaitland, NB., 30, C1.
Penclawdd, LNW., 7, B3.
Pencoed, GW., 8, C5; 43, D4.
Pendlebury, LY., 45, B2.
Pendleton, LY., 45, B3.
Pendleton (Broad St.), LY., 45, B3.
Pendre, Tal., 13, B5.
Pengam (Glam.), Rhy., 8, B4; 43, B2.
Pengam & Fleur-de-lis (Mon) BM., 8, B4; 43, B2.
Penge, LBSC., & SEC., 40, F4.
Penicuik, NB., 30, C2.
Penistone, GC&LYJt., 21, F3; 42, E3.
Penkridge, LNW., 15, E3.
Penmaenmawr, LNW., 19, D3.
Penmaenpool, Cam., 14, A5.
Pen Mill (Yeovil), GW., 3, D2; 8, G2.
Pennington, LNW., 45, C3.
Penns, Mid., 15, F5.
Penpergwm, GW., 8, A3; 43, A1.
Penrhiwceiber, GW. & TV., 8, B5; 43, C2.
Penhiwfelin Goods, Rhy., 43, B3.
Penrhos Jc., Rhy/BRY/AD., 43, B3.
Penrhyndeudraeth, Cam., & Fest., 19, F2.
Penrith, LNW(CKP/NE), 27, E1.
Penruddock, CKP., 26, E1.
Penryn, GW., 1, F1.
Pensford, GW., 3, A2; 8, D1.
Penshaw, NE., 28, C5.
Penshurst, SEC., 5, D4.
Pentir Rhiw, BM., 8, A5; 14, G3; 43, C1.
Penton, NB., 26, B1.
Pentraeth, LNW., 19, D2.
Pentrebach, TV., 8, A5; 43, C2.

Pentre Broughton Halt, GW., 20, E4.
Pentrecourt Plat., GW., 13, F4.
Pentrefelin, Tan., 14, A2; 20, G5.
Pentre Halt, TV., 43, D2.
Pentrepiod Halt, GW., 43, A2
Pentresaeson Halt, GW., 20, E4.
Pentwyn Halt, GW., 43, A2.
Penwithers Jc., GW., 1, E1.
Penwortham Jc., LY., 20, A3; 24, E3.
Penybont, LNW., 14, D3.
Penybontfawr, Tan., 19, G5.
Pen-y-ffordd, GC., 20, E4.
Pen-y-graig, GW., 8, B5; 43, D3.
Penygroes, LNW., 19, E1.
Penyrheol, Rhy., 8, B4; 43, B3.
Penzance, GW., 1, Inset F4.
Peplow, GW., 15, D2; 20, G2.
Percy Main, NE., 28, B5.
Perivale Halt, GW., 39, C2.
Perranporth, GW., 1, D1.
Perranwell, GW., 1, E1.
Perry Barr, LNW., 13, B3; 15, G4.
Pershore, GW., 9, C4.
Persley, GNS., 37, F4.
Perth (General) (Pass.), Cal(NB/HR), 33, F5.
Perth (Goods), Cal. & NB., 33, F5.
Perth (Princes St.), Cal., 33, F5.
Peterborough GE(LNW/Mid), & GN(Mid/MGN/GE), 11, A2; 17, F2.
Peterchurch, GW., 14, F1.
Peterhead, GNS., 37, D5.
Petersfield, LSW., 4, D2.
Peterston, GW., 8, C5; 43, C4.
Petteril Jc. (Carlisle), NE/Mid., 26, Inset.
Petworth, LBSC., 5, E1.
Pevensey & Westham, LBSC., 5, F5.
Pevensey Bay Halt, LBSC., 5, F5.
Pewsey, GW., 4, B5.
Philorth (Private),GNS.,37,C4.
Philorth Bridge Halt, GNS., 37, C4.
Philpstoun, NB., 30, B3.
Pickburn, HB., 21, F4.
Pickering, NE., 22, A5.
Pickhill, NE., 21, A3.
Picton, NE., 28, F5.
Piddington, Mid., 10, B2.
Piel, Fur., 24, B4.
Piercebridge, NE., 27, E5.
Pier Head (Ryde, I. of W.). LBSC&LSWJt(IW/IWC), 4, F3.
Piershill, NB., 30, Inset.
Pill, GW., 3, A2; 8, C2.
Pillbank Jc., GW., 43, A3.
Pilling, KE., 24, C3.
Pilmoor, NE., 21, B4.
Pilning, GW., 8, C2; 9, G1.
Pilsley, GC., 16, B4; 41, D3.
Pilton Jc., Cal., 30, Inset.
Pinchbeck, GN&GEJt., 17, E2.
Pinchinthorpe, NE., 28, E4.
Pinged, BPGV., 7, A2.
Pinhoe, LSW., 2, B3.
Pinmore, G&SW., 25, A3.
Pinner, Met&GCJt., 5, A2; 39, A1.
Pinwherry, G&SW., 25, A3.
Pinxton, GN., 16, C4; 41, E3. See also Kirkby, GC.
Pinxton & Selston, Mid., 16, C4; 41, E3.
Pipe Gate, NS., 15, C2; 20, F2.
Pirbright Jc., LSW., 4, B1; 5, C1.
Pirton, Mid., 9, C3.
Pitlochry, HR., 33, C4.
Pitmedden, GNS., 37, F4.
Pitsea, LTS., 6, A5.
Pitsford & Brampton, LNW., 10, B2.

Pittenweem, NB., 34, G3.
Pittington, NE., 28, D5.
Pitts Hill, NS., 15, C3; 20, E1.
Plains, NB., 30, C5; 44, A4.
Plaidy, GNS., 37, D3.
Plaistow, LTS(Dist), 40, C2.
Plank Lane, LNW., 45, C3.
Plantation Halt, CM., 29, Inset.
Plashetts, NB., 27, A2.
Plas Marl, GW., 7, B4; 43, G2.
Plas Power, GW. & GC., 20, E4.
Platt Bridge, LNW., 45, D2. See also Hindley.
Plawsworth, NE., 27, C5.
Plealey Road, SWP., 14, B1.
Plean, Cal., 30, A5.
Pleasington, LY., 20, A2; 24, E2.
Pleasley, Mid. & GN., 16 B4; 41, D4.
Plessey, NE., 27, B5.
Plex Moss Lane Halt, LY., 20, B4; 24, F4; 45, F2.
Plockton, HR., 33, E1.
Plodder Lane, LNW., 20, B2; 24, F1; 45, C2.
Plowden, BC., 14, C1.
Pluckley, SEC., 6, D4.
Plumbley, CLC., 15, A2; 20, D2; 45, B5.
Plumpton (Cumb.), LNW., 27, D1.
Plumpton (Sussex), LBSC., 5, F3.
Plumpton Jc., Fur., 24, A4.
Plumstead, SEC., 40, D1.
Plumtree, Mid., 16, D3.
Plym Bridge Platform, GW., 2, D5.
Plymouth, GW(LSW), GW. & LSW., 1, D5 and Inset.
Plympton, GW., 2, D5.
Plymstock, LSW(GW), 1, Inset
Pocket Nook Jc., LNW., 45, D3.
Pocklington, NE., 22, C5.
Point Pleasant Jc., LSW., 39, E5.
Pokesdown, LSW., 4, F5.
Polegate, LBSC., 5, F5.
Polesworth, LNW., 16, F5.
Pollok Jc., G&SW/G&P., 44, Inset F1.
Pollokshaws, GBK., 44, E3.
Pollokshaws East, Cal., 44, E3 and Inset F1.
Pollokshields East, Cal., 44, E3 and Inset F1.
Pollokshields West, Cal., 44, E3 and Inset F1.
Polmont, NB., 30, B4.
Polsham, SD., 3, C2; 8, E2.
Polton, NB., 30, C2.
Pomathorn, NB., 30, C2.
Ponder's End, GE., 5, A3; 11, G3.
Pond St. (Sheffield) (Goods), Mid., 16, A5; 21, G3; 41, A2; 42, G2.
Pond St. (Sheffield) (Pass.), Mid(HB/NE/LY), 16, A5; 21, G3; 41, A2; 42, G2.
Ponril Jc., Cal., 30, E5.
Ponfeigh, Cal., 30, E4.
Pontardawe, Mid., 7, A4; 43, F2.
Pontardulais, GW&LNWJt., 7, A3.
Pontcynon Bridge Halt, TV., 43, C3.
Pontdolgoch, Cam., 14, B3.
Pontefract (Baghill), SK(GC/GN), 21, E4; 42, C1.
Pontefract (Monkhill), LY(NE), 21, E4; 42, C1.
Ponteland, NE., 27, B5.
Pontesbury, SWP., 14, B1.
Pontfadog, GVT., 20, F5.
Pontfaen, GVT., 20, F5.
Ponthenry, BPGV., 7, A3.
Ponthir, GW., 8, B3; 43, A3.

Pont Lawrence, LNW., 8, B4; 43, B3.
Pontllanfraith, GW. & LNW., 8, B4; 43, B3.
Pont Llanio, GW., 13, E5.
Pontlliw (Goods), GW., 7, B3; 43, G2.
Pontlottyn, Rhy., 8, A4; 43, C2. *See also* Rhymney, BM.
Pontnewydd, GW., 8, B3; 43, A3.
Pontnewynydd, GW., 43, A2.
Pontrhydyfen, RSB., 43, E3.
Pontrhythallt, LNW., 19, D2.
Pontrilas, GW., 14, G1.
Pont Rug, LNW., 19, D2.
Pontsarn for Vaynor, BM&LNWJt., 8, A5; 43, C1.
Pontsticill Jc., BM., 8, A5; 43, C1.
Pontwalby Halt, GW., 43, E2.
Pontyates, BPGV., 7, A3.
Pontyberem, BPGV., 7, A3.
Pontycymmer, GW(PT), 7, B5; 43, D3.
Pont-y-Pant, LNW., 19, E3.
Pontypool, GW., 8, B3; 43, A2.
Pontypool Road, GW., 8, B3; 43, A2.
Pontypridd, TV(AD), & BRY., 8, B5; 43, C3.
Pontyrhyll, GW(PT), 7, B5; 43, D3.
Pool - in - Wharfedale, NE., 21, C3.
Poole, LSW(SD), 3, F2.
Pool Quay, Cam., 14, A2.
Poplar (Goods), GN., GW., LNW., Mid., & NL., 40, C3/D3 *and* Inset D1/E1.
Poplar (Pass.), GE. & NL., 40, C3 *and* Inset D1.
Poppleton, NE., 21, C4.
Poppleton Jc., NE., 21, C5 *and* Inset A4.
Portbury, GW., 3, A2; 8, C2.
Portbury Rd., WCP., 3, A2; 8, C2.
Port Carlisle, NB., 26, C2.
Portchester, LSW., 4, E2.
Port Clarence, NE., 28, E4.
Portcreek Jc., LSW/LBSC., 4, E2.
Port Dinorwic, LNW., 19, D2.
Port Dundas (Goods) Glasgow Cal. & NB., 44, E4.
Port Eglington Depot, G&SW. 44, Inset F1.
Port Elphinstone (Goods), GNS. 37, F3.
Porterfield (Renfrew) G&P., 44, F4.
Port Erin, IMR., 23, C1.
Port Gordon, GNS., 37, C1.
Portesham, GW., 3, F2.
Portessie, GNS. & HR., 37, C1.
Port Glasgow, Cal., 29, B3.
Port Gordon, GNS., 37, C1.
Porth, TV(BRY), 8, B5; 43, C3.
Porthcawl, GW., 7, C5; 43, E4.
Porthywaen, Tan., 14, A2; 20, G5.
Port Isaac Road, LSW, 1, C3.
Portishead, GW. & WCP., 3, A2; 8, C2.
Portknockie, GNS., 37, C1.
Portland, WP., 3, G3.
Portlethen, Cal., 34, A1; 37, G4
Portmadoc, Cam., Fest. & PCB., 19, F2.
Port Meadow Halt, LNW., 10, E4.
Portobello, NB., 30, Inset.
Portobello Jc., GW., 39, C5 *and* Inset. C1.
Port of Menteith, NB., 29, A5.
Porton, LSW., 4, C5.
Portpatrick, P&W., 25, C1.
Portreath, GW., 1, Inset E5.
Port St. Mary, IMR., 23, C1.
Portskewett, GW., 8, B2; 9, F1.
Portslade, LBSC., 5, F3.

Portsmouth (Yorks.), LY., 20, A1; 21, E1.
Portsmouth Arms, LSW., 7, G3.
Portsmouth Harbour, LSW&LBSCJt., 4, E2.
Portsmouth Town (Hants.), LSW&LBSCJt., 4, E2.
Port Soderick, IMR., 23, C2.
Portsoy, GNS., 37, C2.
Port Sunlight (Goods), BJ., 45, F4.
Port Talbot (Aberavon), RSB., 7, B4; 43, F3.
Port Talbot (Central), PT., 7, B4; 43, F3.
Port Talbot & Aberavon, GW(PT), 7, B4; 43, F3.
Port Victoria, SEC., 6, B4.
Possil Goods, Cal., 44, E4.
Possilpark, NB., 44, E4.
Postland, GN&GEJt., 17, E2.
Potter Hanworth, GN&GEJt., 16, B1; 17, B1.
Potter Heigham, MGN., 18, E2.
Potterhill (Paisley), G&SW., 29, C4; 44, G3.
Potteric Carr. Jc., GN/SYJ., 21, Inset G2.
Potters Bar, GN(NL), 11, G2.
Potto, NE., 28, F4.
Potton, LNW., 11, D2.
Poulton (Lancs.), PWY., 24, D4.
Poulton Curve Halt, PWY., 24, D4.
Pouparts Jc., LBSC., 39, Inset E3.
Powderhall, NB., 30, Inset.
Powerstock, GW., 3, F2.
Poynton, LNW(NS), 15, A3; 20, C1; 45, A4.
Poynton, GC&NSJt., 15, A4.
Praed St. Met(Dist), 39, C5. *See also* Paddington.
Praze, GW., 1, Inset E5.
Prees, LNW., 15, D1; 20, F3.
Preesall, KE., 24, C4.
Preesgweene, GW., 20, F4.
Prescot, LNW., 20, C3; 24, G3; 45, E3.
Prestatyn, LNW., 19, C5.
Prestbury, LNW(NS), 15, A3; 20, D1; 45, A5.
Presteign, GW., 14, D2.
Presthope, GW., 15, F1.
Preston (Goods), LNW., LY., PL. & PWY., 24, E3.
Preston (Pass.), NU. & LY., 24, E3.
Preston Brook, LNW., 15, A1; 20, C3; 45, D5.
Preston Jc., LY., 20, A3; 24, E3.
Prestonpans, NB., 30, B1.
Preston Park, LBSC., 5, F3.
Preston Plat., GW., 2, D3.
Preston Rd., (Lancs.), LY., 20, C4; 24, G4; 45, F3.
Preston Rd. (Mddx.), Met., 39, A3.
Preston St. (Whitehaven) Goods, Fur., 26, E4.
Prestwich. LY., 20, B1; 24, F1; 45, B2.
Prestwick, G&SW., 29, E3.
Priestfield, GW., 13, A1.
Princes Dock (Glasgow), PDJ., 44, E3.
Princes End, GW., 13, A1; 15, F4.
Princes Pier (Greenock), G&SW., 29, B3.
Princes Risborough, GW&GCJt. 10, F2.
Princes St. (Edinburgh), Cal., 30, B2 *and* Inset.
Princes St. (Perth), Cal., 33, F5.
Princetown, GW., 2, C5.
Priory (Dover), SEC., 6, D2.

Priory Rd., Wells (Som.), SD., 3, C2; 8, E2.
Prittlewell, GE., 6, A4.
Privett, LSW., 4, D2.
Probus & Ladock Plat., GW., 1, E2.
Prudhoe, NE(NB), 27, B4.
Pudsey, GN., 21, D2; 42, A4.
Pulborough, LBSC., 5, E1.
Pulford (Goods), GW., 20, E4.
Pulham Market, GE., 12, B3; 18, G3.
Pulham St. Mary, GE., 12, B3; 18, G3.
Puncheston, GW., 13, F1.
Purfleet, LTS., 5, B5.
Purley, LBSC(SEC), 5, C3.
Purley Oaks, LBSC., 5, C3.
Purton, GW., 9, F4.
Putney, LSW., 5, B3; 39, E4.
Putney Bridge, Dist., 39, E4.
Puxton, GW., 3, B1; 8, D3.
Pwllheli, Cam., 19, F1.
Pye Bridge, Mid., 16, C4; 41, E3.
Pye Hill & Somercotes, GN., 16, C4; 41, E3.
Pye Wipe Jc., (Lincoln), GC/GN/GN&GEJt., 16, B1 *and* Inset.
Pyle, GW., 7, C5; 43, E4.
Pylle, SD., 3, C2; 8, E1.
Pylle Hill Goods (Bristol) GW., 3, Inset

Q

Quainton Rd., Met&GCJt., & OAT., 10, E3.
Quaker's Drove (Goods), GE., 11, A3; 17, F3.
Quaker's Yard (H.L.) GW(Rhy)., 8, B5; 43, C2.
Quaker's Yard (L.L.) GW&TVJt., 8, B5; 43, C2.
Quarter, Cal., 29, D5; 44, B1.
Queenborough, SEC., 6, B4.
Queen's Park (Glasgow), Cal., 44, E3.
Queen's Park, West Kilburn, LNW(NL/LE) 39, B5.
Queen's Rd. (Battersea), LSW., 39, D5 *and* Inset E4.
Queen's Rd. (Peckham), LBSC., 40, D4.
Queens Rd. (Sheffield) Goods, Mid., 16, A5; 21, G3; 41, A2; 42, G2.
Queen St. (Cardiff), TV., 8, C4; 43, B4.
Queen St. (Exeter), LSW., 2, B3.
Queen St. (Glasgow), NB., 29, C5; 44, E4.
Queensbury, GN., 21, D2; 42, B5.
Queensferry, LNW., 20, D4.
Quellyn Lake, NWNG., 19. E2.
Quintrell Downs Platform, GW., 1, D1.
Quorn & Woodhouse, GC., 16, E4. *See also* Barrow-on-Soar.
Quy, GE., 11, C4.

R

Racks, G&SW., 26, B3.
Radcliffe, LY., 20, B1; 24, F1; 45, B2. *See also* Black Lane.
Radcliffe Bridge, LY., 45, B2.
Radcliffe - on - Trent, GN(LNW), 16, D3.
Radford, Mid., 16, D4; 41, G4.
Radford & Timsbury Halt, GW., 3, B3; 8, D1.
Radipole Halt, GW., 3, G3.
Radlett, Mid., 11, G1.
Radley, GW., 10, F4.
Radstock, GW. & SD., 3, B3; 8, E1.

Radway Green, NS., 15, C2; 20, E1.
Radyr, TV., 8, C4; 43, C4.
Raglan, GW., 8, A3.
Rainbow Hill Jc., GW., 9, B3.
Rainford Jc., LY(LNW). & LNW., 20, B3; 24, F3; 45, E2.
Rainford Village, LNW., 20, B3; 24, F3; 45, E2.
Rainham (Essex), LTS., 5, A4.
Rainham (Kent), SEC., 6, B5.
Rainhill, LNW., 20, C3 24, G3; 45, E3.
Rampside, Fur., 24, B4.
Ramsbottom, LY., 20, A1; 24, E1; 45, B1.
Ramsden Dock, Fur., 24, B5.
Ramsey (Hunts.), GN. & GE., 11, A2/B2; 17, F3.
Ramsey (I. of M.), IMR. & ME., 23, A3.
Ramsgate |Harbour, SEC., 6, B1.
Ramsgate Town, SEC., 6, B1.
Ramsgill, NV., 21, B2.
Randle Jc., LNW., 20, B3; 24, F3; 45, E2.
Rankinston, G&SW., 29, F4.
Rannoch, NB., 32, C1; 33, D1
Ranskill, GN., 16, A3; 21, G5.
Raskelf, NE., 21, B4.
Ratby, Mid., 16, F4.
Ratgoed Quarry, Corris, 14, A5.
Rathen, GNS., 37, C4.
Ratho, NB., 30, B3.
Rathven, HR., 37, C1.
Rauceby, GN., 16, C1; 17, C1.
Raunds, Mid., 10, A1; 11, B1.
Ravelrig Halt, Cal., 30, C3.
Ravenglass, Fur. & RE., 26, G3.
Ravensbourne, SEC., 40, F3.
Ravenscar, NE., 28, F1.
Ravenscourt Park, LSW(Dist), 39, D4.
Ravenscraig, Cal., 29, B3.
Raven Square, W&L., 14, B2.
Ravensthorpe, LY., 42, C4.
Ravensthorpe & Thornhill, LNW., 42, C3. *See also* Thornhill.
Ravenstonedale, NE., 27, F2. *See also* Kirkby Stephen.
Ravenstone Wood Jc., Mid/SMJ., 10, B2.
Ravenswood Jc., NB., 31, E1.
Rawcliffe, LY., 21, E5. *See also* Airmyn.
Rawtenstall, LY., 20, A1; 24, E1.
Rawyards, NB., 44, A4.
Raydon Wood, GE., 12, D4.
Rayleigh, GE., 6, A5.
Rayne, GE., 11, E5.
Rayner's Lane, Met(Dist), 39, B1.
Raynes Park, LSW., 5, B3; 39, F4.
Raynham Park, MGN., 18, D5
Reading, GW. & SEC(LSW), 4, A2.
Reading West, GW., 4, A2.
Rearsby, Mid., 16, E3.
Rectory Jc., GN., 16, D3. 41, F5.
Rectory Rd., GE., 40, B4.
Redbourn, Mid., 11, F1.
Redbridge, LSW(MSW), 4, E4
Redbrook, GW., 8, A2; 9, E1.
Redcar, NE., 28, E4.
Redcastle, HR., 36, D5.
Redding (Goods), NB., 30, B4.
Reddish, LNW(LY) & GC&MidJt., 21, G1; 45, A3.
Redditch, Mid., 9, B4.
Redheugh (Goods), NE., 28, Inset.
Redhill (Surrey), SEC(LBSC), 5, C3.
Red Hill Jc., (Hereford) GW/LNW., 9, C1.
Red Hills Jc., (Penrith) CKP/NE., 27, E1.

St. Ives (Cornwall), GW., 1,
    Inset E4.
St. Ives (Hunts.),
    GN&GEJt(Mid), 11, B2.
St. James (Cheltenham), GW.,
    9, D4.
St. James (Liverpool), CLC.,
    45, F4.
St. James (Paisley), Cal., 44, G3
St. James's Bridge Jc., NE.,
    28, Inset.
St. James's Park, Dist(Met),
    40, D5.
St. James St. (Walthamstow),
    GE., 40, A3.
St. John's (Bedford), LNW.,
    11, D1.
St. John's (I. of M.), IMR.,
    22, B2.
St. John's (London), SEC.,
    40, E3.
St. John's Chapel, NE., 27, D3.
St. John's Rd. (Ryde, I. of W.),
    IW.LBSC&LSWJt(IWC),
    4, F3.
St. John's Wood Rd., Met.,
    39, C5.
St. Kew Highway, LSW., 1, C2
St. Keyne, LL., 1, D4.
St. Lawrence, IWC., 4, G3.
St. Leonards (Edinburgh)
    (Goods), NB., 30, Inset.
St. Leonards (Sussex), SEC.,
    LBSC. & SEC(LBSC), 6, F5.
St. Luke's (Southport), LY.,
    20, A4; 24, E4; 45, F1.
St. Luke's Jc. (Barrow), Fur.,
    24, B5.
St. Margaret's (Herts.), GE.,
    11, F3.
St. Margaret's (Middx.),
    LSW., 39, E2.
St. Margarets Jc., LBSC.,
    5, D4.
St. Marnock's (Goods),
    G&SW., 29, E4.
St. Mary Church Rd., TV.,
    8, C5; 43, C5.
St. Mary Cray, SEC., 5, B4;
    40, G1.
St. Mary's (Derby) Goods,
    Mid., 41, D2.
St. Mary's (Hunts.), GN.,
    11, A2; 17, G2.
St. Mary's (London),
    Dist&MetJt(H&C), 40, C4.
St. Mary's Crossing Halt, GW.,
    9, F3.
St. Michael's, CLC., 20, C4;
    45, F4.
St. Monan's, NB., 34, G3.
St. Neots, GN., 11, C2.
St. Olave's, GE., 12, A2;18, F1.
St. Pancras Gds., Mid., 40, B5.
St. Pancras (Pass.),
    Mid(LTS/GE), 5, A3;
    40, C5.
St. Pancras Jcs., NL/Mid. &
    NL/GN., 40, B5.
St. Paul's (Halifax), HHL.,
    21, E2; 42, B5.
St. Paul's (London), SEC.,
    40, C5.
St. Paul's Rd.Jc., Mid., 40, B5.
St. Peter's, NE., 28, Inset.
St. Philip's (Bristol), Mid.,
    3, Inset.
St. Philip's Marsh (Bristol)
    (Goods), GW., 3, Inset.
St. Quintin Park & Worm-
    wood Scrubbs, WL., 39, C4.
St. Rollox, Cal., 29, C5; 44, D4
St. Thomas (Exeter), GW.,
    2, B3.
St. Thomas (Swansea), Mid.,
    43, G3.
St. Vigean's Jc.,
    D&A/Cal/NB., 34, D3.
Sale & Ashton-on-Mersey,
    MSJA(CLC), 20, C1; 45, B3.
Salford, LY(Mid), 20, B1;
    24, F1; 45, A3.
Salford Priors, Mid., 9, B4.
Salfords Goods, LBSC., 5, D3.

Salhouse, GE., 18, E2.
Salisbury, LSW(GW), LSW.
    & GW., 4, C5.
Salt, GN., 15, D4.
Saltaire, Mid., 21, D2; 42, A5.
Saltash, GW., 1, D5.
Saltburn, NE., 28, E3.
Saltcoats, G&SW. & Cal.,
    29, D3.
Saltfleetby, GN., 17, A3;22,G1
Saltford, GW., 3, A3; 8, D1.
    See also Kelston.
Salthouse Jc., Fur., 24, B4.
Saltley, Mid., 13, B4; 15, G5.
Saltmarket Jc., G&SW., 44,
    Inset E2.
Saltmarshe, NE(GC), 22, E5.
Saltney, GW., 20, D4.
Saltney Ferry, LNW., 20, D4.
Saltoun, NB., 30, C1.
Salwick, PWY., 24, D3.
Salzcraggie Plat., HR., 38, F4.
Sampford Courtenay, LSW.,
    2, B5.
Sandal, WRG., 21, E3; 42, C2
Sandal & Walton, Mid.,
    21, E3; 42, C2.
Sandbach, LNW. & NS.,
    15, B2; 20, E2.
Sandbach (Wheelock), NS.,
    15, B2; 20, E2.
Sanderstead, CO., 5, C3.
Sandford & Banwell, GW.,
    3, B1; 8, D3.
Sandgate, SEC., 6, D2.
Sandhills, LY., 45, Inset.
Sandholme, HB., 22, D5.
Sandhurst Halt, SEC., 4, B1.
Sandilands, Cal., 30, E4.
Sandling Jc., SEC., 6, D3.
Sandon, NS., 15, D4.
Sandown, IW., 4, F3.
Sandplace, LL., 1, D4.
Sandsend, NE., 28, F2.
Sandside, Fur., 24, A3.
Sandtoft (Goods), AJ., 22, F5.
Sandwich, SEC., 6, C2.
Sandwich Rd., EK., 6, C2.
Sandy, GN. & LNW., 11, D2.
Sandycroft, LNW., 20, D4.
Sandy Lodge, Met&GCJt.,
    5, A2.
Sankey, CLC., 20, C3; 45, D4.
Sankey Bridges, LNW., 45,D4.
Sanquhar, G&SW., 30, F5.
Santon, IMR., 23, C2.
Sarnau, GW., 7, A2; 13, G3.
Sarsden Halt, GW., 10, D5.
Sauchie, NB., 30, A4.
Saughall, GC., 20, D4.
Saughton, NB., 30, B3.
Saughtree, NB., 31, G1.
Saundersfoot, GW., 7, D3.
Saunderton, GW&GCJt.,
    10, F2.
Savernake, GW., 4, A5.
Sawbridgeworth, GE., 11, F3.
Sawdon, NE., 22, A4.
Sawley, Mid., 16, D4.
Sawley Jc., Mid. 16, D4.
Saxby, Mid(MGN), 16, E2.
Saxham & Risby, GE., 11, C5.
Saxilby, GN., 16, A1.
Saxmundham, GE., 12, C2.
Saxondale Jc., GN/LNW.,
    16, C3.
Scafell (Goods), Cam., 14, C3.
Scalby, NE., 22, A4; 28, G1.
Scalford, GN&LNWJt., 16, E2
Scarborough, NE., 22, A3;
    28, G1.
Scarcliffe, GC., 16, B4; 41, C4.
Scawby & Hibaldstow, GC.,
    22, F4.
Scholes, NE., 21, D3; 42, A2.
Schoolhill, GNS., 37, G4.
Scopwick & Timberland, GN.
    & GE., 17, C1.
Scorrier, GW.,
    1, E1 and Inset E5.
Scorton (Lancs.), LNW.,
    24, C3.
Scorton (Yorks.), NE., 27, F5.
Scotby, Mid. & NE., 26, C1.

Scotch Dyke, NB., 26, B1.
Scotland St. (Goods), NB.,
    30, Inset.
Scotland St. Jc., G&SW/Cal.,
    44, Inset F2.
Scotscalder, HR., 38, D3.
Scotsgap, NB., 27, A4.
Scotstoun, Cal., 29, C4; 44, F4
Scotstounhill, NB., 29, C4;
    44, F4.
Scotstoun West, Cal., 29, C4;
    44, F4.
Scotswood, NE(NB), 27, B5.
Scremerston, NE., 31, D4.
Scrooby, GN., 21, G5.
Scruton, NE., 21, A3; 28, G5.
Sculcoates, NE. & HB.,
    22, Inset.
Scunthorpe, GC., 22, F4.
    See also Frodingham.
Seacombe & Egremont,
    Wir(GC), 45, F3.
Seacroft, GN., 17, B4.
Seaford, LBSC., 5, G4.
Seaforth & Litherland,
    LY(LNW/LOR), 20, B4;
    24, G4; 45, F3.
Seaham, NE., 28, C5.
Seaham Colliery, NE., 28, C5.
Seahouses, NSL., 31, E5.
Seamer, NE., 22, A3.
Sea Mills, CE., 3, A2; 8, C2.
Seascale, Fur., 26, F3.
Seaton (Cumb.), CWJ., 26, D3.
Seaton (Devon), LSW., 2, B1.
Seaton (Durham), NE., 28, C5.
Seaton (Rutland), LNW.,
    16, F1.
Seaton Carew, NE., 28, E4.
Seaton Delaval, NE., 28, B5.
Seaton Jc. (Devon), LSW. 2, B1
Seaton Snook, NE., 28, E4.
Sedbergh, LNW., 24, A2;
    27, G2.
Sedgebrook, GN., 16, D2.
Sedgefield, NE., 28, E5.
Sedgeford, GE., 17, D5.
Sedgley Jc., LNW., 13, B1.
Seedley, LNW(BJ), 45, B3.
Seend, GW., 3, B4.
Seer Green Halt, GW&GCJt.,
    5, A1; 10, F1.
Sefton & Maghull, CLC.,
    20, B4; 24, F4; 45, F2.
    See also Maghull.
Sefton Park, LNW., 20, C4;
    45, F4.
Seghill, NE., 28, B5.
Selby, NE(GN/GE/LNW),
    21, D5.
Selham, LBSC., 5, E1.
Selhurst, LBSC., 5, B3; 40, G5.
Selkirk, NB., 30, E1.
Sellafield, Fur., 26, F3.
Selling, SEC., 6, C3.
Selly Oak, Mid., 9, A4; 15, G4
Selsdon Rd., CO/WSC., 5, C3.
Selsey, SL., 4, F1.
Semington Halt, GW., 3, B4.
Semley, LSW., 3, D4.
Senghenydd, Rhy., 8, B4;
    43, C3.
Scrridge Jc., SVW., 8, A1; 9, E2
Sessay, NE., 21, B4.
Settle, Mid., 24, B1.
Settrington, NE., 22, B5.
Seven Kings, GE., 5, A4.
Sevenoaks, SEC., 5, C4.
Seven Sisters (Glam.), N&B.,
    7, A5; 43, E1.
Seven Sisters (Middx.), GE.,
    5, A3; 40, A4.
Seven Stars, W&L., 14, B2.
Severn Bridge, SVW., 8, A1;
    9, E2.
Severn Tunnel Jc., GW.,
    8, B2; 9, F1.
Severus Jc., NE.,
    21, C5 and Inset A4.
Sexhow, NE., 28, F4.
Shackerstone, AN., 16, F5.
Shadwell, GE. & EL., 40, C4.
Shaftholme Jc., GN/NE.,
    21, F5.

Shafton Jc., LY/DV., 21, F4;
    42, D1.
Shalford, SEC., 5, D1.
Shalford Jc., LSW/SEC., 5, D1.
Shandon, NB., 29, A3.
Shankend, NB., 31, F1.
Shanklin, IW., 4, G3.
Shap, LNW., 27, F1.
Shapwick, SD., 3, C1; 8, E3.
Sharlston, LY., 21, E4; 42, C1.
Sharnal Street, SEC., 6, B5.
Sharnbrook, Mid., 10, B1;
    11, C1.
Sharpness, SVW., 8, B1; 9, F2.
Shaugh Bridge Platform, GW.,
    2, D5.
Shaw & Crompton, LY., 21, F1
Shawclough & Healey,
    LY., 20, A1; 45, A1.
Shawford & Twyford,
    LSW(GW), 4, D3.
Shawforth, LY., 20, A1; 45, A1
Shawhill Jc., Cal., 26, B2.
Shawlands, Cal., 44, E3.
Sheepbridge, Mid. 16, A5;
    41, B2.
Sheepbridge & Whittington
    Moor, GC., 16, A5; 41, B2.
Sheerness Dockyard, SEC.,
    6, B4.
Sheerness East, SEC., 6, B4.
Sheerness-on-Sea, SEC., 6, B4.
Sheet Factory Jc., GE., 40, B2.
Sheet Stores Jc., Mid., 16, D4.
Sheffield (Goods), GC., LNW.,
    Mid. & SHD., 16, A5;
    21, G3; 41, A2; 42, G2.
Sheffield (Pass.), GC(LY), &
    Mid(NE/LY), 16, A5;
    21, G3; 41, A2; 42, G2.
Sheffield Park, LBSC., 5, E4.
Shefford, Mid., 11, D1.
Shelford, GE., 11, D3.
Shelwick Jc., S&H/GW., 9 C1.
Shenfield & Hutton, GE.,
    5, A5; 11, G4.
Shenstone, LNW., 15, F5.
Shenton, AN., 16, F5.
Shepherds, GW., 1, D1.
Shepherds Bush, H&C., 39, C4
Shepherd's Well, SEC. & EK.,
    6, D2.
Shepley & Shelley, LY., 21, F2;
    42, D4.
Shepperton, LSW., 5, B2.
Shepreth, GN., 11, D3.
Shepreth Branch Jc., GE.,
    11, C3.
Shepshed, LNW., 16, E4.
Shepton Mallet, GW. & SD.,
    3, C2; 8, E1.
Sherborne, LSW., 3, D3; 8, G1
Sherburn Coll., NE., 28, D5.
Sherburn House, NE., 28, D5.
Sherburn-in-Elmet, NE(GN),
    21, D4.
Sheringham, MGN., 18, D3.
Sherwood, NB., 16, C3; 41, F5
Shettleston, NB., 29, C5; 44, C3
Shide, IWC., 4, F3.
Shieldhall Goods, G&P.,
    44, F4.
Shieldhill, Cal., 26, A3.
Shield Row, NE., 27, C5.
Shields, G&SW., 44, Inset F1.
Shields Jc., Cal/G&P/G&SW.,
    44, Inset F1.
Shields Rd., G&P., 44, Inset F1
Shielmuir Jc., Cal., 44, A2.
Shifnal, GW., 15, E2.
Shildon, NE., 27, E5.
Shillingstone, SD., 3, E4.
Shilton, LNW., 10, A5; 16, G5
Shincliffe, NE., 28, D5.
Shiplake, GW., 10, G2.
Shipley, Mid(NE) & GN.,
    21, D2; 42, A5.
Shipley Gate, Mid., 16, C4;
    41, F3.
Shippea Hill, GE., 11, B4.
Shipston-on-Stour, GW., 9, C5
Shipton, GW., 10, D5.
Shirdley Hill, LY., 20, A4;
    24, F4; 45, F1.

Shirebrook, Mid(GC) & GN., 16, B4; 41, C4.
Shirehampton, CE., 8, A2; 9, G1.
Shireoaks, GC(Mid), 16, A4; 41, A4.
Shirley, GW., 9, A5.
Shobnal Wharf, Mid., 15, Inset D5.
Shoeburyness, LTS., 6, A4.
Sholing, LSW., 4, E3.
Shooters Hill & Eltham Park, SEC., 40, C4.
Shoreditch (Goods), LNW., 40, C4.
Shoreditch, (Pass.) EL. & NL., 40, C4.
Shoreham (Kent), SEC., 5, C4.
Shoreham-by-Sea (Sussex), LBSC., 5, F3.
Shore Rd. Goods (Stirling), NB., 30, A5.
Shorncliffe Camp. SEC., 6, D2.
Short Heath, Mid., 15, F4.
Shortlands, SEC., 5, B4; 40, F2
Shotley Bridge, NE., 27, C4.
Shottle, Mid., 16, C5; 41, F1.
Shotton, LNW., 20, D4.
See also Connah's Quay.
Shotton Bridge, NE., 28, D5.
Shotts, Cal. & NB., 30, B2.
Shrawardine, S&M., 14, A1.
Shrewsbury (Goods), S&H., GW., LNW. & S&M., 15, E1.
Shrewsbury (Pass.), S&H., & S&M., 15, E1.
Shrewsbury West, S&M.,15, E1
Shrivenham, GW., 9, F5.
Shrub Hill (Worcester), GW&MidJt., 9, B3.
Shustoke, Mid., 16, G5.
Sible & Castle Hedingham, CVH., 11, E5.
Sibley's, GE., 11, E4.
Sibsey, GN., 17, C3.
Sidcup, SEC., 5, B4; 40, E1.
Siddick, LNW&CWJJt., 26, D3.
Sidlesham, SL., 4, F1.
Sidley, SEC., 6, F5.
Sidmouth, LSW., 2, B2.
Sidmouth Jc., LSW., 2, B2.
Sigglesthorne, NE., 22, D3.
Sighthill (Goods), NB., 44, D4.
Sileby, Mid., 16, E3.
Silecroft, Fur., 24, A5.
Silian Halt, GW., 13, E5.
Silkstone, GC., 21, F3; 42, E3.
Silkstone Colliery, LY., 21, F3; 42, E3.
Silkstone Jc., LY., 42, D2.
Silloth, NB., 26, C3.
Silverdale (Lancs.), Fur., 24, B3.
Silverdale (Staffs.) NS., 15, C3; 20, F1.
Silvermuir Jc. South, Cal., 30, D4.
Silverton, GW., 2, A3.
Silvertown, GE., 40, C2.
Simonstone, LY., 24, D1.
Sincil Jc., GN/GN&GEJt., 16, B1.
Sinclairtown, NB., 30, A2.
Sinderby, NE., 21, A3.
Sindlesham Halt, SEC., 4, A1.
Singer, NB., 29, C4; 44, F4.
Singleton (Lancs.), PWY., 24, D4.
Singleton (Sussex), LBSC., 4, E1.
Sinnington, NE., 22, A5.
Sirhowy, LNW., 8, A4; 43, B1.
Sirhowy Jc., LNW/GW., 43, B3.
Sittingbourne, SEC., 6, C4.
Six Bells Halt, GW., 43, B2.
Six Mile Bottom, GE., 11, C4.
Skares, G&SW., 29, F4.
Skegby, GN., 16, B4; 41, D4.
Skegness, GN., 17, B4.
Skelbo, HR., 36, A4.
Skellingthorpe, GC., 16, B1.

Skellow Jc., WRG., 21, F4.
Skelmanthorpe, LY., 21, F3; 42, D3.
Skelmersdale, LY(LNW)., 20, B3; 24, F3; 45, E2.
Skewen, GW., 7, B4; 43, F2.
Skinningrove, NE., 28, E3.
Skipton, Mid., 21, C1.
Skipwith, DVL., 21, D5.
Skirlaugh, NE., 22, D3.
Slades Green, SEC., 5, B4;.
Slaggyford, NE., 27, C2.
Slaithwaite, LNW., 21, E2; 42, D5.
Slamannan, NB., 30, B5.
Slateford, Cal., 30, B2.
Sleaford, GN(GN&GEJt), 16, C1; 17, C1.
Sleaford Jc. (Boston), GN., 17, D3.
Sledmere & Fimber, NE., 22, B4.
Sleights, NE., 28, F2.
Slinfold, LBSC., 5, E2.
Sling, SVW., 8, A2; 9, E1.
Slingsby, NE., 21, B5.
Sloane Sq., Dist(Met), 39, D5.
Slough, GW., 5, B1; 10, G1.
Smallbrook Jc., IW/IWC., 4, F3
Smallford, GN., 11, F2.
Small Heath, GW., 15, G5.
Smardale, NE., 27, F2.
Smeafield, NE., 31, D4.
Smeaton, NB., 30, B5.
Smeeth, SEC., 6, D3.
Smeeth Road, GE., 17, F4.
Smethwick, LNW., 13, B2.
See also Handsworth.
Smethwick Jc., GW., 13, B2.
Smitham, SEC., 5, C3.
Smithfield Goods, GW., 40, C5
Smithy Bridge, LY., 20, A1; 21, E1; 45, A1.
Snae Fell, ME., 23, B3.
Snailbeach, SBH., 14, B1.
Snailwell Jc., GE., 11, C4.
Snainton, NE., 22, A4.
Snaith, LY., 21, E5.
Snaith & Pollington, GC&HBJt., 21, E5.
Snape (Goods), GE., 12, C1.
Snapper, LB., 7, F3.
Snaresbrook, GE., 5, A4; 40, A2.
Snarestone, AN., 16, E5.
Snatchwood Halt, GW., 43, A2.
Snelland, GC., 17, A1.
Snell's Nook Halt, LNW., 16, E4.
Snettisham, GE., 17, D5.
Snodland, SEC., 6, C5.
Snowdon, NWNG. & SM., 19, E2.
Snow Hill (Birmingham) GW., 13, C3; 15, G4.
Snydale Jc., Mid., 42, C2.
Soham, GE., 11, B4.
Soho, LNW., 13, C2; 15, G4.
Soho & Winson Green, GW., 13, C3; 15, G4.
Soho Pool, LNW., 13, B3.
Soho Rd., LNW., 13, B3; 15, G4.
Sole Street, SEC., 5, B5.
Solihull, GW., 9, A5.
Somerleyton, GE., 18, F1.
Somerset Rd., Mid., 13, D3; 15, G4.
Somersham, GN&GEJt., 11, B3.
Somers Town Goods, Mid., 40, C5.
Somerton (Som.), GW., 3, D2; 8, F2.
Sorbie, P&W., 25, C4.
South Acton, NSW & Dist., 39, C3.
Southall, GW., 5, B2; 39, C1.
Southam & Long Itchington, LNW., 10, B5.
Southampton (Town), LSW(GW/MSW)., 4, E4.
Southampton (West), LSW(MSW)., 4, E4.

Southam Road & Harbury, GW., 10, B5.
South Bank, NE., 28, E4.
South Beach (Ardrossan), G&SW., 29, D3.
Southborough, SEC., 5, D5.
Southbourne Halt, LBSC., 4, E1.
Southburn, NE., 22, C4.
South Canterbury, SEC., 6, C3.
South Caradon, LC., 1, C4.
South Cave, HB., 22, D4.
Southcoates, NE., 22, Inset.
Southcote Jc., GW., 4, A2.
South Dock (Millwall), GE., 40, D3.
South Ealing, Dist., 39, D2.
Southease & Rodmell Halt, LBSC., 5, F4.
South Eastrington, NE., 22, D5
South Elmsall, WRG., 21, F4; 42, D1. *See also* Moorhouse.
Southend (Glam.), Mum., 43, G3.
Southend-on-Sea, LTS. & GE., 6, A4.
Southerham Jc., LBSC., 5, F4.
Southerndown Road, BRY., 7, C5; 43, D4.
Southern Jc., SY., 16, A4; 21, G4; 41, A4.
Southfield Jc., Cal., 30, D5.
Southfields, LSW(Dist)., 39, E4
Southfleet, SEC., 5, B5.
South Gosforth, NE., 27, B5.
South Harrow, Dist., 5, A2; 39, B1.
South Harrow, GC., 39, B2.
South Hetton, NE., 28, D5.
Southill, Mid., 11, D1.
South Howden, HB., 22, E5.
South Kensington, Dist. & Met(Dist), 39, D5.
South Lambeth Goods, GW., 39, Inset E4; 40, D5.
South Leicester Jc., LNW/Mid., 16, F5.
South Leigh, GW., 10, E5.
South Lynn, MGN., 17, E4.
South Milford, NE., 21, D4.
Southminster, GE., 12, G5.
South Molton, GW., 7, F4.
South Molton Road, LSW., 7, G4.
Southport, LY(LNW) LY., & CLC., 20, A4; 24, E4; 45, F1.
South Queensferry (Goods), NB., 30, B3.
South Renfrew, G&SW., 44, F4
Southrey, GN., 17, B1.
South Rhondda (Goods), GW., 8, C5; 43, D4.
South Shields, NE. & SSM., 28, B5.
South Shore (B'pool), Goods, PWY., 24, D4.
South Side Goods (Glasgow), Cal. & GBK., 44, E2.
South St. Halt, SEC., 6, B3.
South Tottenham, THJ(LTS) 18, F1.
South Town (Yarmouth), GE., 18, F1.
Southwark, LNW., 26 D1.
Southwark Park, SEC., 40, D4
Southwater, LBSC., 5, E2.
Southwell, Mid., 16, C3.
Southwick (Durham) Goods, NE., 28, B5.
Southwick (Kircud.), G&SW., 26, C4.
Southwick (Sussex), LBSC., 5, F3.
South Willingham & Hainton, GN., 17, A2.
South Witham, Mid(MGN). 16, E1.
Southwold, SWD., 12, B1.
Sowerby Bridge, LY., 21, E1; 42, C5.

Spalding, GN(GE/MGN), & Mid., 17, E2.
Sparkford, GW., 3, D2; 8, F1.
Spa Road, SEC., 40, D4.
Sparrowlee, NS., 15, C5.
Spean Bridge, NB., 32, B2.
Speech House Rd., SVW., 8, A1; 9, E1.
Speen, GW., 4, A3.
Speeton, NE., 22, B3.
Speke, LNW., 20, C4; 45, E4.
Spennithorne, NE., 21, A2; 27, G5.
Spennymoor, NE., 27, D5.
Spetchley (Goods), Mid., 9, B3.
Spetisbury, SD., 3, E4.
Spey Bay, GNS., 36, C1.
Spiersbridge (Goods), GBK., 44, E2.
Spilsby, GN., 17, B3.
Spinkhill, GC., 16, A4; 41, B3.
Spital, BJ., 20, C4; 45, F4.
Spitalfields Goods, GE., 40, C4.
Spofforth, NE., 21, C3.
Spondon, Mid., 16, D5; 41, G2
Spon Lane, LNW., 13, B2; 15, G4.
Spooner Row, GE., 12, A4; 18, F4.
Spratton, LNW., 10, A3.
Springbank Jcs. (Hull), HB., 22, Inset.
Springburn, NB., 44, D4.
Springburn Park (Goods), Cal., 29, C5; 44, D4.
Springfield, NB., 34, F5.
Springside, G&SW., 29, E3.
Spring Vale, LY., 20, A2; 24, E2.
Springwood Jc., LNW&LYJt/ LNW/LY., 21, E2; 42, C5.
Sprotborough, HB., 21, F4.
Sprouston, NE., 31, E2.
Stacksteads, LY., 20, A1; 24, E1.
Staddlethorpe, NE(GC/LNW). 22, E5.
Stafford, LNW(NS/GN). 15, E3; 20, G1.
Stafford Common, GN., 15, D3; 20, G1.
Stafford Jc., LNW/SWN., 15, E2.
Staincliffe & Batley Carr, LNW., 42, C3.
See also Batley Carr.
Staincross, GC., 21, F3; 42, D2
Staines, LSW. & GW., 5, B1.
Staines Jc., LSW., 5, B1.
Stainforth & Hatfield, GC(NE), 21, F5.
Stainland & Holywell Green, LY., 21, E2; 42, C5.
Staintondale, NE., 28, G1.
Stairfoot, GC., 42, E2.
Staithes, NE., 28, E2.
Stalbridge, SD., 3, D3; 8, G1.
Staley & Millbrook (Goods), LNW., 21, F1.
Stalham, MGN., 18, E2.
Stallingborough, GC., 22, F2.
Stalybridge, GC&LNWJt., & LY., 21, F1 and Inset A2.
Stamford, Mid(LNW), & GN., 16, F1; 17, F1.
Stamford Bridge (Yorks.), NE., 22, C5.
Stamford Hill, GE., 40, A4.
Stammerham Jc., LBSC., 5, E2.
Stanbridgeford, LNW., 10, D1.
Standish (Lancs.), LNW., 20, B3; 24, F2; 45, D1.
Standish Jc. (Glos.), GW/Mid., 9, E3.
Standon, GE., 11, E3.
Standon Bridge, LNW., 15, D3; 20, F1.
Stanford-le-Hope, LTS., 5, A5.
Stanhoe, GE., 18, D5.
Stanhope, NE., 27, D4.
Stanley (Lancs.), LNW., 45, F3. *See also* Knotty Ash.
Stanley (Yorks.), MJ., 21, E3; 42, B2.

Stanley Bridge Halt. GW., 3, A4.
Stanley Jc. (Perth), Cal.(HR), 33, E5.
Stanmore, LNW., 5, A2.
Stanner, GW., M, E2.
Stannergate (Goods). D&A., 34, Inset E1.
Stanningley, GN(LY), 21, D2; 42, A4.
Stannington, NE., 27, A5.
Stansfield Hall, LY., 21, E1.
Stansted, GE., 11, E4.
Stanton, GW., 9, F5.
Stanton Gate, Mid., 16, D4; 41, G3.
Staple, EK., 6, C2.
Stapleford & Sandiacre (Notts.) Mid., 16, D4; 41, G3.
Staple Hill, Mid., 3, A3; 8, C1.
Staplehurst, SEC., 6, D5.
Stapleton Rd., GW., 3, Inset; 8, C1.
Starbeck, NE., 21, C3.
Starcross, GW., 2, C3.
Staveley (Westmorland), LNW., 27, G1.
Staveley Town (Derbys.), GC. & Mid., 16, A4; 41, B3.
Staveley Works, GC., 16, A4; 41, B3.
See also Barrow Hill.
Staverton (Devon), GW., 2, D4
Staverton Halt (Wilts.), GW., 3, B4.
Staward, NE., 27, C3.
Stechford, LNW., 15, G5.
Steelend (Goods), NB., 30, A3.
Steele Rd., NB., 27, A1.
Steens Bridge, GW., 9, B1.
Steeplehouse (Goods), LNW., 16, C5; 41, E1.
Steer Point, GW., 2, E5.
Steeton & Silsden, Mid., 21, C1
Stenson Jc., Mid/NS., 16, D5.
Stepford, G&SW., 26, A4.
Stepney (Hull), NE., 22, Inset.
Stepney (London), GE(LTS), 40, C3.
Stepney Green, WB., 40, C3.
Stepps Rd., Cal., 29, C5; 44, C4.
Stevenage, GN., 11, E2.
Stevenston, G&SW. & Cal., 29, D3.
Steventon, GW., 10, F4.
Stewarton, GBK., 29, D4.
Stewarts Lane Goods, SEC., 39, Inset E4.
Steyning, LBSC., 5, F2.
Stickney, GN., 17, C3.
Stillington, NE., 28, E5.
Stirchley, GW., 15, F2.
Stirling, Cal. & NB., 30, A5.
Stixwould, GN., 17, B2.
Stobcross, Cal. & Cal&NBJt., 44, E4.
Stobo, Cal., 30, E3.
Stobs, NB., 31, F1.
Stockbridge, LSW(MSW), 4, C4.
Stockcross & Bagnor, GW., 4, A4.
Stockingford, Mid., 16, F5.
Stockport, LNW(NS/LY) & CLC., 20, C1; 45, A4.
Stocksfield, NE(NB), 27, C4.
Stocksmoor, LY., 21, F2; 42, D4.
Stockton (Durham), NE., 28, E5.
Stockton Brook, NS., 15, C3.
Stockwith, GN&GEJt., 22, G5.
Stogumber, GW., 8, F5.
Stoke (Suffolk), GE., 11, D5.
Stoke Bruern (Goods), SMJ., 10, C3.
Stoke Canon, GW., 2, B3.
Stoke Edith, GW., 9, C2.
Stoke Ferry, GE., 11, A4; 17, F5.
Stoke Golding, AN., 16, F5.
Stoke Mandeville, Met&GCJt., 10, E2.

Stoke Newington, GE., 40, B4.
Stoke-on-Trent, NS(LNW), 15, C3; 20, F1.
Stoke Works Goods, Mid., 9, B4.
Stoke Works (Pass.), GW(Mid), 9, B4.
Stokesley, NE., 28, F4.
Stone, NS., 15, D3; 20, F1.
Stonea, GE., 11, A3; 17, G3.
Stonebridge Park, LNW(LE), 39, B3.
Stone Cross Halt, LBSC., 5, F5.
Stoneferry (Goods), NE., 22, D3.
Stonehaven, Cal(NB), 34, A2.
Stonehouse (Glos.), GW. & Mid., 9, E3.
Stonehouse (Lanarks), Cal., 30, D5.
Stonehouse Jc., Cal., 44, A1.
Stonehouse Pool, LSW., 1, Inset.
Stoneywood (Aberdeen), GNS., 37, F4.
Storeton (Goods), GC., 20, C4; 45, F4.
Stottesdon, CMDP., 9, A2; 15, G2.
Stoulton, GW., 9, C3.
Stourbridge, GW., 15, G3.
Stourbridge Jc., GW., 9, A3; 15, G3.
Stourport, GW., 9, A3.
Stourton Jc., Mid/EWY., 21, D3; 42, B2.
Stow (Midlothian), NB., 30, D1.
Stow (Norfolk), GE., 17, F4.
Stow Bedon, GE., 12, A5; 18, F5.
Stowmarket, GE., 12, C4.
Stow-on-the-Wold, GW., 9, D5.
Stow Park, GN&GEJt., 16, A2.
Stracathro, Cal., 34, C3.
Stradbroke, MSL., 12, B3.
Stranraer, P&W., 25, C2.
Strata Florida, GW., 14, D5.
Stratford, GE., 5, A4; 40, B3.
Stratford Market, GE., 40, B2.
Stratford-on-Avon, GW. & SMJ., 9, B5.
Strathaven, Cal., 29, D5.
Strathblane, NB., 29, B5.
Strathbungo, GBK., 44, E3 *and* Inset F1.
Strathcarron, HR., 35, E2.
Strathmiglo, NB., 34, F5.
Strathord, Cal(HR), 33, E5.
Strathpeffer, HR., 35, D5.
Strathyre, Cal., 33, F2.
Stratton, GW., 9, F5.
Stravithie, NB., 34, F3.
Strawberry Hill, LSW., 5, B2; 39, E2.
Strawfrank Jc., Cal., 30, D4.
Streatham, LBSC., 5, B3; 40, F5.
Streatham Common, LBSC., 40, F5.
Streatham Hill, LBSC(LNW), 40, E5.
Streetly, Mid., 15, F5.
Strensall, NE., 21, B5.
Stretford, MSJA(CLC), 45, B3.
Stretford Bridge, BC., 14, C1.
Stretham, GE., 11, B4.
Stretton (Derbys.), Mid., 16, B5; 41, D2.
Stretton & Clay Mills (Staffs.), NS(GN), 15, Inset C5.
Stretton Jc., LNW/NS., 15, Inset C5.
Stretton-on-Fosse, GW., 9, C5.
Strichen, GNS., 37, C4.
Strines, GC&MidJt., 15, A4.
Strome Ferry, HR., 35, E1.
Strood, SEC., 6, B5.
Stroud, GW. & Mid., 9, E3.
Stroud Green, GN(NL), 40, A5
Struan, HR., 33, C3.

Stubbins, LY., 20, A1; 24, E1; 45, B1.
Studland Rd. Jc., LSW/Dist., 39, D4.
Studley & Astwood Bank, Mid., 9, B4.
Sturmer, GE., 11, D5.
Sturminster Newton, SD., 3, E3
Sturry, SEC., 6, C2.
Sturt Lane Jc., LSW., 4, B1.
Sturton (Goods), NE., 21, D4.
Styal, LNW., 20, C1; 45, A4.
Suckley, GW., 9, B2.
Sudbrook, GW., 8, B2; 9, F1.
Sudbury & Harrow Rd., GC., 39, B2.
Sudbury Hill, Dist., 39, B2.
Sudbury Town, Dist., 39, B2.
Sudbury (Staffs.), NS(GN), 15, D5.
Sudbury (Suffolk), GE., 12, D5.
Sulby Bridge, IMR., 23, A3.
Sulby Glen, IMR., 23, A3.
Sully, TV., 8, D4; 43, B5.
Summer Lane, GC., 21, F3; 42, E2.
Summerseat, LY., 20, A1; 24, E1; 45, B1.
Summerston, NB., 29, B5. 44, E5.
Sunbury, LSW., 5, B2.
Sunderland, NE., 28, C5.
Sundridge Park, SEC., 40, F2.
Sunilaws, NE., 31, D2.
Sunningdale, LSW., 5, B1.
Sunnyside (Coatbridge), NB., 44, B4.
Sunnywood Halt, LY., 45, B1.
Surbiton, LSW., 5, B2; 39, G2.
Surfleet, GN., 17, D2.
Surrey Canal Jc., SEC., 40, D3.
Surrey Docks, EL., 40, D4.
Sutton (Cambs.), GE., 11, B3.
Sutton (Surrey), LBSC., 5, C3.
Sutton Bingham, LSW., 3, E2.
Sutton Branch Jc., GE., 11, B4.
Sutton Bridge, MGN., 17, E4.
Sutton Coldfield, LNW., 15, F5.
Sutton-in-Ashfield, Mid., GC. & GN., 16, B4; 41, D4.
Sutton Jc., Mid., 16, B4; 41, D4.
Sutton Oak, LNW., 45, D3.
Sutton-on-Hull, NE., 22, D3.
Sutton-on-Sea, GN., 17, A4.
Sutton Park, Mid., 15, F5.
Sutton Scotney, GW., 4, C3.
Sutton Weaver, LNW., 15, A1; 20, D3; 45, D5.
Swadlincote, Mid., 16, E5.
Swaffham, GE., 18, F5.
Swaffhamprior, GE., 11, C4.
Swainsthorpe, GE., 12, A3; 18, F3.
Swalwell, NE., 27, C5.
Swanage, LSW., 3, G5.
Swanbourne, LNW., 10, D2.
Swanbridge Halt, TV., 43, B5.
Swanley, SEC., 5, B4.
Swannington, Mid., 16, E4.
Swansea, GW., LNW., Mid., RSB. & Mum., 7, B4; 43, G3.
Swansea Bay, LNW., 7, B4; 43, G3.
Swan Village, GW., 13, B2; 15, F4.
Swanwick, LSW., 4, E3.
Swavesey, GE(Mid), 11, C3.
Sway, LSW., 4, E5.
Swaythling, LSW(GW), 4, D4.
Swimbridge, GW., 7, F4.
Swinderby, Mid., 16, B2.
Swindon, GW., 9, F5.
Swindon Town, MSW., 9, G5.
Swine, NE., 22, D3.
Swineshead, GN., 17, D2.
Swinton (Lancs.), LY., 20, B2. 24, F1; 45, B2.
Swinton (Yorks.), Mid(NE) & GC., 21, F4; 42, F1.
Swiss Cottage, Met., 39, B5.

Sydenham, LBSC., 40, F4.
Sydenham Hill, SEC., 40, F4.
Sykehouse, GC&HBJt., 21, E5.
Sykes Jc., GC/GN&GEJt., 16, A2.
Sylfaen, W&L., 14, B2.
Symington, Cal., 30, E4.
Symonds Yat, GW., 8, A2; 9, E1.
Syston, Mid(MGN), 16, E3.

T

Tadcaster, NE., 21, D4.
Tadworth & Walton-on-Hill, SEC., 5, C3.
Taff Bargoed Jc., GW/TBJ., 43, C3.
Taffs Well, TV(Rhy), 8, C4; 43, C4.
Tain, HR., 36, B4.
Takeley, GE., 11, F4.
Talacre, LNW., 20, C5.
Talbot Rd. (Blackpool), PWY., 24, D4.
Talerddig, Cam., 14, B4.
Talgarth, Cam(Mid), 14, F3.
Talley Road, VT., 13, G5.
Tallington, GN., 17, F1.
Talsarn Halt, GW., 13, E5.
Talsarnau, Cam., 19, F2.
Talybont-on-Usk, BM., 14, G3
Tal-y-Cafn & Eglwysbach, LNW., 19, D4.
Talyllyn, BM(Mid/Cam), 14, G3.
Tamerton Foliot, LSW., 1, D5.
Tamworth, LNW. & Mid., 15, F5.
Tanfield, NE., 21, A3.
Tanhouse Lane, GC&MidJt.(CLC)., 45, D4.
Tankerton Halt, SEC., 6, B3.
Tannadice, Cal., 34, C4.
Tanshelf, LY., 21, E4; 42, C1.
Tan-y-Bwlch, Fest., 19, F3.
Tan-y-Grisiau, Fest., 19, F3.
Taplow, GW., 5, B1; 10, G2.
Tapton Jc., Mid., 16,B5; 41, B2.
Tarbolton, G&SW., 29, E4.
Tarff, G&SW., 26, C5.
Tarset, NB., 27, A2.
Tattenhall, LNW., 15, B1; 20, E3.
Tattenhall Road, LNW., 15, B1; 20, E3.
Tattenham Corner, SEC., 5, C3.
Tattershall, GN., 17, C2.
Taunton, GW., 8, F4.
Tavistock, LSW. & GW., 1, C5.
Tavistock Jc., GW., 2, D5.
Tay Bridge (Dundee), NB., 34, Inset.
Taynuilt, Cal., 32, E3.
Tayport, NB., 34, E4.
Tean, NS., 15, D4.
Tebay, LNW&NEJt., 27, F1.
Teddington, LSW., 5, B2; 39, F2.
Teigngrace, GW., 2, C3.
Teignmouth, GW., 2, C3.
Temple, Dist(Met), 40, C5.
Templecombe, LSW&SDJt. & SD., 3, D3; 8, G1.
Temple Hirst, NE., 21, E5.
Temple Meads (Bristol), GW&MidJt., 3, A2 *and* Inset; 8, C2.
Temple Sowerby, NE., 27, E1.
Templeton, GW., 7, C3.
Tempsford, GN., 11, D2.
Tenbury Wells, S&H., 9, A1.
Tenby, GW., 7, D3.
Tennochside Jc., NB., 44, C3.
Tenterden St. Michael's, KES., 6, D4.
Tenterden Town, KES., 6, D4.
Tern Hill, GW., 15, D2; 20, G2.
Terrington, MGN., 17, E4.
Tetbury, GW., 9, F3.
Teversall, Mid. & GN., 16, B4; 41, D3.
Tewkesbury, Mid., 9, D3.

SUPPLEMENTARY ENTRIES

2. INDEX TO TUNNELS

Ampthill, Mid., 10, C1; 11, D1.
Armathwaite, Mid., 27, D1.

Bangor, LNW., 19, D2.
Bodorgan, LNW., 19, D1.
Bo Peep, SEC., 6, F5.
Burdale, NE., 22, B5.

Culgaith, Mid., 27, E1.

Farnworth, LY., 45, B2.

Hadley, GN., 11, G2.
Haltwhistle, NE., 27, B2.
Hastings, SEC., 6, F5.

Lazonby, Mid., 27, D1.
Llandderfel, GW., 19, F5

Ore, SEC., 6, F5.

Penmanshiel, NB., 31, C2.
Polperro, GW., 1, E1.
Potters Bar, GN., 11, G2.

Sandling, SEC., 6, D3.
Selling, SEC., 6, C3.
Stanton, Mid., 16, D3.

Welwyn, GN., 11, F2.
Whitrope, NB., 31, G1.
Wilpshire, LY., 24, D2.
Woolley, LY., 42, D3.

6. INDEX TO STATIONS, JUNCTIONS, ETC.

Ashley Jc., GW., 3, Inset.
Awe Crossing, Cal., 32, F3.

Bangour, NB., 30, C4.
Boston Manor, Dist., 39, D2.
Bridge Street (Banbury), GW(GC), 10, C4.
Brinsley Jc., GN., 41, E3.

Caldew Jc., Cal/GTC., 26, Inset.
Cambusnethan, Cal., 30, C5.
Canfield Place, GC., 39, B5.
Cemetery Jcs. (Hartlepool), NE., 28, D4.
Chiswick & Grove Park, LSW., 39, D3.
Citadel (Carlisle), CJC/(G&SW/M&C/Mid/NE/NB), 26, C1 *and* Inset.
Currock Jc. (Carlisle), M&C., 26, C1 *and* Inset.

Dentonholme Goods, DJ., 26, Inset.
Galton Jc., LNW/GW., 13, B2.
Gavell, NB., 29, B1.
Goldhawk Rd., H&C., 39, D4.
Gorgie, Cal. & NB., 30, Inset.
Grain Crossing Halt., SEC., 6, B4.
Grange, GNS., 37, D1.
Green Lane Jc., GW/H&C., 39, Inset C1.

Hampstead Rd. Jc., LNW/NL., 40, Inset A1.

Hensall Jc., LY/HB., 21, E5.
Heston Hounstow, Dist., 39, D1.

James St. (Liverpool), Mer., 45, F4.
Junction Rd. (Leith), NB., 30, Inset.

Kew Bridge (Goods), NSW., 39, D3.
Kingsland (Dalston), NL., 40, B4.
Kingston Crossing Halt, GW., 10, F3.
Kirklees Jc., LNW., 45, D2.

Ladbroke Grove, H&C., 39, C4.
Langley Jc., GN., 11, E2.
Lewknor Bridge Halt, GW., 10, F3.
London Fields, GE., 40, B4.
Ludgate Hill, SEC., 40, C5.

Merton Street (Banbury), LNW(SMJ), 10, C4.
Monymusk, GNS., 37, F2.
Moor St. (Birmingham), GW., 13, C4.

New Wandsworth Goods, LBSC., 39, E5 *and* Inset F2.
Northfield & Little Ealing, Dist., 39, D2.
North Leith, NB., 30, Inset.
Northolt Halt, GW., 39, B1.
North Walsall, Mid., 15, F4.

Parks Bridge Jc., SEC., 40, E3.
Penarth Curve Jcs., GW/TV., 43, B4.
Pitcaple, GNS., 37, E3.
Pitlurg, GNS., 37, E4.
Plaistow & West Ham Goods, GE., 40, C2.
Port Carlisle Jc., Cal/NB., 26, C1.
Primrose Hill Jc., LNW., 40, Inset A2.
Proof House Jc., LNW., 13, Inset.

Ryecroft Jc., LNW/Mid., 15, F4.

St. Lawrence (Kent), SEC., 6, B1.
Skelton Jc., CLC., 45, B4.
South Bermondsey, LBSC., 40, D4.
South Hampstead, LNW(NL), 39, B5.
South Leith, Cal.&NB., 30, Inset.
Stamford Brook, LSW(Dist), 39, D4.
Strathaven Jc., Cal., 44, C2.
Sun Bank Halt, GW., 20, F5.

Upperby Jc., (Carlisle), LNW., 26, C1.

Watson's Crossing Halt, LY., 21, E1.
Whelley Jc., LNW., 20, B3; 24, F2; 45, D2.
Willington Jc. (Derbys.), Mid/NS., 16, D5.

84